Charles Venable

An elementary algebra

Designed as an introduction to a thorough knowledge of algebraic language

Charles Venable

An elementary algebra
Designed as an introduction to a thorough knowledge of algebraic language

ISBN/EAN: 9783337221720

Printed in Europe, USA, Canada, Australia, Japan

Cover: Foto ©Paul-Georg Meister /pixelio.de

More available books at **www.hansebooks.com**

AN

ELEMENTARY ALGEBRA:

DESIGNED AS

AN INTRODUCTION TO A THOROUGH KNOWLEDGE
OF ALGEBRAIC LANGUAGE, AND TO GIVE
BEGINNERS FACILITY IN THE USE OF
ALGEBRAIC SYMBOLS.

BY

CHARLES S. VENABLE, LL.D.,

PROFESSOR OF MATHEMATICS IN THE UNIVERSITY OF VIRGINIA; AUTHOR OF "FIRST
LESSONS IN NUMBERS," "MENTAL ARITHMETIC," "PRACTICAL
ARITHMETIC," AND "HIGHER ARITHMETIC."

UNIVERSITY PUBLISHING COMPANY,
NEW YORK AND BALTIMORE.
1872.

Entered according to Act of Congress, in the year 1869,

By THE UNIVERSITY PUBLISHING COMPANY,

In the Clerk's office of the District Court of the United States for the Southern District of New York.

PREFACE.

The present Elementary Algebra has been prepared with a view to enable the beginner to obtain a thorough knowledge of Algebraic Language, and to acquire an early facility in the use of Algebraic Symbols. The translation of English into the symbolical language of Algebra, and the interpretation of Algebraic Symbols by arithmetical operations are made prominent from the beginning. Throughout the work I have endeavored, in the Algebraic operations and solutions of problems, to present examples of elegance and conciseness in the transformation of Algebraic expressions. I am convinced by long observation that the difficulties of students in their more advanced mathematical studies are greatly enhanced by their want of knowledge of Algebra as a Language, and their want of facility in the transformation and combination of expressions in the solution of problems. *These things form the basis of any thorough knowledge of Algebraic Analysis, and should be learned well in the beginning.* The demonstrations are, I think, clear and easily intelligible to the young student. The examples for exercise are numerous.

In addition to the fundamental Algebraic operations on Entire Quantities and Fractions, Evolution, Surds, Equations, Arithmetical and Geometrical Progressions, and Proportion, I have treated in an elementary manner the subjects of Fractional Exponents, Permutations and Combinations, the Binomial Theorem for whole-number exponents, Harmonical Progression, Theory of Notation, and Logarithms. I am convinced by long experience that it is important to present these subjects to the young student in a simple and practical manner before he comes in contact with them in their greater extensions and more difficult applications. In the preparation of this book I have consulted many of those works which give a view of the progress and improvement in elementary instruction in Algebra. But three English works —Todhunter's Algebra for Beginners, Colenso's Algebra, and Lund's Wood's Algebra—are made the basis of the work. The demonstrations of Wood, (a standard of more than half a century,) are singularly clear and simple, while those of Colenso are models of elegance and brevity. Todhunter's illustrations are clear and copious. The examples have been selected mainly from the above authors, many of them having been taken by them from the Cambridge Examination papers. I have also used Lund's Easy Algebra, Bobillier's "Principes d'Algèbre," Ritt's Problêmes d'Algèbre, and Wrigley's Collection of Problems.

UNIVERSITY OF VIRGINIA,
    Aug. 1, 1869.

CONTENTS.

		PAGE
I.	Principal Signs	7
II.	Factor—Coefficient—Power—Terms	11
III.	Remaining Signs—Brackets	16
IV.	Change of Order of Terms—Like Terms	20
V.	Addition	24
VI.	Subtraction	28
VII.	Brackets	33
VIII.	Multiplication	38
IX.	General Results of Multiplication	45
X.	Division	52
XI.	Factors	61
XII.	Greatest Common Divisor	67
XIII.	Least Common Multiple	76
XIV.	Fractions	80
XV.	Reduction of Fractions	84
XVI.	Addition and Subtraction of Fractions	88
XVII.	Multiplication of Fractions	94
XVIII.	Division of Fractions	98
XIX.	Complex Fractions, and other Results	101
XX.	Involution	105
XXI.	Evolution	110
XXII.	Simple Equations	128
XXIII.	Simple Equations—continued	137
XXIV.	Problems solved by Simple Equations	145
XXV.	Problems—continued	153

CONTENTS.

XXVI.	Simultaneous Equations of the First Degree	164
XXVII.	Problems Solved by Simultaneous Equations of the First Degree . .	176
XXVIII.	Indices	184
XXIX.	Surds	191
XXX.	Quadratic Equations	200
XXXI.	Equations which may be solved like Quadratic Equations	212
XXXII.	Problems which lead to Quadratic Equations containing One Unknown Quantity	217
XXXIII.	Simultaneous Equations involving Quadratics	221
XXXIV.	Ratio	230
XXXV.	Proportion	233
XXXVI.	Arithmetical Progression . . .	240
XXXVII.	Geometrical Progression . . .	245
XXXVIII.	Harmonical Progression	252
XXXIX.	Permutations and Combinations . .	254
XL.	Binomial Theorem	263
XLI.	Scales of Notation	269
XLII.	Logarithms	275
	Answers to Examples	284

ELEMENTARY ALGEBRA.

I. THE PRINCIPAL SIGNS.

1. ALGEBRA is the science in which we reason about numbers with the aid of letters to denote the numbers, and of certain signs to denote the operations performed on the numbers, and the relations of the numbers to each other. These letters and signs are called *Algebraic Symbols*.

2. *Quantity* signifies anything which admits of increase, or diminution. The word *quantity* is often used with the same meaning as *number*.

3. The sign $+$ placed before a number denotes that this number is to be *added*. Thus $a + b$ denotes that the number represented by b is to be added to the number represented by a. If a represent 9 and b represent 3, then $a + b$ represents 12. The sign $+$ is called the *plus sign*, and $a + b$ is read "a *plus* b."

4. The sign $-$ placed before a number, denotes that the number is to be *subtracted*. Thus $a - b$ denotes that the number represented by b, is to be subtracted from the number represented by a. If a represent 9 and b represent 3, then $a - b$ represents 6. The sign $-$ is called the *minus sign*, and $a - b$ is read thus, "a *minus* b."

5. Similarly, $a + b + c$ denotes that we are to add b to a, and then add c to the result; $a + b - c$ denotes that we

---

Define Algebra; Algebraic Symbols; Quantity. How is Addition indicated? Subtraction?

are to add b to a, and then subtract c from the result; $a - b + c$ denotes that we are to subtract b from a, and then add c to the result; $a - b - c$ denotes that we are to subtract b from a, and then subtract c from the result.

6. The sign $=$ denotes that the numbers between which it is placed are *equal*. Thus $a = b$ denotes that the number represented by a is equal to the number represented by b. And $a + b = c$ denotes that the sum of the numbers represented by a and b is equal to the number represented by c; so that if a represent 9 and b represent 3, then c must represent 12. The sign $=$ is called the *sign of equality*, and $a = b$ is read thus, "a *equals* b," or *a is equal to b*.

7. The sign $\times$ denotes that the numbers between which it stands are to be *multiplied* together. Thus $a \times b$ denotes that the number represented by a is to be multiplied by the number represented by b. If a represent 9 and b represent 3, then $a \times b$ represents 27. The sign $\times$ is called the *sign of multiplication*, and $a \times b$ is read thus, "a *into* b," or "a *multiplied by* b." Similarly, $a \times b \times c$ denotes the product of the numbers represented by a, b, and c.

8. Sometimes a point is used instead of the sign $\times$. Thus $a.b$ instead of $a \times b$. Both of these signs are, however, often omitted for the sake of brevity; thus ab is used instead of $a \times b$, and has the same meaning. So also, abc is used instead of $a \times b \times c$, or $a.b.c$, and has the same meaning. Nor is either the point or the sign $\times$ necessary between a number expressed by a figure and a number expressed by a letter; so that $3a$ is used instead of $3 \times a$, and has the same meaning. The sign of multiplication must not be omitted between numbers expressed in the ordinary way by figures. Thus 45 cannot be used to represent the product of 4 and 5, because the meaning, *forty-five*, has already been assigned to 45. Nor can the point be used between figures to express a product, without producing confusion, as, for example, to 4.5 has already, in Arithmetic, been assigned the meaning $4 + \frac{5}{10}$; still, 4.5 is sometimes written for 4×5.

9. The sign ÷ denotes that the quantity which stands *before* it is to be *divided* by the quantity which *follows* it. Thus $a \div b$ denotes that the number represented by a is to be divided by the number represented by b. If a represent 12, and b represent 4, then $a \div b$ represents 3. The sign ÷ is called the *sign of division*, and $a \div b$ is read thus, "a *divided by* b," or briefly, "a *by* b."

But most frequently to express division the dividend is placed over the divisor, with a line between them. Thus $\frac{a}{b}$ is used for $a \div b$, and has the same meaning.

10. A number or quantity expressed by Algebraic Symbols is called an *Algebraic expression*, or briefly, an *expression*.

11. We shall now give some examples as an exercise in the use of the symbols which have been explained; these examples consist in finding the numerical values of certain Algebraic expressions, and in finding the Algebraic expression for certain quantities expressed in ordinary language.

Suppose $a = 1,\ b = 2,\ c = 3,\ d = 5,\ e = 6,\ f = 0$. Then

$$7a + 3b - 2d + f = 7 + 6 - 10 + 0 = 13 - 10 = 3.$$

$$2ab + 8bc - ae + df = 4 + 48 - 6 + 0 = 52 - 6 = 46.$$

$$\frac{4ac}{b} + \frac{10be}{cd} - \frac{de}{ac} = \frac{12}{2} + \frac{120}{15} - \frac{30}{3} = 6 + 8 - 10 =$$

$$14 - 10 = 4.$$

$$\frac{4c + 5e}{d - b} = \frac{12 + 30}{5 - 2} = \frac{42}{3} = 14.$$

How is Division indicated? What is an Algebraic Expression?

Examples—1.

If $a=1, b=2, c=3, d=4, e=5, f=0$, find the numerical values of the following expressions:

1. $9a+2b+3c-2f$.
2. $4e-3a-3b+5c$.
3. $7ae+3bc+9d-af$.
4. $8abc-bcd+9cde-def$.
5. $abcd+abce+abde+acde+bcde$.
6. $\dfrac{4a}{b}+\dfrac{9b}{c}+\dfrac{8c}{d}-\dfrac{5d}{e}$.
7. $\dfrac{4ac}{b}+\dfrac{8bc}{d}-\dfrac{5cd}{e}$.
8. $\dfrac{12a}{bc}+\dfrac{6b}{cd}+\dfrac{20c}{de}$.
9. $\dfrac{cde}{ab}+\dfrac{5bcd}{ae}-\dfrac{6ade}{bc}$.
10. $7e+bcd-\dfrac{3bde}{2ac}$.
11. $\dfrac{2a+5b}{c}+\dfrac{3b+2c}{d}-\dfrac{a+b+c+d}{2e}$.
12. $\dfrac{b+c+3e}{e+c-d}$.
13. $\dfrac{a+c}{c-a}+\dfrac{b+d}{d-b}+\dfrac{c+e}{e-c}$.
14. $\dfrac{a+b+c+d+e}{e-d+c-b+a}$.

15. What is the difference between $\dfrac{a}{b}+\dfrac{a}{c}$ and $\dfrac{a}{bc}$ when $a=4, b=5, c=10$?   Ans. $\dfrac{28}{25}$.

16. A person who possessed a fortune, expressed by x, receives by inheritance two sums, a and b. Express his whole property.

17. An estate is divided among three heirs: the second obtains a dollars more than the first, and the third b dollars more than the second. Express the value of the estate, the share of the first heir being x.

18. A man who possessed x dollars, lost a of them. How many has he left?

19. The sum of two quantities being represented by s, if one of these quantities is expressed by x, what will be the other?

20. A debtor set out to pay his creditor a part, a, of his debt x; but on the way he met another person, to whom he gave a sum b and carried the remainder to his creditor. Express what remains of the debt.

21. The three figures of a number are such that the tens figure exceeds the units figure by 2, and the hundreds figure exceeds the tens figure by 3. What is the sum of the figures, x being the units figure?

22. Express 45.6 by means of algebraic signs.

23. The figures of a number in the hundreds, tens, and units place respectively are x, y, z. Express the number. Express the number with the figures reversed.

24. A workman whose wages were x dollars a day, receives during n days an increase of wages amounting to b dollars a day. Express the amount of his wages for this time.

25. Express the number which divided by 11 gives 5 for a remainder, x being the quotient.

26. A man travels uniformly a distance s in a number t of hours. What is his rate of travel per hour?

27. Two fountains fill a reservoir, one in a number of hours represented by x, the other in 3 hours more. What part of the reservoir does each one fill in one hour?

28. A number N divided by d gave for remainder the number r. Express the quotient.

II. Factor—Coefficient—Power—Terms.

12. When one number consists of the product of two or more numbers, each of the latter is called a *factor* of the product. Thus, for example, $2 \times 3 \times 5 = 30$; and each of

---

Define Factor.

the numbers 2, 3, and 5 is a factor of the product 30. Or we may regard 30 as the product of the two factors 2 and 15, or as the product of the two factors 3 and 10. So also we may consider $4\,ab$ as the product of the three factors 4, a, and b, or of the two factors $4\,a$ and b; or as the product of the two factors 4 and ab; or as the product of the two factors $4\,b$ and a.

13. When a number consists of the product of two factors, each factor is called the *coefficient* of the other factor; so that *coefficient* means co-factor. Thus, considering $4\,ab$ as the product of 4 and ab, we call 4 the coefficient of ab, and ab the coefficient of 4; and considering $4\,ab$ as the product of $4\,a$ and b, we call $4\,a$ the coefficient of b, and b the coefficient of $4\,a$. In practice, the name *coefficient* is applied to the factor which precedes the other, and usually the *first* factor is called the coefficient. When this *first* factor is a number expressed by a figure, it is called the *numerical coefficient*. Thus 4 is the *numerical coefficient* of ab in the expression $4\,ab$. Since 1 is a factor of every product, when no numerical coefficient is written before an algebraic expression 1 is always understood as its *numerical coefficient*. Thus 1 is the numerical coefficient of the expressions, ab, a, abc. When we use one of the letters of a product as a coefficient it is called a *literal coefficient*. Thus in the expression ax, a is the literal coefficient of x.

14. When all the factors of a product are equal, the product is called a *power* of that factor. Thus 7×7 is called the *second power* of 7; $7 \times 7 \times 7$ is called the *third power* of 7; $7 \times 7 \times 7 \times 7$ is called the *fourth power* of 7, and so on. In like manner, $a \times a$ is called the *second power* of a; $a \times a \times a$ is called the *third power* of a; $a \times a \times a \times a$ is called the *fourth power* of a, and so on. And a itself is called the *first power* of a.

FACTOR—COEFFICIENT—POWER—TERMS.

15. Instead of writing all the equal factors, we express a power more briefly by writing the factor once, and placing over it, and a little to the right, the number which indicates how often the factor is to be repeated. Thus a^2 is used to denote $a \times a$; a^3 denotes $a \times a \times a$; a^4 denotes $a \times a \times a \times a$; $3a^4 b^3 c^2 d$ denotes $3\,aaaa\,bbb\,cc\,d$, and so on. And a^1 may be used to denote the first power of a, that is, a itself; so that a^1 has *the same meaning as* a. The number thus placed over another to indicate how many times the latter occurs as a factor in a power, is called an *index of the power*, or an *exponent of the power*, or briefly an *index* or *exponent*. Thus, for example, in a^3 the exponent is 3; in a^n the exponent is n; in 2^m the exponent is m.

16. The second power of a, that is a^2, is usually called the *square* of a or a *squared*; and a^3 is often called the *cube* of a or a *cubed*. For the powers higher than these there are no similar words in use; a^4 is read thus, "a *to the fourth power*," or "a *to the fourth*;" a^m is read "a to the mth."

17. The student must distinguish carefully between a *coefficient* and an *exponent*. Thus $3c$ means *three times c*, and $m\,a$ stands for m times a. Here 3 and m are coefficients. But c^3 means c times c times c; and c^m stands for c times c times c times c and so on . . . . times c.

18. If an expression contain no parts connected by the signs $+$ and $-$, it is called a *simple* expression or *monomial*. If an expression contain parts connected by the signs $+$ and $-$, it is called a *compound* expression; and the parts connected by the signs $+$ and $-$ are called *terms* of the expression. Thus ax, $4bc$, and $5a^2c^2$ are *simple* expressions; $a^2+b^3-c^4$, $a^4+3a^2b+c^3$, are compound expressions, of which a^2, b^3, and c^4, and a^4, $3a^2b$, and c^3 are the *terms* respectively.

19. Let the student distinguish carefully between *terms*

Index or Exponent. a^2; a^3; a^n. Difference between Coefficient and Exponent. Monomial Terms. Terms and Factors.

and *factors*, recollecting that *factors* are those *parts* of an expression which are connected by Multiplication, and *terms* are those parts of a compound expression which are connected by Addition and Subtraction.

Thus 5, a^2, b, and c are *factors* of the expression $5a^2bc$; while $5a^2$, b, and c are *terms* of the expression $5a^2 + b - c$.

20. When an expression consists of *two* terms it is called a *binomial* expression, or briefly a *binomial*; when it consists of three terms it is called a *trinomial*; any expression consisting of several terms is called a *multinomial* or *polynomial*.

Thus $2a^2 + 3abc$ is a binomial expression; $a - 2b + 5c$ is a trinomial expression; and $a^2 - b^2 + c^2 - 4ab - e$ is a polynomial.

21. Each of the letters or literal factors of a term is called a *dimension* of the term, and the number of these literal factors is called the *degree* of the term. Thus $2a^2b^3c$ or $2aabbbc$ has six dimensions and is said to be of the sixth degree. The numerical coefficient is not counted; thus $9a^3b^4$ and a^3b^4 are of the same dimensions, namely, seven dimensions. The *degree* of a term, that is, the *number of its dimensions*, is evidently the *sum of the exponents of its literal factors*, provided we remember that when no exponent is expressed the exponent 1 must be understood.

22. An expression is said to be *homogeneous* when all its terms are of the same degree.

Thus $7a^3 + 3a^2b + 4abc$ is homogeneous, for each term is of three dimensions, that is, of the third degree.

We shall now give some more examples of finding the numerical values of algebraic expressions.

Suppose $a = 1$, $b = 2$, $c = 3$, $d = 4$, $e = 5$, $f = 0$. Then

$$b^2 = 4, \quad b^3 = 8, \quad b^4 = 16, \quad b^5 = 32.$$

Binomial. Trinomial. Polynomial. Dimension and Degree of Term. When is an expression homogeneous?

$3b^2 = 3 \times 4 = 12$, $5b^3 = 5 \times 8 = 40$, $9b^5 = 9 \times 32 = 288$.

$e^a = 5^1 = 5$, $e^b = 5^2 = 25$, $e^c = 5^3 = 125$.

$a^3 b^3 = 1 \times 8 = 8$, $3b^2 c^2 = 3 \times 4 \times 9 = 108$.

$d^2 + c^2 - 7ab + f^2 = 64 + 9 - 14 + 0 = 59$.

$\dfrac{3c^2 - 4c - 10}{c^3 - 2c^2 + 5c - 23} = \dfrac{27 - 12 - 10}{27 - 18 + 15 - 23} = \dfrac{5}{1} = 5$.

$\dfrac{e^3 + d^3}{e + d} - \dfrac{c^3 - a^3}{c - a} = \dfrac{125 + 64}{5 + 4} - \dfrac{27 - 1}{3 - 1} = \dfrac{189}{9} - \dfrac{26}{2} = 21 - 13 = 8$.

Examples—2.

If $a = 1$, $b = 2$, $c = 3$, $d = 4$, $e = 5$, $f = 0$, find the numerical values of the following expressions.

1. $a^2 + b^2 + c^2 + d^2 + e^2 + f^2$.

2. $e^2 - d^2 + c^2 - b^2 + a^2$.

3. $abc^2 + bcd^2 - dea^2 + f^3$.

4. $c^3 - 2c^2 + 4c - 13$.

5. $a^3 + 3a^2 b + 3ab^2 + b^3$.

6. $e^4 - 4e^3 b + 6e^2 b^2 - 4eb^3 + b^4$.

7. $\dfrac{b^2 c^2}{4a} + \dfrac{de}{b^2} - \dfrac{32}{b^4}$.

8. $\dfrac{2e + 2}{e - 3} + \dfrac{3e - 9}{e - 2} + \dfrac{e^2 - 1}{e + 3}$.

9. $\dfrac{a^2 + b^2}{e} + \dfrac{c^2 + e^2}{b} + \dfrac{e^2 - d^2}{c}$.

10. $\dfrac{8a^2 + 3b^2}{a^2 + b^2} + \dfrac{4c^2 + 6b^2}{c^2 - b^2} - \dfrac{c^2 + d^2}{e^2}$.

11. $\dfrac{28}{a^2 + b^2 + c^2} + \dfrac{12}{d^2 - c^2 - b^2} + \dfrac{4}{a^2 + e^2 - c^2 - d^2}$.

12. $\dfrac{a^4 + 4a^3 b + 6a^2 b^2 + 4ab^3 + b^4}{a^3 + 3a^2 b + 3ab^2 + b^3}$.

13. $\dfrac{d^c}{b^a}$.

14. $\dfrac{e^a + b^a}{c^b - b^c}$.

III. Remaining Signs—Brackets.

23. The sign $>$ stands for *is greater than*, and the sign $<$ denotes *is less than*. Thus $a > b$ denotes that the quantity a is greater than the quantity b, and $b < a$ denotes that the quantity b is less than the quantity a. In this sign the opening is always turned toward the greater quantity.

24. The sign $\therefore$ denotes *then* or *therefore;* the sign $\because$ denotes *since* or *because*.

25. The *square root* of a quantity is that quantity whose *square* or *second power* is equal to the given quantity.

The *cube, fourth*, &c. *root* of a given quantity is that quantity whose cube, fourth, &c. power is equal to the given quantity. Thus since $49 = 7^2$, the square root of 49 is 7; also the square root of a^2 is a. In like manner, since $125 = 5^3$, the cube root of 125 is 5; and so if $a = c^3$, the cube root of a is c.

26. The symbol used to denote a root is $\sqrt{}$ (a corruption of r, the first letter of the word *radix*), which with the proper number as index on the left side of it, a little above, is set before the quantity whose root is expressed.

Thus $\sqrt[2]{a^2} = a$, $\sqrt[3]{64} = 4$, $\sqrt[5]{3125} = 5$, $\sqrt[6]{1} = 1$, $\sqrt[7]{1} = 1$, &c. The index, however, is generally omitted in denoting the *square* root; thus $\sqrt{a}$ is written instead of $\sqrt[2]{a}$.

Examples—3.

1. $\sqrt{4} + 2\sqrt{25} + 3\sqrt{49} - \sqrt{64} = 25$.
2. $3\sqrt{16} - 4\sqrt{36} + 2\sqrt{9} - \sqrt{81} = -15$.
3. $\sqrt[3]{8} + 2\sqrt[3]{125} - 4\sqrt[3]{1} + \sqrt[3]{64} = 12$.
4. $\sqrt[4]{1} + 3\sqrt[4]{16} - 2\sqrt[5]{32} + 3\sqrt[5]{1} = 6$.

If $a = 25$, $b = 9$, $c = 4$, $d = 1$, then

5. $\sqrt{a} + 2\sqrt{b} + 3\sqrt{c} + 4\sqrt{d} = 21$.

Explain the signs $>$ $<$ $\therefore$ $\because$ Square root of a quantity? Cube root? The symbol used to denote a root.

6. $\sqrt{4a} + \sqrt{9b} + \sqrt{16c} - \sqrt{25d} = 22.$

7. $3\sqrt{a} + 2\sqrt{4b} - 4\sqrt{9c} + \sqrt{16d} = 7.$

8. $\sqrt[3]{5a} + 2\sqrt[3]{3b} - \sqrt[3]{2c} + 4\sqrt[3]{d} = 13.$

9. $\sqrt{a^2} - 2\sqrt[3]{b^3} + 3\sqrt[4]{c^4} - 4\sqrt[5]{d} = 15.$

10. $\sqrt{bc} + 3\sqrt{acd} - 4\sqrt{b^2d} + \sqrt{c^2d^2} = 4.$

27. $\sqrt{\dfrac{a}{b}}$ means that the square root of the *fraction* $\dfrac{a}{b}$ is to be taken; but $\dfrac{\sqrt{a}}{b}$ means that the square root of a is to be divided by b.

Examples.

1. What is the difference between $2\sqrt{x}$ and $2 + \sqrt{x}$, when x is 100? Ans. 8.

2. What is the difference between $3\sqrt{x}$, and $\sqrt[3]{x}$, when x is 64? Ans. 20.

3. What is the difference between $\sqrt{a+b}$ and $\sqrt{a} + b$, when a stands for 1, and b for 8? Ans. 6.

4. What is the difference between $\sqrt{\dfrac{a}{b}}$ and $\dfrac{\sqrt{a}}{b}$, when a stands for 16 and b for 4? Ans. 1.

5. What is the difference between $\sqrt{a} + \sqrt{b}$ and $\sqrt{a+b}$, when $a = 16$ and $b = 9$? Ans. 2.

28. *Brackets*, ( ), { }, [ ], are employed to show that all the quantities within them are to be treated as though forming but one quantity. It is of great importance to notice carefully the effect of using them.

Thus $a - (b - c)$ is not the same as $a - b - c$; for, in this last, both b and c are subtracted, whereas in the former it is only the quantity $b - c$ which is subtracted.

Hence, if $a = 4, b = 3, c = 1$, we have

$a - b - c = 4 - 3 - 1 = 0, a - (b - c) = 4 - 2 = 2;$

$2a - 3b + 2c = 8 - 9 + 2 = 1, 2a - (3b + 2c) = 8 - 11 = -3,$

$2a + b - c = 8 + 3 - 1 = 10, 2(a + b) - c = 14 - 1 = 13,$

$2(a + b - c) = 12.$

If we wish to denote that the sum of a and b is to be multiplied by c, we write $(a+b) \times c$ or $\{a+b\} \times c$, or simply $(a+b)c$ or $\{a+b\}c$; here we mean that the whole of $a+b$ is to be multiplied by c. Now if the brackets were omitted we would have $a + bc$, which denotes that b *only* is to be multiplied by c and the result added to a. Similarly $(a + b - c)d$ denotes that the result expressed by $a + b - c$ is to be multiplied by d.

So also $(a - b + c) \times (d + e)$ denotes that the result expressed by $a - b + c$ is to be multiplied by the result expressed by $d + e$. This may also be denoted briefly thus, $(a - b + c)(d + e)$; just as $a \times b$ is shortened into ab.

So also $\sqrt{(a+b+c)}$ stands for the square root of the result expressed by $a+b+c$.

So also $\sqrt{(a+b+c)}$ denotes that we are to obtain the result expressed by $a+b+c$, and then take the square root of this result.

So also $(ab)^2$ denotes $ab \times ab$; and $(ab)^3$ denotes
$$ab \times ab \times ab.$$

So also $(a+b-c) \div (d+e)$ denotes that the result expressed by $a + b - c$ is to be divided by the result expressed by $d + e$.

29. Sometimes instead of using brackets a line is drawn over the numbers which are to be treated as forming one number. Thus $\overline{a-b+c} \times \overline{d+e}$ is used with the same meaning as $(a-b+c)\times(d+e)$. A line used for this purpose is called a *vinculum*. So also $(a+b-c)\div(d+e)$ may be denoted thus, $\dfrac{a+b-c}{d+e}$; and here the line between $a+b-c$ and $d+e$ is really a *vinculum* used in a particular sense.

Thus, too, a vinculum from the top of a radical sign is frequently used, and $\sqrt{a+b+c}$ has the same meaning as $\sqrt{(a+b+c)}$.

30. We have now explained most of the signs used in Algebra. It is well to observe that the word *sign* is applied specially to the two signs $+$ and $-$. Thus the expressions "changing the *signs*," "like signs," and "unlike signs" refer exclusively to $+$ and $-$.

31. We shall now give some more examples of finding the numerical values of expressions.

Suppose $a=1$, $b=2$, $c=3$, $d=5$, $e=8$. Then

$\sqrt{(2b+4c)} = \sqrt{(4+12)} = \sqrt{(16)} = 4$.

$\sqrt[3]{(4c-2b)} = \sqrt[3]{(12-4)} = \sqrt[3]{(8)} = 2$.

$e\sqrt{(2b+4c)} - (2d-b)\sqrt[3]{(4c-2b)} = 8\times 4 - 8\times 2 = 32 - 16 = 16$.

$\sqrt{\{(e-b)(2e-5b)\}} = \sqrt{\{(8-2)(16-10)\}} = \sqrt{(6\times 6)} = 6$.

$\{(e-d)(b+c) - (d-c)(c+a)\}(a+d) = \{3\times 5 - 2\times 4\}6$

$\qquad\qquad\qquad\qquad\qquad = 7\times 6 = 42$.

$\sqrt[3]{(c^3+3c^2b+3cb^2+b^3)} \div \sqrt{(a^2+b^2-2ab)}$

$\qquad = \sqrt[3]{(27+54+36+8)} \div \sqrt{(1+4-4)} = \sqrt[3]{(125)} \div 1 = 5$.

Examples—4.

If $a=1$, $b=2$, $c=3$, $d=5$, $e=8$, find the numerical values of the following expressions.

The word *Sign*, how applied?

1. $a(b+c)$. 2. $b(c+d)$. 3. $c(e-d)$.

4. $b^2(a^2+e^2-c^2)$. 5. $c^2(e^2-b^2-c^2)$. 6. $\dfrac{a^2+c^2+d^2}{a^2+b^2}$.

7. $\dfrac{9a+3d^2+e^2}{2c^2-4b^2}$. 8. $\sqrt{(3bce)}$. 9. $\sqrt{(2b+4d+5e)}$.

10. $(a+2b+3c+5e-4d)(6e-5d-4c-3b+2a)$.

11. $(a^2+b^2+c^2)(e^2-d^2-c^2)$. 12. $(3d^2-7c^2)^2$.

13. $e\sqrt{(d^2-3e)}+d\sqrt{(d^2+3e)}$.

14. $e-\{\sqrt{(e+1)}+2\}+(e-\sqrt[3]{e})\sqrt{(e-4)}$.

If $a=5$, $b=3$, $c=1$, show that the numerical values are equal.

15. Of a^3-b^3 and $(a-b)(a^2+ab+b^2)$.

16. Of b^4-c^4 and $(b+c)(b-c)(b^2+c^2)$.

17. Of $a^4+a^2b^2+b^4$ and $(a^2+ab+b^2)(a^2-ab+b^2)$.

18. Of b^4+4c^4 and $\{b^2+2(b+c)c\}\{b^2-2(b-c)c\}$.

IV. Change of the Order of Terms—Like Terms.

32. The terms in an expression which are preceded by the sign $+$ are called *positive* terms, and the terms which are preceded by the sign $-$ are called *negative* terms.

33. We must now extend the meaning and use of the sign $-$ beyond the strict application of ordinary arithmetical notions. If in the expression $a-b+c$, $a=4$, $b=7$, and $c=8$, then by our first definition of the sign $-$ we should have to subtract 7 from 4, which is impossible. In this case we subtract the 4 from the 7 and write the remainder with the sign $-$. Thus $-7+4=-(7-4)=-3$. Then

---

Positive and Negative Terms. Algebraic meaning and use of the Sign —.

CHANGE OF THE ORDER OF TERMS—LIKE TERMS. 21

we consider $-3+8$ to be the same as $8-3=5$, and 5 is the numerical value of the expression $a-b+c=7-4+8$.

34. It is then indifferent in what order the terms of an Algebraic expression be written. This is clear from the common notions of Arithmetic, and from the *convention* that $-b+a$ is the same as $a-b$. Hence, if *a term is preceded by no sign, the sign $+$ is to be understood*, and such a term is *counted with the positive terms*.

Thus, $7+8-2-3 = 8+7-2-3 = -3+8-2+7$, &c.

$a+b-c = b+a-c = b-c+a = -c+b+a$, &c.

35. Terms are said to be *like* when they do not differ at all or differ only in their numerical coefficients; otherwise they are said to be unlike. Thus a, $4a$, and $7a$ are like terms; a^2bc, $5a^2bc$, and $7a^2bc$ are like terms; $5a^2$, $5ab$, and $5b^2$ are unlike terms; $4a^4$ and bc are unlike terms.

36. An expression which contains like terms may be simplified. For example, consider the expression

$$6a-a+3b+5c-b+3c-2a.$$

This expression, by Art. 34, is equivalent to

$$6a-a-2a+3b-b+5c+3c.$$

Now $6a-a-2a=3a$. For a from $6a$ leaves $5a$; and taking $2a$ from $5a$ we have $3a$ left. Similarly $3b-b=2b$; and $5c+3c=8c$. Thus the expression may be put in the form

$$3a + 2b + 8c.$$

Again, consider the expression $a-3b-4b$. This is equal to $a-7b$. For if we have first to subtract $3b$ from any number a and then to subtract $4b$ from the remainder, we shall obtain the required result in one operation by subtract-

---

The Terms, in what order to be written. Like and unlike terms. Simplification of expressions containing like terms.

ing $7b$ from a; this follows from the common notions of Arithmetic. Thus

$$a - 3b - 4b = a - 7b.$$

37. The statement $-3b - 4b = -7b$ is explained thus: if in the course of an Algebraic operation we have to subtract $3b$ from a number and then to subtract $4b$ from the remainder, we may subtract $7b$ at once instead. It will be seen that by an easy extension of this, the expression $-7b$ has a meaning when standing by itself.

38. It may be noticed (as we have proved in Arithmetic) that it is immaterial in what order the factors of a quantity are arranged. Thus 7×5 is the same as 5×7; $2 \times 6 \times 9$ the same as $6 \times 2 \times 9$ or $9 \times 2 \times 6$, &c.; $a\,b\,c$ the same as $c\,a\,b$ or $c\,b\,a$, &c.; $6x^2a$ and ax^2 are like terms. It is usual, however, to arrange literal factors and terms as much as possible in the order of the letters of the alphabet.

39. The simplifying of expressions by collecting like terms is the essential part of the processes of Addition and Subtraction in Algebra.

Ex. 1. Group together *like* quantities, with their proper signs, from $5a - 3b$, $4a + 7b$, and $-8a - 5b$.

Ans.
$$\begin{array}{c|c} +5a & -3b \\ +4a & +7b \\ -8a & -5b \end{array}$$
Here the quantities in each column are *like*, but the two columns are *unlike*.

Ex. 2. Group together *like* quantities, with their proper signs, from

$$a^3 + 3a^2b + 3ab^2 + 2a^3 + 2b^3 + 5ab^2 - 8ac^2 - a^2b - b^3.$$

Ans.
$$\begin{array}{c|c|c|c|c} +a^3 & +3a^2b & +3ab^2 & -8ac^2 & +2b^3 \\ +2a^3 & -a^2b & +5ab^2 & & -b^3 \end{array}$$

Ex. 3. Group together *like* quantities, with their proper signs, from $2a - 3b + 7bc + b^2c - 5abc + 2xy - 3x^2 + 5b^2 +$

CHANGE OF THE ORDER OF TERMS.—LIKE TERMS. 23

$7b^2c - 9a - 2b^2 + 6b + 10a - 5x^2 - xy + x^2 + abc - 2bc + c^2 - b - 3c^2.$

Ans. $\begin{array}{l}+2a\\-9a\\+10a\end{array}\Big|\begin{array}{l}-3b\\+6b\\-b\end{array}\Big|\begin{array}{l}+7bc\\-2bc\end{array}\Big|\begin{array}{l}+b^2c\\+7b^2c\end{array}\Big|\begin{array}{l}-5abc\\+abc\end{array}\Big|\begin{array}{l}+2xy\\-xy\end{array}\Big|\begin{array}{l}-3x^2\\-5x^2\\+x^2\end{array}\Big|\begin{array}{l}+5b^2\\-2b^2\end{array}\Big|\begin{array}{l}+c^2\\-3c^2\end{array}$

40. We shall close this chapter with some more examples of the conversion of ordinary language into Algebraic language.

Ex. 1. A person makes a mixture of three sorts of wine. The second costs a dollars more per gallon than the first; and the third b dollars more per gallon than the second. There are m gallons of the first sort, n of the second, and p of the third. What is the price of the mixture, x being the price of the first sort?

Ans. $mx + n(x+a) + p(x+a+b).$

Ex. 2. Express algebraically a number of five figures a, b, c, d, e, taken in their order from left to right in the decimal system.

Ans. $10^4 \times a + 10^3 \times b + 10^2 \times c + 10d + e.$

Ex. 3. Three fountains run successively into a reservoir, the first during a hours, the second during b hours, the third during c hours; the second fountain supplies m gallons per hour more than the first, the third n gallons more than the second: how many gallons of water did the three fountains yield, x being the number of gallons per hour which the first yields?

Ans. $ax + b(x+m) + c(x+m+n).$

Ex. 4. A merchant sells a certain number of yards of cloth for a dollars per yard. A second merchant sells b more yards of the same cloth at c dollars more per yard. If x is the number of yards sold by the first, express the difference in the amounts received by the two.

Ans. $(x+b)(a+c) - ax.$

Ex. 5. A mixture is made of 4 substances, A, B, C, D. It is composed of a gallons of A, costing m dollars per gallon, of b gallons of B at n dollars a gallon, of c gallons of C at p dollars a gallon, and of d gallons of D at q dollars a gallon. Express the price of a gallon of the mixture.

Ans. $\dfrac{am + bn + cp + dq}{a + b + c + d}$.

Ex. 6. Three laborers paid at the same rate worked, the first, m days, the second n days, and the third q days. They received altogether a dollars. Express the daily wages of each.

Ans. $\dfrac{a}{m+n+q}$.

Ex. 7. A sum a produced in b years c dollars at simple interest. Express the rate per cent.

Ans. $\dfrac{100c}{ba}$.

Ex. 8. A sum a placed at simple interest amounts in n years to b dollars. What is the rate per cent.?

Ans. $\dfrac{100(b-a)}{an}$.

V. Addition.

41. It is convenient to make three cases in Addition, namely: I. When the terms are all like terms and have the same sign. II. When the terms are all like terms, but have not all the same sign. III. When the quantities to be added consist of both like and unlike terms.

42. I. To add like terms which have the same sign.

Add the numerical coefficients, prefix the common sign to the sum, and annex the common literal factors.

For example:
$$6a + 3a + 7a + 5a = 21a.$$
$$-3b^2c - 5b^2c - 10b^2c = -18b^2c.$$

43. II. To add like terms which have not all the same sign. *Add separately the positive numerical coefficients, and the negative numerical coefficients; take the difference of these two sums, prefix the sign of the greater to this difference, and annex the common literal factors.*

For example:

$7a^2 - 3a^2 + 11a^2 + a^2 - 5a^2 - 2a^2 = 19a^2 - 10a^2 = 9a^2.$

$2bc - 7bc - 3bc + 4bc + 5bc - 6bc = 11bc - 16bc = -5bc.$

44. III. To add expressions which consist of both like and unlike terms. *Add together the like terms by the rule in Case II. Affix to the sums thus obtained the unlike terms, each preceded by its proper sign.*

For example: add together

$$4a+5b-7c+3d, \quad 3a-b+2c+5d, \quad 9a-2b-c-d,$$

and $-a+3b+4c-3d+e.$

It is convenient to arrange the terms in columns, so that like terms shall stand in the same column; thus we have

$$4a+5b-7c+3d$$
$$3a-b+2c+5d$$
$$9a-2b-c-d$$
$$-a+3b+4c-3d+e$$
$$\overline{15a+5b-2c+4d+e.}$$

Here the terms $4a$, $3a$, $9a$, and $-a$ are all like terms; the sum of the positive coefficients is 16; there is one term with a negative coefficient, namely $-a$, of which the coefficient is 1. The difference of 16 and 1 is 15; so that we obtain $+15a$ from these like terms: the sign $+$ may, however, be omitted. Similarly we have $5b - b - 2b + 3b = 5b$. And so on.

45. In the following examples the terms are arranged suitably in columns.

$$x^3 + 2x^2 - 3x + 1$$
$$4x^3 + 7x^2 + x - 9$$
$$-2x^3 + x^2 - 9x + 8$$
$$-3x^3 - x^2 + 10x - 1$$
$$\overline{ 9x^2 - x - 1}$$

$$a^2 + ab + b^2 - c$$
$$3a^2 - 3ab - 7b^2$$
$$4a^2 + 5ab + 9b^2$$
$$a^2 - 3ab - 3b^2$$
$$\overline{9a^2 - c.}$$

In the first example, we have in the first column $x^3 + 4x^3 - 2x^3 - 3x^3$, that is, $5x^3 - 5x^3$, that is, nothing; this is usually expressed by saying *the terms which involve x^3 cancel each other.*

Similarly, in the second example, the terms which involve ab cancel each other; and so also do the terms which involve b^2.

Ex. Add together $a + 2b - c$, $a - 5e + 2c$, and $x + y + 3e$.

Here a and a are *like*,
$-5e$ and $+3e$
$-c$ and $+2c$
the rest are *unlike*.

$$a + 2b - c$$
$$a - 5e + 2c$$
$$3e + x + y$$
$$\text{Sum} = \overline{2a + 2b + c - 2e + x + y.}$$

Ex. Add together $3a^2 - bc$, $2b^2 - ac$, $4c^2 - ab$, and $a^2 + b^2 - c^2$.

Here $3a^2$ and a^2 are *like*,
$2b^2$ and $+b^2$
$4c^2$ and $-c^2$
the rest are *unlike*.

$$3a^2 - bc$$
$$2b^2 - ac$$
$$4c^2 - ab$$
$$a^2 + b^2 - c^2$$
$$\text{Sum} = \overline{4a^2 + 3b^2 + 3c^2 - ab - ac - bc.}$$

Ex. Add together $xy-1$, x^2+2, and y^2+3.

Here the terms are all *unlike*, except -1, $+2$, and $+3$.

$$xy-1$$
$$x^2+2$$
$$y^2+3$$
$$\text{Sum} = \overline{x^2+xy+y^2+4.}$$

46. The Rules above given for the Addition of *like* and *unlike* algebraical quantities are in no wise different from those employed in *Arithmetic*. For, suppose we have to add together 3 hundreds and 4 hundreds, we combine these *like quantities* by taking the sum of the *coefficients* 3 and 4, so as to make 7 hundreds. But if we have to add together 3 hundreds, 5 tens, and 6 units, these, being *unlike quantities*, cannot be added in the same sense, but are merely collected together in one line, 3 hundreds $+5$ tens $+6$ units, which, for convenience, is written shortly 356. It will be observed, however, that algebraical Addition involves the processes both of arithmetical Addition and Subtraction.

Examples—5.

Add together

1. $a+b$ and $a+b$.
2. $a+b$ and $a-b$.
3. $a-b$ and $a-b$.
4. $a-b+c$ and $a+b-c$.
5. $a-b+c$ and $a+b+c$.
6. $1-2m+3n$ and $3m-2n+1$.
7. $5m+3$ and $2m-4$.
8. $3xy-2x$ and $xy+6x$.
9. $4p-2q+1$ and $7-3p+q$.
10. $5ab-2bc$ and $ab+bc$.
11. $3a-2b$, $4a-5b$, $7a-11b$, $a+9b$.
12. $4x^2-3y^2$, $2x^2-5y^2$, $-x^2+y^2$, $-2x^2+4y^2$.

13. $5a+3b+c$, $3a+3b+3c$, $a+3b+5c$.

14. $3x+2y-z$, $2x-2y+2z$, $-x+2y+3z$.

15. $7a-4b+c$, $6a+3b-5c$, $-12a+4c$.

16. $x-4a+b$, $3x+2b$, $a-x-5b$.

17. $a+b-c$, $b+c-a$, $c+a-b$, $a+b-c$.

18. $a+2b+3c$, $2a-b-2c$, $b-a-c$, $c-a-b$.

19. $a-2b+3c-4d$, $3b-4c+5d-2a$, $5c-6d+3a-4b$, $7d-4a+5b-4c$.

20. x^3-4x^2+5x-3, $2x^3-7x^2-14x+5$, $-x^3+9x^2+x+8$.

21. $x^4-2x^3+3x^2$, x^3+x^2+x, $4x^4+5x^3$, $2x^2+3x-4$, $-3x^2-2x-5$.

22. $a^3-3a^2b+3ab^2-b^3$, $2a^3+5a^2b-6ab^2-7b^3$, $a^3-ab^2+2b^3$.

23. $x^3-2ax^2+a^2x+a^3$, x^3+3ax^2, $2a^3-ax^2-2x^3$.

24. $2ab-3ax^2+2a^2x$, $12ab+10ax^2-6a^2x$, $-8ab+ax^2-5a^2x$.

25. $x^2+y^4+z^3$, $-4x^2-5z^3$, $8x^2-7y^4+10z^3$, $6y^4-6z^3$.

26. $3x^2-4xy+y^2+2x+3y-7$, $2x^2-4y^2+3x-5y+8$, $10xy+8y^2+9y$, $5x^2-6xy+3y^2+7x-7y+11$.

VI. Subtraction.

47. Suppose we have to take $5+3$ from 14. The result is the same as if we first take 5 from 14, and 3 from the remainder. This result is denoted by $14-5-3$.

That is, $14-(5+3) = 14-5-3$. The brackets meaning that the whole of the $5+3$ is to be taken from 14.

In like manner, suppose we have to take $b+c+d$ from a. The result is the same as if we first take b from a, and then take c from the remainder, and then d from that remainder; that is, the result is denoted by

$$a-b-c-d.$$

Thus

$$a-(b+c+d) = a-b-c-d.$$

We see in these cases the positive terms of the expression to be subtracted have all been changed to negative terms in the result.

48. Next suppose we have to take $5-3$ from 14. If we take 5 from 14 we get $14-5$; but we have taken too much from 14, for we had to take, not 5, but 5 diminished by 3. Hence we must increase the result by 3. The result is then denoted by $14-5+3$.

Thus

$$14-(5-3) = 14-5+3.$$

In like manner, suppose we have to take $b-c$ from a. If we take b from a, we obtain $a-b$; but we have thus taken too much from a, for we had to take, not b, but b diminished by c. Hence we must increase the result by c. Thus we obtain

$$a-b+c.$$

That is

$$a-(b-c) = a-b+c.$$

By the same reasoning

$$a-(b-c-d) = a-b+c+d.$$

Here the positive term of the expression to be subtracted is negative in the result, and the negative terms are positive.

49. Hence, we have the following rule for Subtraction:

Change the signs of all the terms in the expression to be subtracted, and then proceed as in Addition.

For example: from $4x-3y+2z$ subtract $3x-y+z$.

Change the signs of all the terms to be subtracted; thus we obtain $-3x+y-z$; then collect the terms, and simplify as in Addition. Thus

$$4x-3y+2z-3x+y-z=x-2y+z.$$

From $3x^4+5x^3-6x^2-7x+5$, take $2x^4-2x^3+5x^2-6x-7$.

Change the signs of all the terms to be subtracted, and proceed as in Addition. We thus have

$$3x^4+5x^3-6x^2-7x+5$$
$$-2x^4+2x^3-5x^2+6x+7$$
$$\overline{x^4+7x^3-11x^2-x+12.}$$

The beginner will find it best at first to go through the process fully as above; but he will soon learn to put down the result without actually changing all the signs, but merely doing it mentally.

50. We often have a single negative term to be subtracted from another term or expression. Thus, from a subtract $-c$. Here we can reason thus: Since $a=a+b-b$, if we subtract $-b$ from a, the result is $a+b$, the same as if we add $+b$ to it. Or we can apply our rule, at once considering the result to have a meaning in connection with some other parts of an algebraical operation.

EXAMPLES.

1. From $3a$	2. From $7a$	3. From a
take a	take $6a$	take a
Ans. $2a$	a	0

Rule for Subtraction.

SUBTRACTION.

4. From $3a$
   take $-a$
   Ans. $4a$

5. From $7a$
   take $-6a$
   $13a$

6. From a
   take $-a$
   $2a$

7. From $-3a$
   take a
   Ans. $-4a$

8. From $-7a$
   take $6a$
   $-13a$

9. From $-a$
   take a
   $-2a$

10. From $-3a$
    take $-a$
    Ans. $-2a$

11. From $-7a$
    take $-6a$
    $-a$

12. From $-a$
    take $-a$
    0

13. From $a+b$
    take $a-b$
    Ans. $2b$

14. From $a-b$
    take $a+b$
    $-2b$

15. From $y+ax$
    take $y-ax$
    $2ax$

16. From $3a-4b+6c$
    take $a-2b+9c$
    Ans. $2a-2b-3c$

17. From $7a-2b+4c-2$
    take $6a-6b+4c-1$
    $a+4b-1$

18. From $2a-6ab-\ ac+5$
    take $5a-8ab-2ac-1$
    Ans. $-3a+2ab+ac+6$

19. From $3xy-x^2-\ y^2+a$
    take $2xy+x^2+2y^2-b$
    $xy-2x^2-3y^2+a+b$

20. From $a^2+2ab-3c^2$
    take $2a^2-5ab-7c^2$
    Ans. $-a^2+7ab+4c^2$

21. From $5x^2-\ xy+\ y^2$
    take $-x^2+4xy+3y^2$
    $6x^2-5xy-2y^2$

22. From $8a^2+x^2-5b^2-5c^2$
    take $x^2+2b^2-5c^2$
    Ans. $8a^2-7b^2$

23. From $x^3-3x^2+6x-10$
    take x^3-4x^2+8x-9
    x^2-2x-1

24. From $a+\frac{1}{2}b+1$
    take $\frac{1}{2}a+b+\frac{1}{2}$
    Ans. $\frac{1}{2}a-\frac{1}{2}b+\frac{1}{2}$

25. From $\frac{2}{3}x^2-\frac{5}{4}xy+\frac{3}{2}y^2$
    take $-\frac{1}{3}x^2-\frac{1}{4}xy-\frac{1}{2}y^2$
    $x^2-xy+2y^2$

Examples—6.

1. From $7a+14b$ subtract $4a+10b$.
2. From $6a-2b-c$ subtract $2a-2b-3c$.
3. From $3a-2b+3c$ subtract $2a-7b-c-d$.
4. From $7x^2-8x-1$ subtract $5x^2-6x+3$.
5. From $4x^4-3x^3-2x^2-7x+9$
   subtract $x^4-2x^3-2x^2+7x-9$.
6. From $2x^2-2ax+3a^2$ subtract x^2-ax+a^2.
7. From $x^2-3xy-y^2+yz-2z^2$
   subtract $x^2+2xy+5xz-3y^2-2z^2$.
8. From $5x^2+6xy-12xz-4y^2-7yz-5z^2$
   subtract $2x^2-7xy+4xz-3y^2+6yz-5z^2$.
9. From $a^3-3a^2b+3ab^2-b^3$
   subtract $-a^3+3a^2b-3ab^2+b^3$.
10. From $7x^3-2x^2+2x+2$ subtract $4x^3-2x^2-2x-14$,
    and from the remainder subtract $2x^3-8x^2+4x+16$.

VII. Brackets.

51. On account of the extensive use of brackets in the algebraic language, it is necessary that the student should observe very carefully the rules respecting them.

Since the sign $+$ or $-$ preceding a bracket means that the whole included quantity is to be added or subtracted, if we wish to remove the bracket, we must actually perform the operation indicated by means of it; *i. e.*, we must add or subtract the quantity in question. Now when a quantity is added, the signs of its terms are not altered; but when it is subtracted, the signs of its terms are changed.

Hence,

When an expression is within a pair of brackets preceded by the sign $+$, the brackets may be removed, the signs of the included terms being unchanged.

When an expression is within a pair of brackets preceded by the sign $-$, the brackets may be removed if the sign of every term within the brackets be changed.

Thus, for example:

$$a-b+(c-d+e) = a-b+c-d+e$$
$$a-b-(c-d+e) = a-b-c+d-e.$$

Remember, that if the first term within the brackets has no sign, the $+$ sign is understood before it.

52. In particular, the student must notice such statements as the following:

$$+(-d) = -d \qquad -(-d) = +d$$
$$+(+e) = +e \qquad +(-e) = -e \qquad -(+e) = -e.$$

These are immediate consequences of what we have said of the addition and subtraction of single terms.

53. Expressions may occur with more than one pair of brackets; these may be removed in succession by the preceding rules, *beginning with the inside pair.*

Thus, for example:

$$a+\{b+(c-d)\}=a+\{b+c-d\}=a+b+c-d,$$
$$a+\{b-(c-d)\}=a+\{b-c+d\}=a+b-c+d,$$
$$a-\{b+(c-d)\}=a-\{b+c-d\}=a-b-c+d,$$
$$a-\{b-(c-d)\}=a-\{b-c+d\}=a-b+c-d.$$

Similarly,

$$a-[b-\{c-(d-e)\}]=a-[b-\{c-d+e\}]$$
$$=a-[b-c+d-e]=a-b+c-d+e.$$

It will be seen in these examples that, to prevent confusion between various pairs of brackets, we use brackets of different *shapes;* we might distinguish by using brackets of the same shape but of different *sizes.*

A vinculum is equivalent to a bracket; see Art. 30. Thus, for example:

$$a-[b-\{c-(d-\overline{e-f})\}]=a-[b-\{c-(d-e+f)\}]$$
$$=a-[b-\{c-d+e-f\}]=a-[b-c+d-e+f]$$
$$=a-b+c-d+e-f.$$

54. The beginner is recommended to remove brackets in the order shown in the preceding article, (*i.e.*) by removing first the innermost pair, next the innermost pair of those which remain, and so on. We may, however, vary the order, by removing first the outermost pair, next the outermost pair of those which remain, and so on.

Thus, for example:

$$a+\{b+(c-d)\}=a+b+(c-d)=a+b+c-d,$$

$$a+\{b-(c-d)\}=a+b-(c-d)=a+b-c+d,$$
$$a-\{b+(c-d)\}=a-b-(c-d)=a-b-c+d,$$
$$a-\{b-(c-d)\}=a-b+(c-d)=a-b+c-d.$$

Also,
$$a-[b-\{c-(d-e)\}]=a-b+\{c-(d-e)\}$$
$$=a-b+c-(d-e)=a-b+c-d+e.$$

55. It is often convenient to take up in brackets any given terms of an expression. The rules for thus introducing brackets follow immediately from those of removing brackets.

Any number of terms in an expression may be put within a pair of brackets, and the sign + placed before the bracket, the signs of the terms being unchanged.

Any number of terms in an expression may be put within a pair of brackets, and the sign − placed before the bracket, provided the sign of every term put within the brackets be changed.

In applying this rule, we shall for convenience take the sign of whatever term we choose to set as *first* term within the brackets, as the sign to be placed before the bracket.

Thus $+a-b-c$, collected in a bracket with $+a$ as *first* term, will be $+(a-b-c)$; but, with $-b$ as first term, it will be $-(b-a+c)$, and with $-c$ as first term, it will be $-(c-a+b)$; and now, if we resolve again these last two brackets, the sign $(-)$, preceding each of them, will correct the changes we have made, and the quantities will be reproduced, as at first, $-b+a-c$, $-c+a-b$.

So also we might use an *inner* bracket, and write the quantity $+\{(a-b)-c\}$, or $+\{a-(b+c)\}$, or $-\{(b-a)+c\}$, or $-\{b-(a-c)\}$, &c.

Examples—7.

Reduce to their simplest forms:

1. $(a-x)-(2x-a)-(2-2a)+(3-2x)-(1-x)$.
2. $(a^3-2a^2c+3ac^2)-(a^2c-2a^3+2ac^2)+(a^3-ac^2-a^2c)$.
3. $(2x^2-2y^2-z^2)-(3y^2+2x^2-z^2)-(3z^2-2y^2-x^2)$.
4. $(x^3+ax^2+a^2x)-(y^3-by^2+b^2y)+(z^3+cz^2+c^2z)$
   $-(x^3-y^3+z^3)+(ax^2+by^2+cz^2)-(a^2x-b^2y+c^2z)$.
5. $a^2-(b^2-c^2)-\{b^2-(c^2-a^2)\}+\{c^2-(b^2-a^2)\}$.
6. $\{2a^2-(3ab-b^2)\}-\{a^2-(4ab+b^2)\}+\{2b^2-(a^2-ab)\}$.
7. $\{x^3+y^3-(3x^2y+3xy^2)\}-\{(x^3-3x^2y)-(3xy^2-y^3)\}$.
8. $\{2x-(3y-z)\}-\{y+(2x-z)\}+\{3z-(x-2y)\}$
   $-\{2x-(y-z)\}$.
9. $1-\{1-(1-4x)\}+\{2x-(3-5x)\}-\{2-(-4+5x)\}$.
10. $\{2a-(3b+c-2d)\}-\{(2a-3b)+(c-2d)\}$
    $+\{2a-(3b+c)-2d\}-\{(2a-3b+c)-2d\}$.

Express by brackets, taking the terms (i) *two* together, (ii) *three* together:—

11. $a-2b+3c-d+2e-f$.
12. $-2b+3c-d+2e-f+a$.
13. $3c-d+2e-f+a-2b$.
14. $-d+2e-f+a-2b+3c$.
15. $2e-f+a-2b+3c-d$.
16. $-f+a-2b+3c-d+2e$

56. In Addition and Subtraction we have spoken hitherto only of numerical coefficients; but as any one of the factors of which a term is composed may be considered a coefficient, we often have to apply the rules to these literal

---

Rules for Brackets, as applied to literal coefficients.

coefficients. Thus, when any terms of a quantity contain some common factor, brackets are often employed to collect the *other* factors considered as its literal coefficients into one expression, which is set before or after the common factor.

Thus, just as $3x+2x-x=4x$, that is, $=(3+2-1)x$,

so, likewise, $ax+bx-x=(a+b-1)x$,

$2a-4ax+6ay=2a(1-2x+3y)$,

$(a+2b)x^2-(2b-c)x^2=\{(a+2b)-(2b-c)\}x^2=(a+c)x^2$.

Ex. 1. Add $(a-2p)x^2+(2c-3r)x$
$(2p+a)x^2 \quad -x$
$-(p-a)x^2 \quad -(c-1)x$
$-x^2 \quad -(c-2r)x$
Ans. $(3a-p-1)x^2 \quad -rx$

Ex. 2. From $\quad ax^2 \quad -bx^2 \quad +x$
take $\quad -px^2 \quad -qx^2 \quad +rx$
Ans. $(a+p)x^2-(b-q)x^2+(1-r)x$

Examples—8.

1. Collect coefficients in $ax^2-bx^2-cx-bx^2+cx^2-dx+cx^2-dx^2-ex$.
2. Add together $ax-by$, $x+y$, and $(a-1)x-(b+1)y$.
3. Add together $(a+c)x^2-3(a-b)xy+(b-c)y^2$, and $(b-c)x^2+2(a+b)xy+(a-b)y^2$.
4. Add together $(a+b)x+(b+c)y$ and $(a-b)x-(b-c)y$, and subtract the latter from the former.

5. Add together (i) the first two, (ii) the last two, and (iii) all four together, of $2(a+b)x+3(b+c)y$, $-3(a-b)x+2(a-c)y$, $-(2b+c)x+(a-2b)y$, and $(a-2b)x-(b+2c)y$.

6. In (5) (i) subtract the second quantity from the first, and (ii) the fourth from the third, and (iii) add the two results together.

VIII. Multiplication.

57. It is convenient to make four cases in Multiplication. I. To multiply one positive single term by another; II. To multiply a quantity consisting of two or more terms by a positive single term; III. To multiply one quantity by another when both consist of two or more terms; IV. To multiply one negative single term by another, or by a positive single term.

58. I. Suppose we have to multiply $3a$ by $4b$. The product may be written thus, $3a \times 4b$; or, since the product of any number of factors is the same in whatever order the factors may be taken, we may write it $3 \times 4 \times a \times b$; and it is therefore equal to $12ab$. Here we *multiply together the numerical coefficients* and *put the literal factors after this product*.

Thus, for example:
$$7a \times 3bc = 21abc.$$
Similarly,
$$4a \times 5b \times 3c = 60abc.$$

59. *Powers of the same number are multiplied together by adding the exponents.*

Four Cases in Multiplication. Rule for Case I. Powers of the same number, how multiplied?

Thus, $a^2 \times a^3 = a^5$; for $a^2 = aa$, and $a^3 = aaa$, $\therefore a^2 \times a^3 = aa \times aaa = aaaaa$, or a^5.

In the same manner it may be shown that $a^6 \times a^{10} = a^{16}$; and so on for other powers, always taking the *sum* of the *exponents*. To prove this *generally*, viz., that

$a^m \times a^n = a^{m+n}$, whatever positive whole-numbers m and n may stand for, we have, by definition,

$\qquad a^m = a.a.a.$ &c. to m *factors*,

and $\quad a^n = a.a.a.$ &c. to n *factors*,

$\therefore a^m \times a^n = a.a.a.$ &c. to m *factors* $\times a.a.$ &c. to n *factors*,

$\qquad = a.a.a.$ &c. to $m+n$ *factors*,

$\qquad = a^{m+n}$, by definition.

The reasoning and the rule are the same, if for a we write $a+b$, or $a+b+c$, or any other quantity; that is, the *powers* of such quantities are multiplied together by adding the *exponents* of the powers together. Thus the 2d power of $a+b$ multiplied by the 3d power of the same quantity will produce the 5th power of that quantity.

Ex. 1. $\quad 2x^2 \times 3x^3 = 2 \times 3 \times x^2 x^3 = 6x^5.$

Ex. 2. $\quad 7ax \times 2axy = 7 \times 2 \times aaxxy = 14a^2x^2y.$

Ex. 3. $\quad 5a^6b \times abc = 5a^6abbc = 5a^7b^2c.$

Ex. 4. $\quad 3x^2y^2z^2 \times 4x^2y^2z = 3 \times 4 \times x^2x^2y^2y^2z^2z = 12x^4y^4z^3.$

Ex. 5. $\quad mnx^2y \times py = mnpx^2yy = mnpx^2y^2.$

Ex. 6. $\quad 2a^m \times 3a^3 = 2 \times 3 \times a^m a^3 = 6a^{m+3}.$

Ex. 7. $\quad ax^m \times bx^n = abx^m x^n = abx^{m+n}.$

Ex. 8. $\quad ax^m \times bx^n \times cx^p = abcx^m x^n x^p = abcx^{m+n+p}.$

60. II. Suppose we have to multiply $a+b$ by 3. We have,

$\qquad 3(a+b) = a+b+a+b+a+b = 3a+3b.$

Similarly,
$$c(a+b) = ca + cb.$$

In the same manner we have,

$$3(a-b) = 3a - 3b \qquad c(a-b) = ca - cb$$

$$8a^2(b-c) = 8a^2 b - 8a^2 c.$$

Thus, to multiply an expression consisting of two or more terms by a single positive term: *Multiply each term of the expression by the single term, and put before each product the sign of the term which produced it; then collect these results to form the complete product.*

Ex. 1. $a+b-c$ multiplied by $2 = 2a+2b-2c$.

Ex. 2. $a-b+c$ .... $d = ad - bd + cd$.

Ex. 3. $ax+by$ .... $c = acx + bcy$.

Ex. 4. $ax+by-cz$ .... $2p = 2apx + 2bpy - 2cpz$.

Ex. 5. $2a+3b-4c$ .... $2x = 4ax + 6bx - 8cx$.

Ex. 6. $ax+by$ .... $ax = a^2x^2 + abxy$.

Ex. 7. $ax+by$ .... $by = abxy + b^2y^2$.

Ex. 8. $7x-4y+6$ .... $3x = 21x^2 - 12xy + 18x$.

Ex. 9. $6x^2-13x+1$ .... $5 = 30x^2 - 65x + 5$.

Ex. 10. x^2-px+q .... $px = px^3 - p^2x^2 + pqx$.

Ex. 11. $\frac{1}{2}ab + \frac{3}{2}cd$ .... $4ab = 2a^2b^2 + 6abcd$.

61. III. Let it be required to multiply $a+b$ by $c+d$; this means that $a+b$ is to be taken $c+d$ times, that is, c times *and* d times. Now $a+b$ taken c times produces, by rule of Art. 60, $ac+bc$; and $a+b$ taken d times produces, by the same rule, $ad+bd$; ∴ $a+b$ taken c times *and* d times, that is, $c+d$ times, produces $ac+bc+ad+bd$, which is the product required.

Or, if the quantities be $a+b$ and $c-d$, $a+b$ multiplied by $c-d$ means that $a+b$ is to be taken d times less than c times. Now $a+b$ taken c times produces $ac+bc$; but this is too much by d times $a+b$, that is, by $ad+bd$; ∴ $ad+bd$ is to be *subtracted* from $ac+bc$. Hence the product required is $ac+bc-ad-bd$, following the rule of Subtraction.

Or, if the quantities be $a-b$, and $c-d$, the product of these is, as in the last case, c times $a-b$ wanting d times $a-b$, that is, $ad-bd$ *subtracted* from $ac-bc$, which leaves $ac-bc-ad+bd$ (changing the *signs* in the quantity to be subtracted, according to rule).

Collecting these results, we have,

$$(a+b)(c+d) = ac+bc+ad+bd$$
$$(a+b)(c-d) = ac+bc-ad-bd$$
$$(a-b)(c-d) = ac-bc-ad+bd.$$

Considering these results, we see, for example, that corresponding to $+a$ in the multiplicand, and $+c$ in the multiplier, there is a term $+ac$ in the product; corresponding to the terms $+a$ and $-d$ there is a term $-ad$ in the product; corresponding to the terms $-b$ and $+c$, there is a term $-bc$ in the product; and corresponding to the terms $-b$ and $-d$ there is a term $+bd$ in the product.

These observations are briefly collected in the following important rule in Multiplication: *Like signs produce* $+$, *and unlike signs* $-$. This rule is called the *Rule of Signs*.

62. IV. Let it be proposed to multiply $2a$ by $-4b$, or

$-4c$ by $3a$, or $-4c$ by $-4b$. We apply the *Rule of Signs*, above established, to these single terms. Thus, we have,

$$2a \times -4b = -8ab$$
$$-4c \times 3a = -12ac$$
$$-4c \times -4b = +16bc.$$

We attach a meaning to these operations on single terms, after the same manner as in Addition and Subtraction. Thus, the statement $-4c \times -4b = +16bc$, means that if $-4c$ occur among the terms of a multiplicand, and $-4b$ among the terms of a multiplier, there will be a term $+16bc$ in the product corresponding to them.

As particular cases of examples of this sort, we have,

$$2a \times -4 = -8a, \quad 2 \times -4 = -8, \quad -2 \times -1 = +2.$$

Remark.—If several single terms are to be multiplied together the product will be $+$ or $-$, according as the number of *negative* factors is even or odd.

Thus,
$$4a \times -2b \times 3c \text{ is } -24abc$$
$$4a \times -2b \times -3c \text{ is } +24abc$$
$$4a \times -2b \times -3c \times -2d \text{ is } -48abcd.$$

63. The rules for Multiplication may now be conveniently presented thus:

To multiply single terms: *Multiply together the numerical coefficients, put the literal factors after this product, and determine the sign by the Rule of Signs.*

To multiply quantities of two or more terms: *Multiply each term of the multiplicand by each term of the multiplier, according to the rule for single terms, and the sum of these separate products will be the product required.*

The process is generally conducted as in the following examples.

Two General Rules of Multiplication.

EXAMPLES.

Ex. 1. Multiply $\quad -2a^2b^2 + \quad 5ab^3 \quad - \quad 7b^4$
$\qquad\qquad$ by $\quad -4ab$
$\qquad$ Prod. $\quad 8a^3b^3 - 20a^2b^4 + 28ab^5.$

Ex. 2. Multiply $\;2a + 3b - 4c$
$\qquad\qquad$ by $\;\;a + \;b - \;c$
Prod. by $\;\;a = 2a^2 + 3ab - 4ac$
$\quad$ by $+b = \quad\;\; +2ab + 3b^2 - 4bc$
$\quad$ by $-c = \qquad\qquad -2ac - 3bc + 4c^2$
Whole prod. $= 2a^2 + 5ab - 6ac + 3b^2 - 7bc + 4c^2.$

Ex. 3. $\;a + b\qquad\quad$ **Ex. 4.** $\;a + b\qquad\quad$ **Ex. 5.** $\;a - b$
$\qquad\;\;\;a + b\qquad\qquad\qquad\;\;\;a - b\qquad\qquad\qquad\;\;\;a - b$
$\qquad\;\;\overline{a^2 + ab}\qquad\qquad\quad\;\overline{a^2 + ab}\qquad\qquad\quad\;\overline{a^2 - ab}$
$\qquad\quad\;\; + ab + b^2\qquad\qquad\quad\;\; - ab - b^2\qquad\qquad\quad\;\; -ab + b^2$
$\qquad\;\;\overline{a^2 + 2ab + b^2.}\qquad\;\;\overline{a^2 \;\; * \;\; - b^2.}\qquad\;\;\overline{a^2 - 2ab + b^2.}$

Ex. 6. $\;x + a\qquad\quad$ **Ex. 7.** $\;x^2 + (a + b)x + ab$
$\qquad\;\;\;x + b\qquad\qquad\qquad\;\;\;x + c$
$\qquad\;\;\overline{x^2 + ax}\qquad\qquad\quad\;\overline{x^3 + (a+b)x^2 + abx}$
$\qquad\quad\;\; + bx + ab\qquad\qquad\quad\; + \quad c\,x^2 + (ac+bc)x + abc$
Ans. $\;\;\overline{x^2 + (a+b)\,x + ab}\quad\;\overline{x^3 + (a+b+c)\,x^2 + (ab+ac+bc)\,x + abc}$

Ex. 8. $\;x^3 - ax^2 + \;bx \;\;-\;\; c$
$\qquad\;\;\;x^2 + mx + \;\;n$
$\qquad\;\;\overline{x^5 - ax^4 + \;bx^3 \;\;-\; cx^2}$
$\qquad\qquad\;\; + mx^4 - amx^3 + bmx^2 - cmx$
$\qquad\qquad\qquad\quad + nx^3 - anx^2 + bnx - cn$
Ans. $\;\;x^5 - (a-m)x^4 + (b-am+n)x^3 - (c-bm+an)x^2 - (cm-bn)x - cn.$

64. We arrange the terms of the partial products so that *like terms may stand in the same column.* This enables us to collect the terms easily, in order to get the final result. With the view of bringing the like terms of the product into

---

The order of Arrangement of Terms of Multiplicand and Multiplier.

the same column, we arrange the terms of the multiplicand and multiplier in a certain order. We fix on some letter which occurs in many of the terms, and arrange the terms *according to the powers of that letter.*

Thus, taking the last example, we fix on the letter x; we put first in the multiplicand the term containing the third power of x; next we put the term which contains the next power of x; next the term which contains the first power of x; and last we put the term which does not contain x at all. The multiplicand is said now to be arranged *according to descending powers of x*. We arrange the multiplier always in the same way as the multiplicand. It would have done as well to arrange them both *according to ascending powers of x*.

Examples—9.

1. Multiply ax^2y^3 by bxy; mx^2 by $-nx^3$; $-acx$ by $-2axy$; abc by bc; $-abc$ by $-ac$; x^2y by $-xy^2$.

2. Multiply x^2-xy+y^2 by x, and a^2-ax+x^2 by $-ax$; x^2-ax+b by $-abx$; $x^3-3x^2y+3xy^2-y^3$ by xy.

3. Multiply $2a+b$ by $a+3b$, and $2a-b$ by $c-3d$.

4. Multiply $3x+2y$ by $2x+3y$, and $3ab+4b^2$ by $2ab-3b^2$.

5. Multiply x^2+3x-2 by $x+3$, and x^2-4x+3 by $x-2$.

6. Multiply a^2+2a-1 by a^2-a+1, and by a^2-3a-1.

7. Multiply $27x^3+9x^2y+3xy^2+y^3$ by $3x-y$.

8. Multiply $a^4-2a^3b+4a^2b^2-8ab^3+16b^4$ by $a+2b$.

9. Multiply $x^2+2ax+3a^2$ by $x^2-2ax+a^2$.

10. Multiply $9a^2-3ab+b^2-6a-2b+4$ by $3a+b+2$.

11. Multiply $x^2+y^2+z^2+xy-xz+yz$ by $x-y+z$.

12. Multiply a^3+2a^2+2a+1 by a^3-2a^2+2a-1.

13. Multiply $a^2+4b^2+9c^2+2ab+3ac-6bc$ by $a-2b-3c$.

14. Multiply $a^4-2a^3b+3a^2b^2-2ab^3+b^4$ by $a^2+2ab+b^2$.

15. Multiply x^2-ax+b by $x-c$, and by x^2+ax-c.

16. Multiply $1-ax+bx^2-cx^3$ by $1+x-x^2$.

IX. General Results in Multiplication.

65. N.B.—The rules for the management of *Brackets*, given in VII., apply only to the *addition* and *subtraction* of quantities so enclosed. If a collection of quantities within brackets is to be *multiplied* or *divided* by any quantity or collection of quantities, the brackets must not be struck out until the multiplication or division is actually performed. Thus $(a+b) \times (c+d)$ signifies that $a+b$ is to be taken $c+d$ times, and is obviously not the same as either $a+b(c+d)$, or $(a+b)c+d$. Again, $(a+b) \div (c+d)$ is not equivalent to either $a+b \div (c+d)$, or $(a+b) \div c+d$; but it may be written $\dfrac{a+b}{c+d}$, the line which separates the numerator and denominator serving as a vinculum to *both*.

The learner would do well to practise multiplication of quantities by means of *brackets* as early as possible.

Thus,

Ex. 1. $(a-b)(c-d) = (a-b)c - (a-b)d,$
$= ac - bc - (ad - bd),$
$= ac - bc - ad + bd.$

Ex. 2. $(x+a)(x+b) = (x+a)x + (x+a)b,$
$$= x^2 + ax + bx + ab,$$
$$= x^2 + (a+b)x + ab.$$

Ex. 3. $(x+1)(x+2)(x+3) = (x^2 + \overline{2+1}.x + 2)(x+3),$
$$= (x^2 + 3x + 2)x + (x^2 + 3x + 2)3,$$
$$= x^3 + 3x^2 + 2x + 3x^2 + 9x + 6,$$
$$= x^3 + 6x^2 + 11x + 6.$$

Ex. 4.
$(a+b-c)(a+b-c) = (a+b-c)a + (a+b-c)b - (a+b-c)c,$
$$= a^2 + ab - ac + ab + b^2 - bc - ac - bc + c^2,$$
$$= a^2 + 2ab + b^2 - 2ac - 2bc + c^2.$$

66. The student should notice some results in Multiplication, so as to be able to apply them when similar cases occur, and write down at once the corresponding products.

Ex. 3, Art. 63, gives $(a+b)(a+b)$ or $(a+b)^2$
$$= a^2 + 2ab + b^2 \text{ (i)}. \quad \text{Thus,}$$

The square of the sum of two quantities is equal to the sum of the squares of the two quantities increased by twice their product.

Ex. 5, Art. 63, gives $(a-b)(a-b)$, or $(a-b)^2$
$$= a^2 - 2ab + b^2 \text{ (ii)}. \quad \text{Thus,}$$

The square of the difference of two quantities is equal to the sum of the squares of the two quantities diminished by twice their product.

Ex. 4, Art. 63, gives $(a+b)(a-b) = a^2 - b^2$ (iii). Thus,

The product of the sum and difference of two quantities is equal to the difference of their squares.

The square of the sum of two quantities. The square of the difference of two quantities. The product of the difference of two quantities.

67. General results expressed by symbols, as in the equations (i), (ii), and (iii), are called *formulas*.

In these formulas, a and b indicate any quantities or expressions whatever.

Remark.—We may express the two formulas,

$$(a+b)^2 = a^2 + 2ab + b^2; \text{ and } (a-b)^2 = a^2 - 2ab + b^2,$$

in one formula. Thus,

$$(a \pm b)^2 = a^2 \pm 2ab + b^2,$$

where $\pm$ indicates that we may take either the sign $+$ or the sign $-$ *keeping throughout the upper sign or the lower sign.* $a \pm b$ is read thus "*a plus or minus b.*" $\pm$ is called the *double sign*.

As applications of these rules or formulas, we have,

$$(x+y)^2 = x^2 + 2xy + y^2, \ (x-2)^2 = x^2 - 4x + 4,$$

$$(2x+y)^2 = 4x^2 + 4xy + y^2,$$

$$(2ax - 3by)^2 = 4a^2x^2 - 12abxy + 9b^2y^2,$$

$$(29)^2 = (30-1)^2 = 900 - 60 + 1,$$

$$(54)^2 = (50+4)^2 = 2500 + 400 + 16 = 2916,$$

$$(x+2)(x-2) = x^2 - 4,$$

$$(2ax - 3by)(2ax + 3by) = 4a^2x^2 - 9b^2y^2,$$

$$(127)^2 - (123)^2 = (127 + 123)(127 - 123) = 250 \times 4$$

$$= 1000.$$

68. Ex. 6, Art. 63, gives

$$(x+a)(x+b) = x^2 + (a+b)x + ab \text{ (iv)},$$

where the coefficient of x is the *sum* of the two latter terms of the factors, $x+a$, $x+b$, and the last term, $+ab$, is their *product*. In like manner, we shall have,

$$(x-a)(x-b) = x^2 - (a+b)x + ab,$$

$$(x-a)(x+b) = x^2 + (b-a)x - ab,$$

Thus,

$$(x+5)(x+2)=x^2+(5+2)x+10=x^2+7x+10,$$
$$(x-5)(x+2)=x^2+(2-5)x-10=x^2-3x-10,$$
$$(x-6)(x-5)=x^2-(5+6)x+30=x^2-11x+30,$$
$$(x+2)(x-2)(x+3)(x-3)=(x^2-4)(x^2-9),$$
$$=x^4-(9+4)x^2+36=x^4-13x^2+36.$$

69. By a little ingenuity the formulas (i), (ii), (iii), and (iv), may be extensively applied to lighten the labor of Multiplication.

Suppose we require the square of $x+y+z$. Denote $x+y$ by a.

Then $x+y+z=a+z$; and by the use of (1) we have,
$$(a+z)^2=a^2+2az+z^2=(x+y)^2+2(x+y)z+z^2$$
$$=x^2+2xy+y^2+2xz+2yz+z^2.$$

Thus, $(x+y+z)^2=x^2+y^2+z^2+2xy+2yz+2xz.$

Suppose we require the square of $p-q+r-s$. Denote $p-q$ by a, and $r-s$ by b; then $p-q+r-s=a+b$.

By the use of (i) we have,
$$(a+b)^2=a^2+2ab+b^2=(p-q)^2+2(p-q)(r-s)+(r-s)^2.$$

Then by the use of (ii) we express $(p-q)^2$ and $(r-s)^2$.

Thus, $(p-q+r-s)^2$
$$=p^2-2pq+q^2+2(pr-ps-qr+qs)+r^2-2rs+s^2$$
$$=p^2+q^2+r^2+s^2+2pr+2qs-2pq-2ps-2qr-2rs.$$

Suppose we require the product of $p-q+r-s$ and $p-q-r+s$.

Let $p-q=a$, and $r-s=b$; then
$$p-q+r-s=a+b, \text{ and } p-q-r+s=a-b.$$

What are the Formulas (i), (ii), (iii), and (iv)?

Then by the use of (iii) we have,
$$(a+b)(a-b) = a^2 - b^2 = (p-q)^2 - (r-s)^2;$$
and by the use of (ii) we have,
$$(p-q+r-s)(p-q-r+s) = p^2 - 2pq + q^2 - (r^2 - 2rs + s^2)$$
$$= p^2 + q^2 - r^2 - s^2 - 2pq + 2rs.$$

As the student becomes more familiar with the subject, he may dispense with some of the work. Thus, in the last example, he will be able to omit that part relating to a and b, and simply put down the following process:

$$(p-q+r-s)(p-q-r+s) = (p-q+(r-s))(p-q-(r-s)).$$
$$= (p-q)^2 - (r-s)^2$$
$$= p^2 - 2pq + q^2 - (r^2 - 2rs + s^2)$$
$$= p^2 - 2pq + q^2 - r^2 + 2rs - s^2.$$

70. Ex. 1. $(ax+b+cy+d)^2 = (\overline{ax+b} + \overline{cy+d})^2,$
$$= (ax+b)^2 + (cy+d)^2 + 2(ax+b)(cy+d),$$
$$= a^2x^2 + b^2 + 2abx + c^2y^2 + d^2 + 2cdy$$
$$+ 2acxy + 2adx + 2bcy + 2bd.$$

Ex. 2. $(a^2 - ax + x^2)(a^2 - ax - x^2) =$ by (ii) $(a^2 - ax)^2 - x^4$
$$= a^4 - 2a^3x + a^2x^2 - x^4.$$

Ex. 3. $(a^2 + ax - x^2)(a^2 - ax - x^2)$
$$= \{(a^2 - x^2) + ax\}\{(a^2 - x^2) - ax\}$$
$$= (a^2 - x^2)^2 - a^2x^2 = a^4 - 2a^2x^2 + x^4 - a^2x^2$$
$$= a^4 - 3a^2x^2 + x^4.$$

N.B.—The formula here employed, $(a+b) \times (a-b) = a^2 - b^2$, may be always applied, whenever it is seen that the two quantities to be multiplied consist of terms which differ only (some of them) in sign, by taking for a those terms which are found *with their signs unaltered* in each of the given quantities, and the others for b. Thus, in Ex. 3, $a^2 - x^2$ appear in both the given quantities, whereas in the one we have $+ax$, in the other $-ax$; hence, the product required is $(a^2-x^2)^2 - a^2x^2$, as above.

Ex. 4. $(a^2+ax+x^2)(a^2-ax+x^2)=(a^2+x^2)^2-a^2x^2$
$\qquad =a^4+a^2x^2+x^4.$

Ex. 5. $(a^2+ax-x^2)(a^2-ax+x^2)=a^4-(ax-x^2)^2$
$\qquad =a^4-a^2x^2+2ax^3-x^4.$

Ex. 6. $(a^2-ax+x^2)(ax+x^2-a^2)=x^4-(a^2-ax)^2$
$\qquad =x^4-a^4+2a^3x-a^2x^2.$

Ex. 7. $(a+b+c+d)(a+b-c-d)=(a+b)^2-(c+d)^2$
$\qquad =a^2+2ab+b^2-c^2-2cd-d^2.$

Ex. 8. $(a+2b-3c-d)(a-2b+3c-d)$
$\qquad =(a-d)^2-(2b-3c)^2$
$\qquad =a^2-2ad+d^2-4b^2+12bc-9c^2.$

Examples—10.

1. Write down the squares of $a-x$, $1+2x^2$, $2a^2+3$ $3x-4y$.

2. Write down the squares of $3+2x$, $2x-3y$, a^2-3ax, bx^2-cxy.

3. Write down the products of $(2a+1)\times(2a-1)$, $(3ax+b)\times(3ax-b)$, $(x-1)(x+1)(x^2+1)$.

4. Write down the products of $(x+3)\times(x+1)$, $(x^2+4)\times(x^2-1)$, $(ab-3)(ab+2)$, $(2ax-3b)(2ax-b).$

5. Find the continued product of $x+a$, $x-a$, $x+2a$, and $x-2a$.

6. Obtain the product of $mx+2ny$, $mx-2ny$, $mx-3ny$, and $mx+3ny$.

7. Simplify $3(a-2x)^2 + 2(a-2x)(a+2x)$
   $+ (3x-a)(3x+a) - (2a-3x)^2$.

8. Multiply $x^2+2xy+2y^2$ by $x^2-2xy+2y^2$,
   and $2a^2-3ab+b^2$ by $2a^2+3ab+b^2$.

9. Multiply $a+b+c$ by $a+b-c$, by $a-b+c$,
   and by $a-b-c$.

10. Multiply $a-b+c$ by $a-b-c$, by $b+c-a$,
    and by $c-b-a$.

11. Multiply $2a+b-3c$ by $2a-b+3c$, and by $b+3c-2a$.

12. Multiply $2a-b-3c$ by $2a+b+3c$, and by $b-3c-2a$.

13. Multiply $a+b+c+d$ by $a-b+c-d$, by $a-b-c+d$,
    and by $b+c-d-a$.

14. Multiply $a-2b+3c+d$ by $a+2b-3c+d$,
    by $2b-a+3c+d$, and by $a+2b+3c-d$.

71. There are other results in Multiplication which are of less importance than the four formulas given in Art. 66, but which are deserving of attention. We place them here in order that the student may be able to refer to them when they are wanted; they can be easily verified by actual multiplication.

$$(a+b)(a^2-ab+b^2) = a^3+b^3,$$
$$(a-b)(a^2+ab+b^2) = a^3-b^3,$$
$$(a+b)^3 = (a+b)(a^2+2ab+b^2) = a^3+3a^2b+3ab^2+b^3,$$
$$(a-b)^3 = (a-b)(a^2-2ab+b^2) = a^3-3a^2b+3ab^2-b^3.$$

X. DIVISION.

72. Division, as in Arithmetic, is the inverse of Multiplication. In Division we have given the product and one of the factors, and we have to determine the other factor. The factor to be determined is the *quotient*.

73. I. The rule for the division of simple expressions follows at once from the corresponding case in Multiplication.

For example, we have,

$$4ab \times 3c = 12abc;$$

therefore $\quad \dfrac{12abc}{4ab} = 3c, \qquad \dfrac{12abc}{3c} = 4ab.$

Also $\quad 4ab \times -3c = -12abc;$

therefore $\quad \dfrac{-12abc}{4ab} = -3c, \qquad \dfrac{-12abc}{-3c} = 4ab.$

Also $\quad -4ab \times 3c = -12abc;$

therefore $\quad \dfrac{-12abc}{-4ab} = 3c, \qquad \dfrac{-12abc}{3c} = -4ab.$

Also $\quad -4ab \times -3c = 12abc;$

therefore $\quad \dfrac{12abc}{-4ab} = -3c, \qquad \dfrac{12abc}{-3c} = -4ab.$

Hence, we have the following rule for dividing one *single term* by another: *Divide respectively the coefficient and literal parts of the dividend by those of the divisor; and then, if the two quantities have like signs, prefix to the quotient the sign $+$, if different, the sign $-$.*

What is Division? Rule for dividing one single term by another.

This division is the familiar process of cancelling like factors in Arithmetic. Hence the rule may be given briefly thus:

Strike out from the dividend the factors which occur in the divisor; the rest of the dividend is the quotient, whose sign is determined by the Rule of Signs, viz.: Like signs give +, unlike signs —.

Thus,

$-7b \div b = -7$, $-ax \div -a = x$, $14ab \div 7b = 2a$, $7b \div 7b = 1$,

$abc \div ab = c$.

74. *One power of a quantity is divided by another power of the same quantity by subtracting the index of the latter from that of the former.*

For example, suppose we have to divide a^5 by a^3.

$$\frac{a^5}{a^3} = \frac{a^3 \cdot a^2}{a^3} = a^2 = a^{5-3}.$$

Or we may show the truth of the rule thus:

$$a^3 \times a^2 = a^5.$$

Therefore, $\quad \dfrac{a^5}{a^3} = a^2, \quad\quad \dfrac{a^5}{a^2} = a^3.$

And generally, if m and n be positive integers, and $m > n$,

$$a^m \div a^n = a^{m-n}.$$

Similarly,

$$\frac{6a^4b^5}{3a^2b^3} = 2a^2b^2, \qquad \frac{x^3y^2z^3}{xyz} = x^2yz^2.$$

$$\frac{5a^4b^3c^5}{a^2bc^2} = 5a^3b^2c^3, \qquad \frac{a^m b^n}{a^p b^q} = a^{m-p}b^{n-q}.$$

Division of one power of a quantity by another power of the same quantity.

$$\frac{(a+b)^5}{(a+b)^3}=(a+b)^2, \quad \frac{(c-d)^7}{(c-d)^3}=(c-d)^4.$$

75. It may happen that the factors of the divisor do not occur in the dividend. In this case we can only indicate the division. Thus, if $5a$ is to be divided by $3c$, the quotient is indicated by $5a \div 3c$, or by $\dfrac{5a}{3c}$.

Again, it may happen that *some* of the factors of the divisor occur in the dividend, but not *all* of them; or that a power of a quantity occurs in the dividend, and a higher power of the same quantity in the divisor. In this case the indicated quotient is a fraction, which can be simplified by striking out common factors, as in Arithmetic.

Suppose, for example, $15a^2b$ is to be divided by $6bc$; we have,

$$\frac{15a^2b}{6bc}=\frac{5a^2 \times 3b}{2c \times 3b}=\frac{5a^2}{2c},$$

striking out the common factor $3b$.

Again, if $4ab^2$ is to be divided by $3cb^5$, the quotient is indicated by $\dfrac{4ab^2}{3cb^5}$. Remove the factor b^2 which occurs in both dividend and divisor,

$$\frac{4ab^2}{3cb^5}=\frac{4a}{3cb^3}.$$

76. II. To divide a quantity consisting of two or more terms by a single term:

Divide each term of the dividend by the divisor, and collect the results to form the complete quotient.

For, since $a+b-c+$ &c. *multiplied* by m produces
$$ma+mb-mc+\&c.,$$
$\therefore ma+mb-mc+$ &c. *divided* by m, gives
$$a+b-c+ \&c.$$

Hence, the rule is as above stated.

Rule for Case II.

DIVISION.

Ex. 1. $\dfrac{4a^3-3abc+a^2}{a} = \dfrac{4a^3}{a} - \dfrac{3abc}{a} + \dfrac{a^2}{a} = 4a^2 - 3bc + a.$

Ex. 2. $\dfrac{a^3x^2-5abx^3+6ax^4}{ax^2} = \dfrac{a^3x^2}{ax^2} - \dfrac{5abx^3}{ax^2} + \dfrac{6ax^4}{ax^2}$

$= a^2 - 5bx + 6x^2.$

Ex. 3. $(a+b+c) \div abc = \dfrac{a}{abc} + \dfrac{b}{abc} + \dfrac{c}{abc} = \dfrac{1}{bc} + \dfrac{1}{ac} + \dfrac{1}{ab}.$

Ex. 4. $\dfrac{a^2c^2-2abc^2+3ac^3}{-4abc^2} = -\dfrac{a^2c^2}{4abc^2} + \dfrac{2abc^2}{4abc^2} - \dfrac{3ac^3}{4abc^2}$

$= -\dfrac{a}{4b} + \dfrac{1}{2} - \dfrac{3c}{4b}.$

77. III. To divide one expression by another when the divisor consists of two or more terms, we must proceed as in the operation called Long Division in Arithmetic. The following rule may be given:

Arrange both dividend and divisor according to ascending powers of some common letter, or both according to descending powers of some common letter. Divide the first term of the dividend by the first term of the divisor, and put the result for the first term of the quotient; multiply the whole divisor by this term and subtract the product from the dividend. To the remainder join as many terms of the dividend, taken in order, as may be required, and repeat the whole operation. Continue the process until all the terms of the dividend have been taken down.

The reason for this rule is the same as that for the rule of Long Division in Arithmetic, namely, that we may break the dividend up into parts and find how often the divisor is contained in each part, and then the aggregate of these results is the complete quotient.

Rule for Case III.

78. We shall now give some examples of Division arranged in a convenient form.

Ex. 1. $1-x$) $1-2x+x^2$ ($1-x$
$\underline{1-x}$
$\underline{-x+x^2}$
$-x+x^2$

Ex. 2. $3x-4y$) $6x^3-17x^2y+16y^3$ ($2x^2-3xy-4y^2$
$\underline{6x^3-8x^2y}$
$\underline{-9x^2y+16y^3}$
$-9x^2y+12xy^2$
$\underline{-12xy^2+16y^3}$
$-12xy^2+16y^3$

Ex. 3. $a-x$) a^3-x^3 (a^2+ax+x^2
$\underline{a^3-a^2x}$
$\underline{a^2x-x^3}$
a^2x-ax^2
$\underline{ax^2-x^3}$
ax^2-x^3

Ex. 4. $a+x$) a^3+x^3 (a^2-ax+x^2
$\underline{a^3+a^2x}$
$\underline{-a^2x+x^3}$
$-a^2x-ax^2$
$\underline{ax^2+x^3}$
ax^2+x^3

Ex. 5.

$a^2-2ab+3b^2$) $3a^4-10a^3b-22a^2b^2+22ab^3+15b^4$ ($3a^2-4ab+5b^2$
$\underline{3a^4-6a^3b+9a^2b^2}$
$\underline{-4a^3b+13a^2b^2-22ab^3}$
$-4a^3b+8a^2b^2-12ab^3$
$\underline{5a^2b^2-10ab^3+15b^4}$
$5a^2b^2-10ab^3+15b^4$

Consider the last example. The dividend and divisor are both arranged according to descending powers of a. The first term in the dividend is $3a^4$, and the first term in the divisor is a^2; dividing the former by the latter we obtain $3a^2$ for the first term of the quotient. We then multiply the whole divisor by $3a^2$, and place the result so that each term comes below the term of the dividend which contains the same power of a; we subtract, and obtain $-4a^3b+13a^2b^2$; and we bring down the next term of the dividend, namely, $-22ab^3$. We divide the first term, $-4a^3b$, by the first term of the divisor, a^2; thus we obtain $-4ab$ for the next term in the quotient. We then multiply the whole divisor by $-4ab$ and place the result in order under those terms of the dividend with which we are now occupied; we subtract, and obtain $5a^2b^2-10ab^3$; and we bring down the next term of the dividend, namely, $15b^4$. We divide $5a^2b^2$ by a^2, and thus we obtain $5b^2$ for the next term in the quotient. We then multiply the whole divisor by $5b^2$, and place the terms as before; we subtract, and there is no remainder. As all the terms in the dividend have been brought down, the operation is completed; and the quotient is $3a^2-4ab+5b^2$.

It is of great importance to arrange both dividend and divisor according to the same order of some common letter; and to attend to this order in every part of the operation.

79. It may happen that the division *cannot be exactly performed*. Thus, for example, if we divide $a^2+2ab+2b^2$ by $a+b$ we shall obtain $a+b$ in the quotient, and there will *then be a remainder,* b^2. This result we place, as in Arithmetic, in the quotient over the divisor, in the form of a fraction, thus indicating that b^2 remains still to be divided by $a+b$. Thus,

$$\frac{a^2+2ab+2b^2}{a+b}=a+b+\frac{b^2}{a+b}.$$

Ex. 6. $\quad a+x)\ a^2+x^2\ (a-x+\dfrac{2x^2}{a+x}$

$$\begin{array}{r} a^2+ax \\ \hline -ax+x^2 \\ -ax-x^2 \\ \hline 2x^2 \end{array}$$

Ex. 7. $\quad a-x)\ a^2+x^2\ (a+x+\dfrac{2x^2}{a-x}$

$$\begin{array}{r} a^2-ax \\ \hline ax+\ x^2 \\ ax-\ x^2 \\ \hline 2x^2 \end{array}$$

Important principle in Division. Division with a remainder.

80. We give some more examples:

Ex. 8. $1-x$) 1 $\quad (1+x+x^2+x^3+\&c.+\dfrac{Remainder}{1-x}$

$$\dfrac{1-x}{+x}$$
$$\dfrac{+x-x^2}{+x^2}$$
$$\dfrac{+x^2-x^3}{+x^3}$$
$$\dfrac{+x^3-x^4}{+x^4} \&c.$$

Ex. 9. Divide $x^7-5x^5+7x^3+2x^2-6x-2$ by $1+2x-3x^2+x^4$.

Arrange both dividend and divisor according to descending powers of x.

x^4-3x^2+2x+1) $x^7-5x^5 \quad\quad +7x^3+2x^2-6x-2$ (x^3-2x-2
$\underline{x^7-3x^5+2x^4+\ x^3}$
$\quad\quad -2x^5-2x^4+6x^3+2x^2-6x$
$\underline{\quad\quad -2x^5\quad\quad +6x^3-4x^2-2x}$
$\quad\quad\quad\quad\quad -2x^4\quad\quad +6x^2-4x-2$
$\underline{\quad\quad\quad\quad\quad -2x^4\quad\quad +6x^2-4x-2}$

Ex. 10. Divide $64-a^6$ by $2-a$.

$2-a$) $64-a^6$ $\quad(32+16a+8a^2+4a^3+2a^4+a^5$
$\underline{64-32a}$
$\quad 32a-a^6$
$\underline{\quad 32a-16a^2}$
$\quad\quad 16a^2-a^6$
$\underline{\quad\quad 16a^2-8a^3}$
$\quad\quad\quad 8a^3-a^6$
$\underline{\quad\quad\quad 8a^3-4a^4}$
$\quad\quad\quad\quad 4a^4-a^6$
$\underline{\quad\quad\quad\quad 4a^4-2a^5}$
$\quad\quad\quad\quad\quad 2a^5-a^6$
$\underline{\quad\quad\quad\quad\quad 2a^5-a^6}$

DIVISION.   59

Ex. 11. Divide $a^3+b^3+c^3-3abc$ by $a+b+c$.

Arrange the dividend according to descending powers of a.

$$a+b+c)a^3-3abc+b^3+c^3(a^2-ab-ac+b^2-bc+c^2$$

$$\underline{a^3+a^2b+a^2c}$$
$$-a^2b-a^2c-3abc$$
$$\underline{-a^2b-ab^2-abc}$$
$$-a^2c+ab^2-2abc$$
$$\underline{-a^2c-abc-ac^2}$$
$$ab^2-abc+ac^2+b^3$$
$$\underline{ab^2+b^3+b^2c}$$
$$-abc+ac^2-b^2c$$
$$\underline{-abc-b^2c-bc^2}$$
$$ac^2+bc^2+c^3$$
$$\underline{ac^2+bc^2+c^3}$$

The above is the easier method in such a case, but the following, in which the coefficients of the different powers of a are collected in brackets, is the neater and more compendious:

$$a+(b+c)\Big)a^3-3abc+(b^3+c^3)\Big(a^2-(b+c)a+(b^2-bc+c^2)$$

$$\underline{a^3+(b+c)a^2}$$
$$-(b+c)a^2-3bca$$
$$\underline{-(b+c)a^2-(b^2+2bc+c^2)a}$$
$$+(b^2-bc+c^2)a+(b^3+c^3)$$
$$\underline{+(b^2-bc+c^2)a+(b^3+c^3)}$$

EXAMPLES—11.

Divide

1. $15x^5$ by $3x^2$.   2. $24a^6$ by $-8a^3$.   3. $18x^3y^2$ by $6x^2y$.

4. $24a^4b^3c^6$ by $-3a^2b^3c^4$.   5. $20a^5b^4x^3y^3$ by $5b^2x^2y$.

6. $4x^3 - 8x^2 + 16x$ by $4x$.   7. $3a^4 - 12a^3 + 15a^2$ by $-3a^2$.
8. $x^3y - 3x^2y^2 + 4xy^3$ by xy.
9. $-15a^3b^3 - 3a^2b^2 + 12ab$ by $-3ab$.
10. $60a^5b^3c^2 - 48a^4b^4c^3 + 36a^3b^3c^4 - 20abc^6$ by $4abc^2$.
11. $x^2 - 7x + 12$ by $x - 3$.   12. $x^2 + x - 72$ by $x + 9$.
13. $2x^3 - x^2 + 3x - 9$ by $2x - 3$.
14. $6x^3 + 14x^2 - 4x + 24$ by $2x + 6$.
15. $9x^3 + 3x^2 + x - 1$ by $3x - 1$.
16. $7x^3 - 24x^2 + 58x - 21$ by $7x - 3$.
17. $x^5 - 1$ by $x - 1$.   18. $a^2 - 2ab^2 + b^4$ by $a - b$.
19. $x^4 - 81y^4$ by $x - 3y$
20. $x^4 - 2x^3y + 2x^2y^2 - xy^3$ by $x - y$.
21. $x^5 - y^5$ by $x - y$.   22. $a^5 + 32b^5$ by $a + 2b$.
23. $2a^4 + 27ab^3 - 81b^4$ by $a + 3b$.
24. $x^5 + x^4y + x^3y^2 + x^2y^3 + xy^4 + y^5$ by $x^2 + y^2$.
25. $x^5 + 2x^4y + 3x^3y^2 - x^2y^3 - 2xy^4 - 3y^5$ by $x^2 - y^2$.
26. $x^4 - 5x^3 + 11x^2 - 12x + 6$ by $x^2 - 3x + 3$.
27. $x^4 + x^3 - 9x^2 - 16x - 4$ by $x^2 + 4x + 4$.
28. $x^4 - 13x^2 + 36$ by $x^2 + 5x + 6$.
29. $x^4 + 64$ by $x^2 + 4x + 8$.
30. $x^4 + 10x^3 + 35x^2 + 50x + 24$ by $x^2 + 5x + 4$.
31. $x^3 - (a+b+c)x^2 + (ab+ac+bc)x - abc$
    by $x^2 - (a+b)x + ab$.
32. $x^3 - (a+p)x^2 + (q+ap)x - aq$ by $x - a$.
33. $y^5 - my^4 + ny^3 - ny^2 + my - 1$ by $y - 1$.

34. $a^3-b^3+c^3+3abc$ by $a-b+c$, and $a^3-b^3-c^3-3abc$ by $a-b-c$.

35. a by $1+x$, and $1+2x$ by $1-3x$, each to four terms in the quotient.

36. 1 by $1-2x+x^2$, to four terms.

XI. Factors.

81. We shall now notice some general results in Division, in connection with those already given in Multiplication; and we shall apply some of these to find what expressions will divide a given expression, or, in other words, to *resolve algebraic expressions into their factors*.

82. For example, by the use of formula (iii) of Art. 66, we have,
$$a^4-b^4=(a^2+b^2)(a^2-b^2)=(a^2+b^2)(a+b)(a-b)$$
$$a^8-b^8=(a^4+b^4)(a^4-b^4)=(a^4+b^4)(a^2+b^2)(a+b)(a-b).$$

Hence, we see that a^8-b^8 is the product of the four factors a^4+b^4, a^2+b^2, $a+b$, and $a-b$. Thus, a^8-b^8 is divisible by any of these factors, or by the product of any two of them, or by the product of any three of them.

Again, in Art. 70, we have,
$$(a^2+ab+b^2)(a^2-ab+b^2)=(a^2+b^2)^2-(ab)^2=a^4+a^2b^2+b^4.$$

Thus, $a^4+a^2b^2+b^4$ is the product of the two factors a^2+ab+b^2 and a^2-ab+b^2, and is therefore divisible by either of them.

83. The following results in Division may be easily verified, and will enable us to write out with ease the quotients in many similar cases.
$$\frac{x-y}{x-y}=1,$$

How to resolve Algebraic quantities into their Factors.

$$\frac{x^2-y^2}{x-y}=x+y,$$

$$\frac{x^3-y^3}{x-y}=x^2+xy+y^2,$$

$$\frac{x^4-y^4}{x-y}=x^3+x^2y+xy^2+y^3.$$

Also,

$$\frac{x^2-y^2}{x+y}=x-y,$$

$$\frac{x^4-y^4}{x+y}=x^3-x^2y+xy^2-y^3,$$

$$\frac{x^6-y^6}{x+y}=x^5-x^4y+x^3y^2-x^2y^3+xy^4-y^5,$$

and so on.

Also,

$$\frac{x+y}{x+y}=1,$$

$$\frac{x^3+y^3}{x+y}=x^2-xy+y^2,$$

$$\frac{x^5+y^5}{x+y}=x^4-x^3y+x^2y^2-xy^3+y^4,$$

and so on.

The student can carry on these operations as far as he pleases, and he will thus gain confidence in the truth of the statements which we shall now make, and which are strictly demonstrated in larger works on Algebra. The following are the statements:

x^n-y^n is divisible by $x-y$ if n be *any* whole number;

x^n-y^n is divisible by $x+y$ if n be any *even* whole number;

x^n+y^n is divisible by $x+y$ if n be any *odd* whole number.

We might also put into words a statement of the forms of the quotient in the three cases; but the student will most readily learn these forms by looking at the above examples, and, if necessary, carrying the operations still farther.

We may add that $x^n + y^n$ is never divisible by $x+y$ or $x-y$, when n is an *even* whole number.

84. The student will be assisted in remembering the results of the preceding Article by noticing the simplest case in each of the four results, and referring other cases to it. For example, suppose we wish to consider whether $x^7 - y^7$ is divisible by $x-y$ or by $x+y$; the index 7 is an *odd* whole number, and the simplest case of this kind is $x-y$, which is divisible by $x-y$, but not by $x+y$; so we infer that $x^7 - y^7$ is divisible by $x-y$ and not by $x+y$. Again, take $x^8 - y^8$; the index 8 is an *even* whole number, and the simplest case of this kind is $x^2 - y^2$, which is divisible both by $x-y$ and $x+y$; so we infer that $x^8 - y^8$ is divisible both by $x-y$ and $x+y$.

Now, in every case the quotient will consist (as above, Art. 83) of terms in which the exponents of x decrease, and of y increase continually by 1; but when the divisor is $x-y$, these terms are all plus; when it is $x+y$, they are alternately $+$ and $-$.

We shall now apply these results to some examples.

Thus,

$$\frac{8a^3x^3 - 1}{2ax - 1} = 4a^2x^2 + 2ax + 1.$$

$$\frac{x^3 + 27y^3}{x + 3y} = x^2 - 3xy + 9y^2.$$

$$\frac{x^4 - 16}{x - 2} = x^3 - 2x^2 + 4x - 8.$$

Law for the exponents and signs of the quotient.

Examples—12.

Divide

1. a^2-x^2 by $a+x$, a^3-x^3 by $a-x$, and a^6-x^6 by $a+x$.

2. $9x^2-1$ by $3x-1$, $25x^2-1$ by $5x+1$, and $4x^2-9$ by $2x+3$.

3. $9m^2n^2-25$ by $3mn+5$, and $16m^4-n^4$ by $4m^2+n^2$.

4. $1+8x^3$ by $1+2x$, $27x^3-1$ by $3x-1$, and $1-16x^4$ by $1+2x$.

5. x^4-81y^4 by $x-3y$, a^5+32b^5 by $a+2b$, and $x^{18}-y^{18}$ by x^2+y^2.

6. $\tfrac{1}{8}a^3+b^3$ by $\tfrac{1}{2}a+b$, and $x^4y^4-z^4$ by $xy+z$.

7. $(a+b)^2-c^2$ by $a+b-c$, and $a^2-(b-c)^2$ by $a-b+c$.

8. $(x+y)^3+z^3$ by $x+y+z$, and $x^3-(y-z)^3$ by $x-y+z$.

85. The above results and those of (66) may also be applied to resolve algebraical quantities into their elementary factors, a process which is often required.

Ex. 1. $4x^2-y^2=(2x+y)(2x-y)$.

Ex. 2. $x^3+8=(x+2)(x^2-2x+4)$.

Ex. 3. $(2a-b)^2-(a-2b)^2=(2a-b+a-2b)(2a-b-a+2b)$
$=3(a-b)(a+b)$.

Ex. 4. $x^6-a^6=(x^3+a^3)(x^3-a^3)$
$=(x+a)(x^2-ax+a^2)(x-a)(x^2+ax+a^2)$.

Ex. 5. $(a^3-x^3)^2=\{(a-x)(a^2+ax+x^2)\}^2$
$=(a-x)^2\times(a^2+ax+x^2)^2$.

Examples—13.

Resolve into elementary factors

1. $1-4x^2$, a^2-9x^2, $9m^2-4n^2$, $25a^2x^2-4x^2$, $16x^4y^2-25x^2y^4$.

2. x^2+y^2, x^2-y^2, $1+x^2y^2$, x^4-1, $a^2xy^2-x^5y$, $2a^2b^2c-8ab^2c^3$.

3. $25x^6-a^2x^2$, $a^6-9a^4b^6$, $8x^3-27$, a^3-8b^3, $a^3x^2y+27x^2y^4$.

4. x^3+32, $a^3x^3+27x^6$, $8x^9+y^6$, $a^4b^{12}-c^8$, $a^2bc+2a^2bc^2+abc^3$.

5. $81x^4-1$, x^6-64, $x^4-2bx^3+b^2x^2$, $x^6-2a^2x^4+a^4x^2$.

6. $(3x-2)^2-(x-3)^2$, $(a+b)^2-4b^2$, $(4x+3y)^2-(3x+4y)^2$.

7. $(x^2+y^2)^2-4x^2y^2$, $c^2-(a-b)^2$, $(2a+b)^2-(2a-b)^2$.

8. $x^3+y^3+3xy\,(x+y)$, $m^3-n^3-m\,(m^2-n^2)+n(m-n)^2$,
$a^2-ab+2\,(b^2-ab)+3\,(a^2-b^2)-4\,(a-b)^2$.

9. $5\,(x^2-y^2)+3\,(x+y)^2$, $3\,(x^2-y^2)-5\,(x-y)^2$,
$(x+y)^2+2\,(x^2+xy)-3(x^2-y^2)$.

10. $2\,(a^3+a^2b+ab^2)-(a^3-b^3)$, $a^3-b^3-3ab\,(a-b)$,
$a^4-b^4+(a^2-b^2)^2-2a^4+2a^2b^2$.

86. So, too, we may often apply (68, iv) to resolve a trinomial into factors when it is of the form ax^2+bx+c. We repeat formulas (iv):

$$x^2+(a+b)x+ab=(x+a)(x+b);$$
$$x^2-(a+b)x+ab=(x-a)(x-b);$$
$$x^2+(a-b)x-ab=(x+a)(x-b).$$

Ex. 1. $x^2+7x+12=(\ x+3)(\ x+4)$.

Ex. 2. $x^2-9x+14=(\ x-2)(\ x-7)$.

Ex. 3. $x^2-5x-14=(\ x-7)(\ x+2)$.

Ex. 4. $6x^2+x-12=(3x-4)(2x+3)$.

Resolution of Trinomials into factors.

The student may notice that, if the last term of the given trinomial be *positive* (Ex. 1, 2), then the last terms of the two factors will have the same sign as the middle term of the trinomial; but if *negative* (Ex. 3, 4), they will have, one the sign $+$, the other $-$.

In Ex. 4, it is clear that the first terms of the two factors might be $6x$ and x, or $3x$ and $2x$, since the product of either of these pairs is $6x^2$, and so the last two terms might be 12 and 1, 6 and 2, or 4 and 3; it is easily seen on trial which are to be taken, that is, which serve also to produce the *middle* term of the trinomial.

Examples—14.

Resolve into elementary factors

1. x^2+6x+5, $x^2+9x+20$, x^2-5x+6, $x^2-8x+15$, x^2+8x+7, $x^2-10x+9$.

2. x^2+x-6, x^2-x-6, x^2-2x-3, $x^2+2x-15$, x^2+7x-8, x^2-8x-9.

3. $4x^2+8x+3$, $4x^2+13x+3$, $4x^2+11x-3$, $4x^2-4x-3$, $3x^2+4x-4$, $6x^2+5x-4$.

4. $12x^2-5x-2$, $12x^2-14x+2$, $12x^2-x-1$, x^2+x-12, $3x^2-2x-5$.

5. $a^2x^2-3a^2x+2a^4$, $a^3-a^2x-6ax^2$, $3a^2b+a^2b^2-2ab^3$, $12a^4+a^2x^2-x^4$.

6. $2x^3y+5x^2y^2+2xy^3$, $9x^2y^2-3xy^3-6y^4$, $6a^4x^2+a^2x-a^2$, $6b^2x^2-7bx^3-3x^4$.

87. We shall now give a few examples of multiplication and division of expressions in which factors or terms occur with letters for their exponents.

Ex. 1. Multiply $a^{2-2m}b^{2p+1}c^3$ by $a^{5m-2}b^2c$.

Ans. $a^{3m}b^{2p+3}c^4$.

Ex. 2. Multiply $x^{3p}+ax^{2p}-a^2x^p$ by $a^m x^p$.

Ans. $a^m x^{4p}+a^{m+1}x^{3p}-a^{m+2}x^{2p}$.

Ex. 3. Multiply $a^{n-1}b-a^{n-2}b^2+ab^{n-1}$ by ab.

Ans. $a^n b^2-a^{n-1}b^3+a^2 b^n$.

Ex. 4. Find the continued product of
$$a^{n+1}b^{n-1} \times c^{2p}d^n \times a^{p-1}b^{p+1} \times c^{n-p}d^p.$$

Ans. $a^{n+p}b^{n+p}c^{n+p}d^{n+p}$.

Ex. 5. Multiply a^m-2c^n by a^m-c^n.

Ans. $a^{2m}-3a^m c^n+2c^{2n}$.

Ex. 6. Divide $115a^m b^n c^{2p+q}d^{2r-1}$ by $-69a^n b^n c^{p+q}d$.

Ans. $-\tfrac{5}{3}a^{m-n}c^p d^{2r-2}$.

Ex. 7. Divide $a^m b-a^{m-1}b^2+a^{m-2}b^3-a^{m-3}b^4+a^{m-4}b^5$ by ab.

Ans. $a^{m-1}-a^{m-2}b+a^{m-3}b^2-a^{m-4}b^3+a^{m-5}b^4$.

Ex. 8. Divide $x^{m+n}+x^n y^n+x^m y^m+y^{m+n}$ by x^n+y^m.

Ans. x^m+y^n.

Ex. 9. Divide $a^{2m}-3a^m c^n+2c^{2n}$ by a^m-c^n.

Ans. a^m-2c^n.

XII. Greatest Common Divisor.

88. In Arithmetic, a whole number which divides another whole number exactly is said to be a *divisor* or *measure* of it, or to *divide* or *measure* it. A whole number which divides two or more whole numbers exactly is said to be a *common divisor* or *common measure* of them.

Divisor or Measure. Common Divisor or Measure.

In Algebra, an expression which divides another expression exactly is said to be a *divisor* or *measure* of it. An expression which divides two or more expressions exactly is said to be a *common measure* or *common divisor* of them.

NOTE.—The English use the word *measure*; the French, the words *divisor* and *divide* in the same sense. We shall use the latter, as they have been generally adopted in this country.

89. In Arithmetic, the *greatest common divisor* of two or more whole numbers is the greatest whole number which will divide them all. The expression *Greatest Common Divisor*, in Algebra, must be understood as applying, not to the *numerical* magnitude of the quantity, but to its *dimensions* only; on which account it is sometimes called the *Highest Common Divisor*.

The expression *Greatest* Common Divisor is, however, retained in accordance with established usage, and we shall use the letters G.C.D. for shortness, to indicate it.

90. The following is the rule for finding the G.C.D. of monomials:

Find by Arithmetic the G.C.D. *of the Numerical Coefficients; after this number put every letter which is common to all the monomials, giving to each letter respectively the least exponent which it has in the monomials.*

91. For example: required the G.C.D. of $16a^4b^2c$ and $20a^3b^2d$. Here the numerical coefficients are 16 and 20, and their G.C.D. is 4. The letters common to both the expressions are a and b; the least index of a is 3, and the least index of b is 2. Thus we obtain $4a^3b^2$ as the required G.C.D.

Again: required the G.C.D. of $8a^2b^3c^2x^5yz^3$, $12a^4bcx^2y^3$, and $16a^3c^3x^2y^4$. Here the numerical coefficients are 8, 12, and 16; and their G.C.D. is 4. The letters common to all the expressions are a, c, x, and y; and their least indices are respectively 2, 1, 2, and 1. Thus we obtain $4a^2cx^2y$ as the required G.C.D.

92. The following statement gives the best practical idea of what is meant by the term greatest common divisor, in Algebra, as it shows the sense of the word *greatest* here. *When two or more expressions are divided by their greatest common divisor, the quotients have no common divisor.*

Take the first example of Art. 91, and divide the expressions by their G.C.D.; the quotients are $4ac$ and $5bd$, and these quotients have no common measure.

Again, take the second example of Art. 91, and divide the expressions by their G.C.D.; the quotients are $2b^2cx^2z^2$, $3a^3by^2$, and $4ac^2y^3$, and these quotients have no common measure.

93. The idea which is supplied by the preceding Article, with the aid of the Chapter on Factors, will enable the student to determine in many cases the G.C.D. of *compound expressions*. For example: required the G.C.D. of $4a^2(a+b)^2$ and $6ab(a^2-b^2)$. Here $2a$ is the G.C.D. of the factors $4a^2$ and $6ab$; and $a+b$ is a factor of $(a+b)^2$ and of a^2-b^2, and is the only common factor. The product $2a(a+b)$ is then the G.C.D. of the given expressions.

The rule in this case is similar to that given in Art. 90:

Put down every factor common to all the expressions, giving to each factor respectively the least exponent which it has in the expressions. The product of these factors will be the Greatest Common Divisor of the expressions.

Ex. 1. The G.C.D. of $15x^4$ and $18x^2$, is $3x^2$.

Ex. 2. The G.C.D. of $36x^4y^2z^6$ and $48x^6y^5z^4$, is $12x^4y^2z^4$.

Ex. 3. The G.C.D. of $35a^2b^3x^2y^4$ and $49a^3b^4x^4y^3$, is $7a^2b^3x^2y^3$.

Ex. 4. The G.C.D. of $3ax^2-2a^2x$ and a^2x^2-3abx, is ax.

The G.C.D. of Compound Expressions.

Ex. 5. The G.C.D. of $6x^2y - 12x^2y^2 + 3xy^2$

and $4ax^2 + 4axy + 4a^2x$, is x.

Ex. 6. The G.C.D. of $6a^2x^2(a^2-x^2)$ and $4a^2x(a+x)^2$,
is $2a^2x(a+x)$.

Ex. 7. The G.C.D. of $a^2(a^2x^2 - 3ax^3 + 2x^4)$ and $x^2(a^4 - 4a^2x^2)$, that is, of $a^2x^2(a^2 - 3ax + 2x^2)$ or $a^2x^2(a-2x)(a-x)$ and $a^2x^2(a^2 - 4x^2)$, is $a^2x^2(a-2x)$.

Examples—15.

Find by inspection the G.C.D. of

1. $4x^2(a+x)^2$ and $10(a^2x-x^3)^2$.

2. $x^2(a^2-x^2)^2$ and $(a^2x+ax^2)^2$.

3. $(a^2b-ab^2)^2$ and $ab(a^2-b^2)^2$.

4. $6(x^2-1)$ and $8(x^2-3x+2)$.

5. $(x^2+x)^2$ and $x^3(x^2-x-2)$.

6. $4(x^2+a^2)$ and $6(x^2-2ax-3a^2)$.

7. $a^2(x^2+12x+11)$ and $a^2x^2-11a^2x-12a^2$.

8. $9(a^2x^2-4)$ and $12(a^2x^2+4ax+4)$.

9. $x^2-9x+14$ and $x^2-11x+28$.

10. $x^2+8x+15$ and $x^2+9x+20$.

11. $x^2+2x-120$ and $x^2-2x-80$.

12. $4(x^2-x+1)$ and $3(x^4+x^2+1)$.

13. $x^2-xy-12y^2$ and $x^2+5xy+6y^2$.

94. The G.C.D. of two polynomials cannot be generally found, however, thus by inspection. Hence, for more complex examples it is necessary to adopt another method—the same given in Arithmetic for two numbers.

95. Let there be given then two algebraic quantities of which it is required to find the G.C.D.

RULE.—*Arrange the quantities according to powers of some common letter, and divide the one of higher dimensions by the other; or, if the highest exponent happen to be the same in each, take either of them for dividend. Take now, as in Arithmetic, the remainder after this division for divisor, and the preceding divisor for dividend, and so on until there is no remainder; then the last divisor will be the* G.C.D. *of the two given quantities.*

Ex. Find the G.C.D. of $x^2-7x+10$ and $4x^3-25x^2+20x+25$

$$x^2-7x+10 \overline{)4x^3-25x^2+20x+25} (4x+3$$
$$\underline{4x^3-28x^2+40x}$$
$$3x^2-20x+25$$
$$\underline{3x^2-21x+30}$$
$$x-5 \overline{)x^2-7x+10} (x-2$$
$$\underline{x^2-5x}$$
$$-2x+10$$
$$\underline{-2x+10} \quad \text{Ans. } x-5.$$

EXAMPLES—16.

Find the G.C.D.

1. Of $3x^2+x-2$ and $3x^2+4x-4$.

2. Of $6x^2+7x-3$ and $12x^2+16x-3$.

3. Of $9x^2-25$ and $9x^2+3x-20$.

4. Of $8x^2+14x-15$ and $8x^3+30x^2+13x-30$.

5. Of $4x^2+3x-10$ and $4x^3+7x^2-3x-15$.

6. Of $2x^4+x^3-20x^2-7x+24$ and $2x^4+3x^3-13x^2-7x+15$.

Rule for the G.C.D. of Polynomials.

96. In order to prove the Rule above given, it will be necessary to show first the truth of the following statement

If a quantity c be a common divisor of a *and* b, *it will also divide the sum or difference of any multiples of* a *and* b, *as* $ma \pm nb$.

For let c be contained p times in a and q times in b; then $a = pc$, $b = qc$, and $ma \pm nb = mpc \pm nqc = (mp \pm nq)c$; hence c is contained $mp \pm nq$ times in $ma \pm nb$, and therefore c divides $am \pm nb$.

Thus, since 6 will divide 12 and 18 without remainder, it will also divide any number such as $7 \times 12 + 5 \times 18$, $11 \times 12 - 8 \times 18$, 12 (or 1×12) $+ 7 \times 18$, $5 \times 12 - 18$, &c., *i. e.*, any number found by adding or subtracting any multiples of 12 and 18.

97. *To prove the Rule for finding the Greatest Common Divisor of two quantities.*

First, let the two given quantities, denoted by a and b, have neither of them any monomial factor.

Let a be that which is not of lower dimensions than the other; and suppose a divided by b, with quotient p and remainder c; b by c, with quotient q and remainder d, &c.

```
  b ) a ( p             546 ) 672 ( 1
      pb                      546
      ─                       ───
   c ) b ( q            126 ) 546 ( 4
       qc                     504
       ──                     ───
    d ) c ( r            42 ) 126 ( 3
        rd                    126
        ──                    ───
```

Then, by (96), all the common divisors of a and b are also divisors of $a - pb$ or c, and are therefore common divisors of b and c; and conversely, all the common divisors of b and c are also divisors of $pb + c$ or a, and are therefore common divisors of a and b. Hence it is plain that b and c have precisely the *same* common divisors as a and b.

In like manner it may be shown that c and d have the same common divisors as b and c, and therefore the same as a and b.

And so we might proceed if there were more remainders, the quantities a, b, c, d, &c. getting lower and lower, yet still being such that a and b, b and c, c and d, &c. have the same common divisors.

But, if d divides c without remainder, then d is itself the greatest quantity that divides both c and d; that is, d is the *greatest* of the common divisors of c and d, and therefore is the *Greatest Common Divisor* of a and b.

Thus, in the numerical example, the common divisors of 546 and 672 are precisely the same as those of 126 and 546, and these again are the same as those of 42 and 126; but 42 is the G.C.D. of 42 and 126, and is therefore the G.C.D. of 126 and 546, and also of 546 and 672.

(See Venable's Arithmetic, Arts. 82, 83.)

98. If the original expressions contain a common factor F, which is obvious on inspection, then this factor F will be a factor of the G.C.D. We strike it out from both the quantities and apply the rule to the resulting quantities. The G.C.D. thus found must be multiplied by F to get the G.C.D. of the original quantities.

99. If either of the quantities contain a factor which is obviously not a factor of the other, this must be struck out, and the G.C.D. of the resulting quantities is the G.C.D. of the original quantities.

So, whenever we take a Remainder for a Divisor in applying the rule, we may strike out any simple factor it may contain.

100. Again, if after having thus prepared the divisor, at any step of the process we find that the first term of the dividend is not *exactly* divisible by the first of the divisor, then,

---

Other features of the process of finding the G.C.D.

in order to avoid fractions in the quotient, we may multiply the whole dividend by such a simple factor as will make its first term so divisible.

In general, *we may divide the divisor by any expression which has no factor common to the two quantities whose G.C.D. we are seeking; or we may multiply the dividend by any expression which has no factor common to the divisor.*

Ex. Find the G.C.D. of

$$2x^5 - 8x^4 + 12x^3 - 8x^2 + 2x \text{ and } 3x^5 - 6x^3 + 3x.$$

Here, striking out of the first the factor $2x$ (which is common to all its terms), and of the second the factor $3x$, we reduce the quantities to $x^4 - 4x^3 + 6x^2 - 4x + 1$ and $x^4 - 2x^2 + 1$; but as $2x$ and $3x$ have themselves a common factor x, it is plain that the original quantities have a common factor x, which these latter quantities have not; hence the G.C.D. of these, when found, must be multiplied by x to produce that of the given quantities.

$$\begin{array}{r} x^4 - 2x^2 + 1) \overline{x^4 - 4x^3 + 6x^2 - 4x + 1} (1 \\ \underline{x^4 - 2x^2 + 1} \\ -4x \underline{| -4x^3 + 8x^2 - 4x} \\ x^2 - 2x + 1 \end{array}$$

$$\begin{array}{r} x^2 - 2x + 1) \overline{x^4 - 2x^2 + 1} (x^2 + 2x + 1 \\ \underline{x^4 - 2x^3 + x^2} \\ 2x^3 - 3x^2 + 1 \\ \underline{2x^3 - 4x^2 + 2x} \\ x^2 - 2x + 1 \\ x^2 - 2x + 1 \end{array}$$

In this example, the first remainder is reduced by dividing it by $-4x$; and, the G.C.D. of these two quantities being $x^2 - 2x + 1$, that of the two given quantities will be $x\,(x^2 - 2x + 1)$ or $x^3 - 2x^2 + x$.

Ex. Find the G.C.D. of

$$6x^2y + 4xy^2 - 2y^3 \text{ and } 8x^3 + 4x^2y - 4xy^2.$$

Stripping them of their simple factors $2y$ and $4x$ (and noting that these contain the common factor 2), we have $3x^2 + 2xy - y^2$ and $2x^2 + xy - y^2$, and proceed with these quantities as follows:

$$\begin{array}{r}3x^2+2xy-y^2\\2\hphantom{xxxxxxx}\\\hline\end{array}$$

$$2x^2+xy-y^2\overline{)6x^2+4xy-2y^2}(3$$
$$6x^2+3xy-3y^2$$
$$\overline{y)xy+y^2}$$
$$x+y)2x^2+xy-y^2(2x-y$$
$$2x^2+2xy$$
$$\overline{-xy-y^2}$$
$$-xy-y^2$$

The G.C.D. then will be $2(x+y)$; it being plain that the G.C.D. of $2(3x^2+2xy-y^2)$ and $2x^2+xy-y^2$ will be the same as that of $3x^2+2xy-y^2$ and $2x^2+xy-y^2$, because the 2 introduced into the first is no factor of the second quantity.

Examples—17.

Find the G.C.D.

1. Of $15x^2-x-6$ and $9x^2-3x-2$.

2. Of $6x^2-x-2$ and $21x^3-26x^2+8x$.

3. Of $2x^3+6x^2+6x+2$ and $6x^3+6x^2-6x-6$.

4. Of $2y^3-10y^2+12y$ and $3y^4-15y^3+24y^2-24$.

5. Of $x^3-6ax^2+12a^2x-8a^3$ and $x^4-4a^2x^2$.

6. Of $2x^3+10x^2+14x+6$ and $x^3+x^2+7x+39$.

7. Of $3x^3+3x^2-15x+9$ and $3x^4+3x^3-21x^2-9x$.

8. Of $x^3+x^2y+xy^2+y^3$ and $x^4+x^3y+xy^3-y^4$.

9. Of $2a^4+a^3b-4a^2b^2-3ab^3$ and $4a^4+a^3b-2a^2b^2+ab^3$.

10. Of $3a^5+15a^4b-3a^2b^2-15a^2b^3$

and $10a^5-30a^4b-10a^2b^2+30ab^3$.

11. Of $x^4-2x^3y+2xy^3-y^4$ and $x^4-2x^3y+2x^2y^2-2xy^3+y^4$.

12. Of $x^4+6x^3+11x^2+4x-4$ and $x^4+2x^3-5x^2-12x-4$.

XIII. Least Common Multiple.

101. When one quantity *contains* another as a divisor without remainder, it is said to be a *multiple* of it; and a *common multiple* of two or more quantities is one that contains each of them without remainder.

Thus, $6x^2y$ is a common multiple of $2x^2$, $3xy$, $6x^2$, &c., and any quantity is a multiple of any of its divisors.

102. The Least Common Multiple of two or more algebraic expressions is a term not appropriate if we use it in the arithmetical sense. We must understand it to mean the quantity of lowest dimensions which is exactly divisible by these expressions. As in Arithmetic, we will use the letters L.C.M. for shortness.

103. To find the L.C.M. of *simple expressions* or *monomials*:

Find by Arithmetic the L.C.M. *of the numerical coefficients; after this number put every letter which occurs in the expressions, and give to each letter respectively the greatest exponent which it has in the expressions.*

Ex. Find the L.C.M. of $16a^4bc$ and $20a^3b^3d$. Here the L.C.M. of 16 and 20 is 80. The letters which occur in the expressions are a, b, c, d; and their greatest exponents are 4, 3, 1, and 1. The required L.C.M. is, therefore, $80a^4b^3cd$.

Meaning of Least Common Multiple in Algebra. Rule for L.C.M. of Monomials.

LEAST COMMON MULTIPLE.   77

Ex. Find the L.C.M. of $8a^2b^3c^2x^5yz^2$, $12a^4bcx^2y^3$ and $16a^3c^2x^2y^4$.

Here the L.C.M. of the numerical coefficients is 48. The letters which occur are $a, b, c, x, y,$ and z; and their greatest exponents are, respectively, 4, 3, 3, 5, 4, and 3. Thus we obtain $48a^4b^3c^2x^5y^4z^3$ as the required L.C.M.

104. We shall now show how to find the L.C.M. of two compound expressions or polynomials.

Let a and b represent the two quantities, d their G.C.D.: and let $a=pd$, $b=qd$, so that p and q will have no common factor. Then the least quantity which contains p and q will be pq, and therefore the least quantity which contains pd and qd will be pqd, which is consequently the L.C.M. required of a and b.

Since $pqd = \dfrac{pd \times qd}{d} = \dfrac{a \times b}{d}$, it appears that the L.C.M of a and b may be found by *dividing their product by their* G.C.D.; or, which is more simple in practice, *by dividing either of them by their* G.C.D., *and multiplying the quotient by the other.*

For example: required the L.C.M. of x^2-4x+3 and $4x^3-9x^2-15x+18$.

The G.C.D. is $x-3$; see Art. 95. Divide x^2-4x+3 by $x-3$; the quotient is $x-1$. Therefore the L.C.M. is $(x-1)(4x^3-9x^2-15x+18)$; and this gives, by multiplying out, $4x^4-13x^3-6x^2+33x-18$.

It is, however, often convenient to have the L.C.M. expressed in factors, rather than multiplied out. We know that the G.C.D., which is $x-3$, will divide the expression $4x^3-9x^2-15x+18$; by division we obtain the quotient. Hence the L.C.M. is

$$(x-3)(x-1)(4x^2-3x-6).$$

105. The principle of the rule in Art. 103, with the aid of

L.C.M. by Inspection.

the Chapter on Factors, will enable us in many cases to determine, by inspection, the L.C.M. of polynomial expressions; as we have only to *set down the factors which compose them, each affected with the highest exponent which it has in the expressions; and the product of these is the* L.C.M. *required.*

Ex. 1. Find the L.C.M. of $2bx$, $6abxy$, $3acx$.

Here the factors are $2bx$, $3ay$, c; and the L.C.M. is $6abcxy$.

Ex. 2. Find the L.C.M. of $2a^2(a+x)$, $4ax(a-x)$, $6x^2(a+x)$.

Here the L.C.M. of the simple factors is $12a^2x^2$, and that of the compound factors is a^2-x^2; therefore the L.C.M. required is $12a^2x^2(a^2-x^2)$.

106. *Every common multiple of two quantities A and B, is a multiple of their* L.C.M. For, let M denote the L.C.M. of A and B, and N some other multiple. Suppose that if possible when N is divided by M there is a remainder R; let q denote the quotient. Then,

$$N = Mq + R, \text{ and } R = N - Mq.$$

Now since A and B divide both M and N, they divide, also, $N - Mq$ or R. Therefore R, which from the nature of division is of *lower dimensions* than M, is a multiple of A and B less than the L.C.M. This is absurd. Therefore there can be no remainder R. That is, N is a multiple of M.

107. Hence to find the L.C.M. of several expressions, we may find the L.C.M. of two of them; then find the L.C.M. of this first L.C.M. and the third expression, and so on.

Examples—18.

Find the L.C.M.

1. Of $4a^2bc$ and $6ab^2c$; of $9x^2y$ and $12xy^3$; of axy and $a(xy-y^2)$; of $ab+ad$ and $ab-ad$.

2. Of $8a^4$, $10a^3b$, and $12a^2b^2$; of a^5, $5a^4b$, $10a^3b^2$, $10a^2b^3$, $5ab^4$, and b^5; of $9x^2$, $6ax$, $8a^2$, $36x^2$, $3ax^2$, $50a^2x$, and $24a^3$.

3. Of $2(a+b)$ and $3(a^2-b^2)$; of $4(a^2-a)$ and $6(a^2+a)$; of $6(x^2+xy)$, $8(xy-y^2)$, and $10(x^2-y^2)$.

4. Of $4(a^3-ab^2)$, $12(ab^2+b^3)$, $8(a^3-a^2b)$; and of $6(x^2y+xy^2)$, $9(x^3-xy^2)$, $4(y^3+xy^2)$.

5. Of x^2-3x-4, x^2-x-12.

6. Of x^3+5x^2+7x+2, x^2+6x+8.

7. Of $12x^2+5x-3$, $6x^3+x^2-x$.

8. Of $x^3-6x^2+11x-6$, $x^3-9x^2+26x-24$.

9. Of x^3-7x-6, $x^3+8x^2+17x+10$.

10. Of $x^4+x^3+2x^2+x+1$, x^4-1.

11. Of $4a^2b^2c$, $6ab^3c^2$, $18a^2bc^3$.

12. Of $8(a^2-b^2)$, $12(a+b)^2$, $20(a-b)^2$.

13. Of $4(a+b)$, $6(a^2-b^2)$, $8(a^3+b^3)$.

14. Of $15(a^2b-ab^2)$, $21(a^3-ab^2)$, $35(ab^2+b^3)$.

15. Of x^2-1, x^2+1, x^3-1.

16. Of x^2-1, x^2+1, x^4+1, x^8-1.

17. Of x^2-1, x^2+1, x^3-1, x^6+1.

18. Of x^2+3x+2, x^2+4x+3, x^2+5x+6.

XIV. Fractions.

108. Algebraical fractions are for the most part precisely similar, both in their nature and treatment, to common arithmetical fractions. Hence, the student will find the rules and demonstrations in the chapters on Fractions are little more than a repetition of those with which he is already familiar in Arithmetic.

109. The expression $\frac{a}{b}$, we have agreed shall denote that a is divided by b. We now say $\frac{a}{b}$ means that the unit is divided into b equal parts, a of which are taken: a is called the numerator, and b the denominator, and the expression $\frac{a}{b}$ is a fraction. (We shall show, as in Arithmetic, that a fraction does also express the quotient of the numerator divided by the denominator.)

Every integral quantity may be considered as a fraction whose denominator is 1. Thus,

$$a = \frac{a}{1}, \quad b + c = \frac{b+c}{1}.$$

110. To *multiply* a fraction by an integer: *Either multiply the numerator, or divide the denominator by the integer;* and conversely, to *divide* a fraction by an integer: *Either divide the numerator, or multiply the denominator by the integer.*

Thus, $\frac{a}{b} \times x = \frac{ax}{b}$; for in each of the fractions $\frac{a}{b}$, $\frac{ax}{b}$, the unit is divided into b equal parts, and x times as many of them are taken in the latter as in the former; hence the lat-

---

Algebraic Fractions. To multiply or divide a fraction by an integer.

ter fraction is x times the former, that is, $\dfrac{ax}{b}=\dfrac{a}{b}\times x$; and, by similar reasoning, $\dfrac{ax}{b}\div x=\dfrac{a}{b}$.

Again, $\dfrac{a}{b}\div x=\dfrac{a}{bx}$; for in each of the fractions $\dfrac{a}{b}$, $\dfrac{a}{bx}$, the same number of parts is taken, but each of the parts in the latter is $\dfrac{1}{x}$th of each in the former, since the unit in the latter case is divided into x times as many parts as in the former; hence the latter fraction is $\dfrac{1}{x}$th part of the former, that is, $\dfrac{a}{bx}=\dfrac{a}{b}\div x$; and, similarly, $\dfrac{a}{bx}\times x=\dfrac{a}{b}$.

111. If any quantity be *both* multiplied and divided by the same quantity, its value will, of course, remain unaltered. Hence, *if the numerator and denominator of a fraction be both multiplied or divided by the same quantity, its value will remain unaltered.*

Thus, $\dfrac{a}{b}=\dfrac{ax}{bx}=\dfrac{a^2}{ab}=$ &c., and $\dfrac{a^3b}{a^2bc}=\dfrac{a}{c}=\dfrac{ac}{c^2}=$ &c.

This result is of great importance, and many of the operations in Fractions depend on it.

112. To reduce an integer to a fraction with a given denominator: *Multiply it by the given denominator, and the product will be the numerator of the required fraction.*

The truth of this is evident from (110).

Thus, a expressed as a fraction with denominator x is $\dfrac{ax}{x}$; or with denominator $b-c$, is $\dfrac{ab-ac}{b-c}$.

113. Since $a=\dfrac{a}{1}$, and therefore a divided by $b=\dfrac{a}{1}\div b=\dfrac{a}{b}$ (109), it follows, as stated in (108), that a fraction represents the quotient of the numerator by the denominator. In fact we get $\frac{1}{b}$th of a units (or $a \div b$) by taking $\frac{1}{b}$th of *each* of the a units, and this is the same as a such parts of one unit which we have expressed (108) by $\frac{a}{b}$.

Thus, in Arithmetic, $\frac{1}{4}$ of \$3 is the same as $\frac{3}{4}$ of \$1.

114. The demonstrations given in the preceding Articles are based on the assumption that every letter denotes some *positive whole number*. By the *Rule of the Signs* established in Multiplication and Division, we have the following:

Since $\frac{a}{b} = \frac{ac}{bc}$, by putting -1 for c we have $\frac{a}{b} = \frac{-a}{-b}$. Hence, we may *change the signs of all the terms in both the numerator and denominator of a fraction without altering its value*.

Ex. $\frac{x^2 - 2ax - a^2}{3ax - x^2}$ is identical with $\frac{a^2 + 2ax - x^2}{x^2 - 3ax}$.

So also, $\frac{a}{-b} = +\frac{-a}{b} = -\frac{a}{b}$;

And $-\frac{a}{-b} = -\frac{-a}{b} = \frac{a}{b}$.

In like manner, by assuming that $\frac{a}{b} \times c$ is equal to $\frac{ac}{b}$, whatever be the sign of c, we obtain such results as the following:

$$\frac{a}{b} \times -1 = \frac{-a}{b} = -\frac{a}{b}, \quad \frac{a}{b} \times -2 = \frac{-2a}{b} = -\frac{2a}{b}.$$

115. If the numerator of a fraction be of *lower dimensions* than the denominator, the fraction may be considered in the light of a *proper* fraction in Arithmetic: if the numerator be of *higher dimensions* than the denominator, it may be considered in the light of an *improper* fraction, which (Art. 112) in Algebra, as in Arithmetic, may be expressed as a mixed quantity by the rule:

Divide the numerator by the denominator as far as the division is possible, and annex to the quotient a fraction having the remainder for numerator and the divisor for the denominator.

Thus,
$$\frac{24a}{7} = 3a + \frac{3a}{7}.$$

$$\frac{a^2 + 3ab}{a+b} = a + 2b - \frac{2b^2}{a+b}.$$

$$\frac{x^2 - 6x + 14}{x^2 - 3x + 4} = x + 3 + \frac{-x+2}{x^2 - 3x + 4}, \text{ or } = x + 3 - \frac{x-2}{x^2 - 3x + 4}.$$

This last step the student should particularly notice, as an example of the use of brackets, namely:

$$+(-x+2) = -(x-2).$$

Examples—19.

Express the following fractions as mixed quantities.

1. $\dfrac{25x}{7}.$ 2. $\dfrac{36ac + 4c}{9}.$ 3. $\dfrac{8a^2 + 3b}{4a}.$

4. $\dfrac{12x^2 - 5y}{6x}.$ 5. $\dfrac{x^3 + 3x + 2}{x+3}.$ 6. $\dfrac{2x^2 - 6x - 1}{x - 3}.$

7. $\dfrac{x^3 + ax^2 - 3a^2x - 3a^3}{x - 2a}.$ 8. $\dfrac{x^3 - 2x^2}{x^2 - x + 1}.$

To reduce improper fractions to whole or mixed quantities.

9. $\dfrac{x^4+1}{x-1}$. 10. $\dfrac{x^4-1}{x+1}$.

Multiply

11. $\dfrac{4a^2}{9b^2}$ by $3b$. 12. $\dfrac{8(a^2+b^2)}{9(a^2-b^2)}$ by $3(a-b)$.

13. $\dfrac{3(a-b)}{8(a^3+b^3)}$ by $4(a^2-ab+b^2)$.

14. $\dfrac{x^2}{(x^2-1)^2}$ by $x+1$.

Divide

15. $\dfrac{8x^2}{3y}$ by $2x$. 16. $\dfrac{9a^2-4b^2}{a+b}$ by $3a-2b$.

17. $\dfrac{10(a^3-b^3)}{3(a+b)}$ by $5(a^2+ab+b^2)$.

18. $\dfrac{x^6-1}{x^2+1}$ by x^2-x+1.

XV. Reduction of Fractions.

116. The result contained in Art. 110 will now be applied to the reduction of a fraction to its lowest terms, and the reduction of fractions to a common denominator.

117. Rule for reducing a fraction to its lowest terms:

Divide the numerator and denominator of the fraction by their Greatest Common Divisor.

For example: reduce $\dfrac{16a^4b^2c}{20a^2b^3d}$ to its lowest terms.

Dividing both numerator and denominator by $4a^3b^2$, which is their G.C.D., we obtain for the required result $\dfrac{4ac}{5bd}$. That is, $\dfrac{4ac}{5bd}$ is equal to $\dfrac{16a^4b^2c}{20a^3b^3d}$ (110), but it is expressed in a more simple form.

Again: reduce $\dfrac{x^2-4x+3}{4x^3-9x^2-15x+18}$ to its lowest terms.

Dividing both numerator and denominator by $x-3$, which is their G.C.D., we obtain for the required result $\dfrac{x-1}{4x^2+3x-6}$.

118. In many examples we may apply the results of the chapter on Factors, and strike out the common factors from the numerator and denominator without using the rule for finding the G.C.D.; or rather, we *may by mere inspection find the* G.C.D. (Art. 93), *and strike it out from the numerator and denominator.*

Ex. 1. $\dfrac{a^2x^2y^2}{a^2xy+axy^2} = \dfrac{a^2x^2y^2}{axy(a+y)} = \dfrac{axy}{a+y}$.

Ex. 2. $\dfrac{a^3+x^3}{a^2-x^2} = \dfrac{(a+x)(a^2-ax+x^2)}{(a+x)(a-x)} = \dfrac{a^2-ax+x^2}{a-x}$.

Ex. 3. $\dfrac{x^2+4x+3}{x^2+5x+6} = \dfrac{(x+3)(x+1)}{(x+3)(x+2)} = \dfrac{x+1}{x+2}$.

Ex. 4. $\dfrac{x^3+x^2+3x-5}{x^2-4x+3} = \dfrac{(x-1)(x^2+2x+5)}{(x-1)(x-3)} = \dfrac{x^2+2x+5}{x-3}$.

Ex. 5. $\dfrac{(a-b)^2-c^2}{a^2-(b+c)^2} = \dfrac{(a-b+c)(a-b-c)}{(a+b+c)(a-b-c)} = \dfrac{a-b+c}{a+b+c}$.

119. Rule for reducing fractions to a common denominator:

Multiply the numerator of each fraction by all the denom-

inators except its own for the numerator corresponding to that fraction; and multiply all the denominators together for a common denominator.

The truth of this rule is evident; since the numerator and denominator of each fraction are *both* multiplied by the same quantities (viz. the denominators of the other fractions), its value will not be altered, though all the fractions will now appear with the same denominator.

For example: reduce $\frac{a}{b}$, $\frac{c}{d}$, and $\frac{e}{f}$, to a common denominator.

$$\frac{a}{b} = \frac{adf}{bdf}, \quad \frac{c}{d} = \frac{cbf}{dbf}, \quad \frac{e}{f} = \frac{ebd}{fbd}.$$

Thus, $\frac{adf}{bdf}$, $\frac{cbf}{dbf}$, and $\frac{ebd}{fbd}$ are fractions of the same value, respectively, as $\frac{a}{b}$, $\frac{c}{d}$, and $\frac{e}{f}$, and they have the common denominator bdf.

We often wish to reduce fractions to their *lowest* common denominator, which the above process will not effect if there are any common factors in the denominators. It is therefore often convenient, as in Arithmetic, to use another rule.

120. Rule for reducing fractions to the lowest common denominator

Find the L.C.M. *of the denominators. This will be the Lowest Common Denominator. Then for the new numerators multiply the numerator of each of the given fractions by the quotient which is obtained by dividing the* L.C.M. *by its denominator.*

For example: reduce $\frac{a}{yz}$, $\frac{b}{zx}$, $\frac{c}{xy}$, to their lowest common denominator. The L.C.M. of the denominators is xyz; and,

REDUCTION OF FRACTIONS.

$\dfrac{a}{yz} = \dfrac{ax}{xyz}$, $\dfrac{b}{zx} = \dfrac{by}{xyz}$, $\dfrac{c}{xy} = \dfrac{cz}{xyz}$. The numerator and denominator of each fraction has been multiplied by the same quantity.

EXAMPLES—20.

Reduce the following fractions to their lowest terms.

1. $\dfrac{12a^4 b^2 x}{18a^2 b^3 y}$.

2. $\dfrac{a^2 + ab}{2ab}$.

3. $\dfrac{a^2 + ab}{a^2 - ab}$.

4. $\dfrac{10a^2 x}{5a^2 x - 15ay^2}$.

5. $\dfrac{4(a+b)^2}{5(a^2 - b^2)}$.

6. $\dfrac{a^3 + b^3}{a^2 - b^2}$.

7. $\dfrac{x^2 + 3x + 2}{x^2 + 6x + 5}$.

8. $\dfrac{x^2 + 10x + 21}{x^2 - 2x - 15}$.

9. $\dfrac{2x^2 + x - 15}{2x^2 - 19x + 35}$.

10. $\dfrac{x^2 + (a+b)x + ab}{x^2 + (a+c)x + ac}$.

11. $\dfrac{x^2 - (a+b)x + ab}{x^2 + (c-a)x - ac}$.

12. $\dfrac{3x^2 + 23x - 36}{4x^2 + 33x - 27}$.

13. $\dfrac{(x+a)^2 - (b+c)^2}{(x+b)^2 - (a+c)^2}$.

14. $\dfrac{x^2 + 5x + 6}{x^3 + x + 10}$.

15. $\dfrac{x^2 - 10x + 21}{x^3 - 46x - 21}$.

16. $\dfrac{x^2 + 9x + 20}{x^3 + 7x^2 + 14x + 8}$.

17. $\dfrac{x^4 + a^2 x^2 + a^4}{x^6 - a^6}$.

18. $\dfrac{x^{m-1} y^{2n}}{x^{2m} y^{n+1}}$.

19. $\dfrac{x^2 - 1}{ax + a}$, $\dfrac{x^4 - a^4}{x^3 - a^2 x^3}$, $\dfrac{a^6 - b^6}{a^4 - b^4}$, $\dfrac{x^3 - b^2 x}{x^2 + 2bx + b^2}$, $\dfrac{a^2 - ab + ax - bx}{a^2 + ab + ax + bx}$.

Reduce the following fractions to their lowest common denominator.

20. $\dfrac{3}{4x}$, $\dfrac{4}{6x^2}$, $\dfrac{5}{12x^3}$.

21. $\dfrac{1}{x+1}$, $\dfrac{3}{4x+4}$, $\dfrac{x}{x^2-1}$.

22. $\dfrac{a}{x-a}$, $\dfrac{x}{a-x}$, $\dfrac{a^2}{x^2-a^2}$, $\dfrac{ax}{a^2-x^2}$.

23. $\dfrac{a}{a-b}$, $\dfrac{b}{a+b}$, $\dfrac{ab}{a^2-b^2}$, $\dfrac{b^2}{a^2+b^2}$.

24. $\dfrac{1}{(x-1)}$, $\dfrac{x}{(x-1)^2}$, $\dfrac{3}{x+1}$, $\dfrac{4}{(x+1)^2}$, $\dfrac{5}{x^2-1}$.

25. $\dfrac{a}{x-a}$, $\dfrac{a+x}{x^2+ax+a^2}$, $\dfrac{ax}{x^3-a^3}$.

26. $\dfrac{1}{x^2-ax+a^2}$, $\dfrac{1}{x^2+ax+a^2}$, $\dfrac{a^2}{x^4+a^2x^2+a^4}$.

XVI. Addition and Subtraction of Fractions.

121. To add or subtract fractions: *Reduce them to a common denominator* (if necessary), *and add or subtract the numerators for a new numerator and retain the common denominator.*

Ex. 1. Add $\dfrac{a+c}{b}$ and $\dfrac{a-c}{b}$.

Here the sum is $\dfrac{a+c+a-c}{b} = \dfrac{2a}{b}$.

Ex. 2. From $\dfrac{4a-3b}{c}$ take $\dfrac{3a-4b}{c}$.

$\dfrac{4a-3b}{c} - \dfrac{3a-4b}{c} = \dfrac{4a-3b-(3a-4b)}{c} = \dfrac{4a-3b-3a+4b}{c}$

$= \dfrac{a+b}{c}$.

To add or subtract fractions.

ADDITION AND SUBTRACTION OF FRACTIONS.   89

Ex. 3. Add $\dfrac{c}{a+b}$ and $\dfrac{c}{a-b}$.

Here the common denominator will be the product of $a+b$ and $a-b$, that is, a^2-b^2.

$$\frac{c}{a+b}=\frac{c(a-b)}{a^2-b^2};\quad \frac{c}{a-b}=\frac{c(a+b)}{a^2-b^2}.$$

Therefore, $\quad \dfrac{c}{a+b}+\dfrac{c}{a-b}=\dfrac{c(a-b)+c(a+b)}{a^2-b^2}$

$$=\frac{ca-cb+ca+cb}{a^2-b^2}=\frac{2ca}{a^2-b^2}.$$

Ex. 4. From $\dfrac{a+b}{a-b}$ take $\dfrac{a-b}{a+b}$.

The common denominator is a^2-b^2.

$$\frac{a+b}{a-b}=\frac{(a+b)^2}{a^2-b^2};\quad \frac{a-b}{a+b}=\frac{(a-b)^2}{a^2-b^2}.$$

Therefore, $\quad \dfrac{a+b}{a-b}-\dfrac{a-b}{a+b}=\dfrac{(a+b)^2-(a-b)^2}{a^2-b^2}$

$$=\frac{a^2+2ab+b^2-(a^2-2ab+b^2)}{a^2-b^2}=\frac{4ab}{a^2-b^2}.$$

Ex. 5. Add $\dfrac{1+x}{1+x+x^2}+\dfrac{1-x}{1-x+x^2}$.

Ans. $\dfrac{(1+x)(1-x+x^2)+(1-x)(1+x+x^2)}{(1+x+x^2)(1-x+x^2)}=\dfrac{2}{1+x^2+x^4}.$

Ex. 6. From $\dfrac{1+x}{1+x+x^2}$ take $\dfrac{1-x}{1-x+x^2}$.

Ans. $\dfrac{(1+x)(1-x+x^2)-(1-x)(1+x+x^2)}{(1+x+x^2)(1-x+x^2)}=\dfrac{2x^3}{1+x^2+x^4}.$

122. We have sometimes to *reduce a mixed quantity to a fraction*; this is a simple case of addition or subtraction of fractions.

For example:

$$a + \frac{b}{c} = \frac{a}{1} + \frac{b}{c} = \frac{ac}{c} + \frac{b}{c} = \frac{ac+b}{c};$$

$$a - \frac{b}{c} = \frac{a}{1} - \frac{b}{c} = \frac{ac}{c} - \frac{b}{c} = \frac{ac-b}{c}.$$

Hence,

Multiply the entire part by the denominator of the fraction, add to or subtract from this the numerator of the fraction, and place the result over the denominator.

Ex. 1. $a + \dfrac{2ab}{a+b} = \dfrac{a}{1} + \dfrac{2ab}{a+b} = \dfrac{a(a+b)}{a+b} + \dfrac{2ab}{a+b} = \dfrac{a^2 + 3ab}{a+b}.$

Ex. 2. $x + 3 - \dfrac{x-2}{x^2 - 3x + 4} = \dfrac{x+3}{1} - \dfrac{x-2}{x^2 - 3x + 4}$

$= \dfrac{(x+3)(x^2 - 3x + 4)}{x^2 - 3x + 4} - \dfrac{x-2}{x^2 - 3x + 4}$

$= \dfrac{x^3 - 5x + 12 - (x-2)}{x^2 - 3x + 4} = \dfrac{x^3 - 5x + 12 - x + 2}{x^2 - 3x + 4} = \dfrac{x^3 - 6x + 14}{x^2 - 3x + 4}.$

Ex. 3. $1 + \dfrac{a^2 + b^2 - c^2}{2ab} = \dfrac{2ab + a^2 + b^2 - c^2}{2ab} = \dfrac{(a+b)^2 - c^2}{2ab}$

$= \dfrac{(a+b+c)(a+b-c)}{2ab}.$

Ex. 4. Show that $1 - \dfrac{a^2 + b^2 - c^2}{2ab} = \dfrac{(a-b+c)(b-a+c)}{2ab}.$

ADDITION AND SUBTRACTION OF FRACTIONS. 91

Ex. 5. Show that

$$a^2 - \left(\frac{a^2+b^2-c^2}{2b}\right)^2 = \frac{(a+b+c)(a+b-c)(a+c-b)(b+c-a)}{4b^2}.$$

The attention of the student is again called to the fact that the line which separates the numerator from the denominator of a fraction is a vinculum or bracket. Hence, he will apply the rules of brackets, Arts. 51 and 55.

123. Expressions may occur involving both addition and subtraction.

Ex. Find the value of $2 + \dfrac{a^2+b^2}{a^2-b^2} - \dfrac{a-b}{a+b}$.

Ans. $\dfrac{2(a^2-b^2)+(a^2+b^2)-(a-b)(a-b)}{a^2-b^2} = \dfrac{2a^2+2ab-2b^2}{a^2-b^2}.$

EXAMPLES—21.

Find the value of

1. $\dfrac{a}{2b} - \dfrac{(a-b)}{2(a+b)}$; $\dfrac{a}{2b} + \dfrac{(a+b)}{3(a-b)}$; $\dfrac{3a-4b}{2} - \dfrac{2a-b-c}{3} + \dfrac{15a-4c}{12}.$

2. $\dfrac{a^2}{a-b} - a$; $\dfrac{a}{a+b} + \dfrac{b}{a-b}$; $\dfrac{a}{a-b} - \dfrac{b}{a+b}$; $\dfrac{a-b}{a+b} + \dfrac{ab}{a^2-b^2}.$

3. $\dfrac{a}{c} - \dfrac{(ad-bc)x}{c(c+dx)}$; $\dfrac{a^2+b^2}{a^2-b^2} \pm \dfrac{a-b}{a+b}$; $\dfrac{2x^2-2xy+y^2}{x^2-xy} - \dfrac{x}{x-y}.$

4. $\dfrac{1}{2(a-x)} + \dfrac{1}{2(a+x)} + \dfrac{a}{a^2+x^2}$; $\dfrac{a-b}{ab} + \dfrac{c-a}{ac} + \dfrac{b-c}{bc}.$

5. $\dfrac{1}{2(x-1)} - \dfrac{1}{2(x+1)} - \dfrac{1}{x^2}.$ 6. $\dfrac{1}{2a+b} + \dfrac{1}{2a-b} - \dfrac{3a}{4a^2-b^2}.$

7. $\dfrac{a}{b} - \dfrac{(a^2-b^2)x}{b^2} + \dfrac{a(a^2-b^2)x^2}{b^2(b+ax)}$.   8. $\dfrac{1}{x^2} - \dfrac{1}{(x^2+1)^2} + \dfrac{x-1}{x^2+1}$.

9. $\dfrac{x^2+y^2}{x^2-y^2} - \dfrac{y}{x-y} + \dfrac{x}{x+y}$.   10. $1 - \dfrac{x-y}{x+y} + \dfrac{y^2}{x^2-y^2} + \dfrac{2xy}{x^2+y^2}$.

11. $\dfrac{x}{a^2} - \dfrac{a+x}{a(a+x)}$.   12. $2 - \dfrac{x^2-y^2}{x^2+y^2} + \dfrac{x^2+y^2}{x^2-y^2}$.

13. $\dfrac{x}{a^2} - \dfrac{a+x}{a(a-x)}$.   14. $\dfrac{x+y}{y} - \dfrac{2x}{x+y} + \dfrac{x^2y-x^2}{x^2y-y^2}$.

15. $\dfrac{x}{1-x} - \dfrac{x^2}{(1-x)^2} + \dfrac{x^3}{(1-x)^3}$.

16. $\dfrac{3}{8(1-x)} + \dfrac{1}{8(1+x)} - \dfrac{1-x}{4(1+x^2)}$.

Remark.—In the preceding examples we have combined two or more fractions in a single fraction. On the other hand, we may if we please break up a single fraction into two or more fractions. For example:

$$\dfrac{3bc - 4ac + 5ab}{abc} = \dfrac{3bc}{abc} - \dfrac{4ac}{abc} + \dfrac{5ab}{abc} = \dfrac{3}{a} - \dfrac{4}{b} + \dfrac{5}{c};$$

but the beginner must not confound $\dfrac{a}{b-c}$ with $\dfrac{a}{b} - \dfrac{a}{c}$.

124. The addition and subtraction of fractions can often be much simplified by observing closely the factors of the denominators, and avoiding unnecessary multiplications in reducing the fractions to a common denominator.

Ex. Find the value of

$$\dfrac{a}{(a-b)(a-c)} + \dfrac{b}{(b-c)(b-a)} + \dfrac{c}{(c-a)(c-b)}.$$

Here the beginner is liable to take the product of the denominators for the common denominator, and thus to render the operations laborious.

The second fraction contains the factor $b-a$ in its denominator, and this factor differs from the factor $a-b$, which occurs in the denominator of the first fraction only, in the sign of each term; and by Art. 110:

$$\frac{b}{(b-c)(b-a)} = -\frac{b}{(b-c)(a-b)}.$$

Also, in the denominator of the third fraction, by the Rule of Signs we have,

$$(c-a)(c-b) = (a-c)(b-c).$$

Hence, the given expression may be written,

$$\frac{a}{(a-b)(a-c)} - \frac{b}{(b-c)(a-b)} + \frac{c}{(a-c)(b-c)};$$

And in this form we see at once that the L.C.M. of the denominators is $(a-b)(a-c)(b-c)$.

By reducing the fractions to this lowest common denominator, we get

$$\frac{a(b-c) - b(a-c) + c(a-b)}{(a-b)(a-c)(b-c)} = \frac{ab-ac-ab+bc+ac-bc}{(a-b)(a-c)(b-c)} = 0.$$

Examples—22.

Find the value of

1. $\dfrac{a}{(x-a)(a-b)} + \dfrac{b}{(x-b)(b-a)}.$

2. $\dfrac{a^2}{(x-a)(a-b)} + \dfrac{b^2}{(x-b)(b-a)}.$

3. $\dfrac{1}{(a-b)(a-c)} + \dfrac{1}{(b-a)(b-c)}.$

4. $\dfrac{b}{(a-b)(a-c)} + \dfrac{a}{(b-a)(b-c)}.$

5. $\dfrac{1}{(a-b)(a-c)} + \dfrac{1}{(b-a)(b-c)} + \dfrac{1}{(c-a)(c-b)}.$

6. $\dfrac{1}{a(a-b)(a-c)} + \dfrac{1}{b(b-a)(b-c)} - \dfrac{1}{abc}.$

7. $\dfrac{a^2}{(a-b)(a-c)} + \dfrac{b^2}{(b-a)(b-c)} + \dfrac{c^2}{(c-a)(c-b)}.$

XVII. Multiplication of Fractions.

125. To multiply fractions together:

Multiply the numerators together for a new numerator, and the denominators for a new denominator.

Suppose that we have to multiply $\dfrac{a}{b}$ by $\dfrac{c}{d}$: let $\dfrac{a}{b} = x$, $\dfrac{c}{d} = y$; $\therefore a = bx$, $c = dy$, and $ac = bdxy$; hence (dividing each of these equals by bd), $\dfrac{ac}{bd} = xy$; but $xy = \dfrac{a}{b} \times \dfrac{c}{d}$, and $\dfrac{ac}{bd} = \dfrac{a \times c}{b \times d} = \dfrac{\text{product of numerators}}{\text{product of denominators}}$, whence the truth of the rule is manifest.

Similarly we may proceed for any number of fractions.

Ex. $\dfrac{a+b}{c+d} \times \dfrac{a-b}{c-d} \times \dfrac{3}{2} = \dfrac{3(a+b)(a-b)}{2(c+d)(c-d)} = \dfrac{3(a^2-b^2)}{2(c^2-d^2)}.$

126. The Rule of Signs (Art. 61) gives the following results in the multiplication of fractions:

MULTIPLICATION OF FRACTIONS.

$$\frac{a}{b} \times -\frac{c}{d} = \frac{a}{b} \times \frac{-c}{d} = \frac{-ac}{bd} = -\frac{ac}{bd};$$

$$-\frac{a}{b} \times \frac{c}{d} = \frac{-a}{b} \times \frac{c}{d} = \frac{-ac}{bd} = -\frac{ac}{bd};$$

$$-\frac{a}{b} \times -\frac{c}{d} = \frac{-a}{b} \times \frac{-c}{d} = \frac{ac}{bd}.$$

127. We shall now give some examples. Before multiplying the factors of the new numerator together, and the factors of the new denominator together, examine if any factor occurs in *both* the numerator and denominator; in which case *it may be struck out of both, and the result will be more simple.* Art. 116. (See method of cancelling in Arithmetic—Vulgar Fractions.)

Ex. 1. Multiply a by $\frac{b}{c}$.

$$a = \frac{a}{1};\ \frac{a}{1} \times \frac{b}{c} = \frac{ab}{c}.$$

Hence $a\frac{b}{c}$ and $\frac{ab}{c}$ are equivalent; so, for example,

$$4\frac{x}{5} = \frac{4x}{5};\ \text{and}\ \frac{1}{4}(2x-3) = \frac{2x-3}{4}.$$

Ex. 2. Multiply $\frac{x}{y}$ by $\frac{x}{y}$.

$$\frac{x}{y} \times \frac{x}{y} = \frac{x \times x}{y \times y} = \frac{x^2}{y^2};$$

thus

$$\left(\frac{x}{y}\right)^2 = \frac{x^2}{y^2}.$$

Application of the Rule of Signs. Cancellation.

Ex. 3. Multiply $\dfrac{3a}{4b}$ by $\dfrac{8c}{9a}$.

$$\dfrac{3a}{4b}\times\dfrac{8c}{9a}=\dfrac{3a\times 8c}{4b\times 9a}=\dfrac{2c\times 12a}{3b\times 12a}=\dfrac{2c}{3b}.$$

Ex. 4. Multiply $\dfrac{3a^2}{(a+b)^2}$ by $\dfrac{4(a^2-b^2)}{3ab}$.

$$\dfrac{3a^2}{(a+b)^2}\times\dfrac{4(a^2-b^2)}{3ab}=\dfrac{4a(a-b)\times 3a(a+b)}{b(a+b)\times 3a(a+b)}=\dfrac{4a(a-b)}{b(a+b)}.$$

Ex. 5. $\dfrac{a}{bx}\times\dfrac{cx}{d}=\dfrac{a}{b}\times\dfrac{c}{d}=\dfrac{ac}{bd}.$

Ex. 6. $\dfrac{5ax}{3cy}\times\dfrac{xy+y^2}{x^2-xy}=\dfrac{5a(x+y)}{3c(x-y)}=\dfrac{5ax+5ay}{3c(x-y)}.$

Ex. 7. $\dfrac{4ax}{3by}\times\dfrac{a^2-x^2}{c^2-x^2}\times\dfrac{bc+bx}{a^2-ax}=\dfrac{4x(a+x)}{3y(c-x)}=\dfrac{4ax+4x^2}{3y(c-x)}.$

Remark.—The student should leave the denominators of fractions with their factors *unmultiplied*, as in Ex. 6 and 7, unless they combine very simply. The convenience of this will be found in practice.

Ex. 8. Multiply $\dfrac{a}{b}+\dfrac{b}{a}+1$ by $\dfrac{a}{b}+\dfrac{b}{a}-1$.

$$\dfrac{a}{b}+\dfrac{b}{a}+1=\dfrac{a^2}{ab}+\dfrac{b^2}{ab}+\dfrac{ab}{ab}=\dfrac{a^2+b^2+ab}{ab};$$

$$\dfrac{a}{b}+\dfrac{b}{a}-1=\dfrac{a^2}{ab}+\dfrac{b^2}{ab}-\dfrac{ab}{ab}=\dfrac{a^2+b^2-ab}{ab}.$$

$$\dfrac{a^2+b^2+ab}{ab}\times\dfrac{a^2+b^2-ab}{ab}=\dfrac{(a^2+b^2+ab)(a^2+b^2-ab)}{a^2b^2}$$

$$=\dfrac{(a^2+b^2)^2-a^2b^2}{a^2b^2}=\dfrac{a^4+b^4+a^2b^2}{a^2b^2}.$$

Or we may proceed thus:

$$\left(\frac{a}{b}+\frac{b}{a}+1\right)\left(\frac{a}{b}+\frac{b}{a}-1\right)=\left(\frac{a}{b}+\frac{b}{a}\right)^2-1;$$

$$\left(\frac{a}{b}+\frac{b}{a}\right)^2=\left(\frac{a}{b}\right)^2+2\frac{a}{b}\frac{b}{a}+\left(\frac{b}{a}\right)^2=\frac{a^2}{b^2}+2+\frac{b^2}{a^2};$$

therefore,

$$\left(\frac{a}{b}+\frac{b}{a}+1\right)\left(\frac{a}{b}+\frac{b}{a}-1\right)=\frac{a^2}{b^2}+2+\frac{b^2}{a^2}-1=\frac{a^2}{b^2}+\frac{b^2}{a^2}+1.$$

The two results agree, for $\dfrac{a^2}{b^2}+\dfrac{b^2}{a^2}+1=\dfrac{a^4+b^4+a^2b^2}{a^2b^2}.$

Examples—23.

Find the value of the following:

1. $\dfrac{2a}{3b}\times\dfrac{6bc}{5a^2}.$ 2. $\dfrac{a^2}{bc}\times\dfrac{b^2}{ac}\times\dfrac{c^2}{ab}.$

3. $\dfrac{a^2b}{x^2y}\times\dfrac{b^2c}{y^2z}\times\dfrac{c^2a}{z^2x}.$ 4. $\dfrac{x+1}{x-1}\times\dfrac{x+2}{x^2-1}\times\dfrac{x-1}{(x+2)^2}.$

5. $\dfrac{xa}{x+a}\times\left(\dfrac{x}{a}-\dfrac{a}{x}\right).$ 6. $\left(b+\dfrac{a^2}{b}\right)\left(a-\dfrac{b^2}{a}\right).$

7. $\left(a+\dfrac{ab}{a-b}\right)\left(b-\dfrac{ab}{a+b}\right).$

8. $\dfrac{x(a-x)}{a^2+2ax+x^2}\times\dfrac{a(a+x)}{a^2-2ax+x^2}.$

9. $\dfrac{x^6-y^6}{x^4+2x^2y^2+y^4}\times\dfrac{x^2+y^2}{x^2-xy+y^2}\times\dfrac{x+y}{x^3-y^3}.$

10. $\dfrac{x^2-(a+b)x+ab}{x^2-(a+c)x+ac}\times\dfrac{x^2-c^2}{x^2-b^2}.$

11. $\dfrac{x^2+xy}{x^2+y^2} \times \left(\dfrac{x}{x-y} - \dfrac{y}{x+y}\right).$

12. $\left(\dfrac{a}{bc} - \dfrac{b}{ac} - \dfrac{c}{ab} - \dfrac{2}{a}\right) \times \left(1 - \dfrac{2c}{a+b+c}\right).$

13. $\left(\dfrac{x^2}{a^2} + \dfrac{a^2}{x^2} - \dfrac{x}{a} - \dfrac{a}{x} + 1\right) \times \left(\dfrac{x}{a} - \dfrac{a}{x}\right).$

14. $\left(\dfrac{x}{a} - \dfrac{a}{x} + \dfrac{y}{b} - \dfrac{b}{y}\right) \times \left(\dfrac{x}{a} - \dfrac{a}{x} - \dfrac{y}{b} + \dfrac{b}{y}\right).$

15. $\dfrac{x^2-2x+1}{x^2-5x+6} \times \dfrac{x^2-4x+4}{x^2-4x+3} \times \dfrac{x^2-6x+9}{x^2-3x+2}.$

XVIII. Division of Fractions.

128. Rule for dividing one fraction by another:

Invert the divisor, and proceed as in Multiplication.

The following is the usual demonstration of the rule. Suppose we have to divide $\dfrac{a}{b}$ by $\dfrac{c}{d}$; put $\dfrac{a}{b} = x$, and $\dfrac{c}{d} = y$;

then, $\qquad a = bx$, and $c = dy$;

and, $\qquad ad = bdx$, and $bc = bdy$;

therefore, $\qquad \dfrac{ad}{bc} = \dfrac{bdx}{bdy} = \dfrac{x}{y}.$

But $\qquad \dfrac{x}{y} = x \div y = \dfrac{a}{b} \div \dfrac{c}{d};$

therefore, $\qquad \dfrac{a}{b} \div \dfrac{c}{d} = \dfrac{ad}{bc} = \dfrac{a}{b} \times \dfrac{d}{c}.$

To divide one fraction by another.

DIVISION OF FRACTIONS.

129. The results given in Art. 125 give us the following in connection with Division of Fractions:

Since $\dfrac{a}{b} \times -\dfrac{c}{d} = -\dfrac{ac}{bd}$, and $-\dfrac{a}{b} \times \dfrac{c}{d} = -\dfrac{ac}{bd}$,

we have $-\dfrac{ac}{bd} \div -\dfrac{c}{d} = \dfrac{a}{b}$, and $-\dfrac{ac}{bd} \div \dfrac{c}{d} = -\dfrac{a}{b}$.

Also, since $-\dfrac{a}{b} \times -\dfrac{c}{d} = \dfrac{ac}{bd}$, we have $\dfrac{ac}{bd} \div -\dfrac{c}{d} = -\dfrac{a}{b}$.

130. The student should, in the division of fractions, endeavor to simplify the operations as much as possible by striking out factors which occur in both numerator and denominator.

Ex. 1. Divide a by $\dfrac{b}{c}$.

$$a = \dfrac{a}{1};\quad \dfrac{a}{1} \div \dfrac{b}{c} = \dfrac{a}{1} \times \dfrac{c}{b} = \dfrac{ac}{b}.$$

Ex. 2. Divide $\dfrac{3a}{4b}$ by $\dfrac{9a}{8c}$.

$$\dfrac{3a}{4b} \div \dfrac{9a}{8c} = \dfrac{3a}{4b} \times \dfrac{8c}{9a} = \dfrac{2c}{3b}.$$

Ex. 3. Divide $\dfrac{ab - b^2}{(a+b)^2}$ by $\dfrac{b^2}{a^2 - b^2}$.

$$\dfrac{ab - b^2}{(a+b)^2} \div \dfrac{b^2}{a^2 - b^2} = \dfrac{ab - b^2}{(a+b)^2} \times \dfrac{a^2 - b^2}{b^2}$$

$$= \dfrac{b(a-b)(a+b)(a-b)}{b^2(a+b)^2} = \dfrac{(a-b)^2}{b(a+b)}.$$

Ex. 4. $\dfrac{x^2 + xy}{x - y} \div \dfrac{x^4 - y^4}{(x-y)^2} = \dfrac{x^2 + xy}{x - y} \times \dfrac{(x-y)^2}{x^4 - y^4} = \dfrac{x}{x^2 + y^2}.$

Examples—24.

Divide

1. $\dfrac{4a^2b}{5x^2y}$ by $\dfrac{2ab^2}{15xy^2}$. 2. $\dfrac{3a^2b^3c^4}{4x^2y^3z^4}$ by $\dfrac{4a^4b^2c^3}{3x^4y^3z^2}$.

3. $\dfrac{1}{x^2-y^2}$ by $\dfrac{1}{x-y}$. 4. $\dfrac{6(ab-b^2)}{a(a+b)^2}$ by $\dfrac{2b^2}{a(a^2-b^2)}$.

5. $\dfrac{a^2-4x^2}{a^2+4ax}$ by $\dfrac{a^2-2ax}{ax+4x^2}$. 6. $\dfrac{8x^3}{x^3-y^3}$ by $\dfrac{4x^2}{x^2+xy+y^2}$.

7. $\dfrac{a^3+3a^2x+3ax^2+x^3}{x^3+y^3}$ by $\dfrac{(a+x)^2}{x^2-xy+y^2}$.

8. $\dfrac{x^2+(a+c)x+ac}{x^2+(b+c)x+bc}$ by $\dfrac{x^2-a^2}{x^2-b^2}$.

9. $\dfrac{a^2+b^2+2ab-c^2}{c^2-a^2-b^2+2ab}$ by $\dfrac{a+b+c}{b+c-a}$.

10. $\dfrac{x^2+xy+y^2}{x^3+y^3}$ by $\dfrac{x^3-y^3}{x^2-xy+y^2}$.

11. $\dfrac{x^2-3x+2}{x^2-6x+9}$ by $\dfrac{x^2-5x+6}{x^2-2x+1}$.

12. $\left(1+\dfrac{x}{y}\right)\left(1-\dfrac{x}{y}\right)$ by $\dfrac{y}{x^2+y^2}$.

13. $5x^2-\dfrac{1}{5}$ by $x+\dfrac{1}{5}$. 14. $a^2-\dfrac{1}{a^2}$ by $a-\dfrac{1}{a}$.

15. $\dfrac{x^4}{a^4}-\dfrac{a^4}{x^4}$ by $\dfrac{x}{a}-\dfrac{a}{x}$. 16. $\dfrac{x^3}{a}-8a+\dfrac{12a^3}{x^2}$ by $x-\dfrac{2a^2}{x}$.

17. $\dfrac{x^2}{y^2}-\dfrac{1}{x}$ by $\dfrac{x}{y^2}+\dfrac{1}{y}+\dfrac{1}{x}$. 18. $\dfrac{x^2}{a^2}+1+\dfrac{a^2}{x^2}$ by $\dfrac{x}{a}-1+\dfrac{a}{x}$.

XIX. Complex Fractions and other Results.

131. Hitherto we have supposed, in the chapters on Fractions, that the letters represented whole numbers, but when we come to interpret the multiplication of fractions we must extend the meaning of the term, as we have done in Arithmetic. Thus, to multiply $\frac{a}{b}$ by $\frac{c}{d}$, the fraction $\frac{a}{b}$ is divided into d equal parts, and c such parts are taken. Now if $\frac{a}{b}$ be divided into d equal parts, each of these parts is $\frac{a}{bd}$; and if c such parts be taken, the result is $\frac{ac}{bd}$. Then, too, to divide $\frac{a}{b}$ by $\frac{c}{d}$ *means* to find a quantity such, that if it be multiplied by $\frac{c}{d}$ the product shall be $\frac{a}{b}$.

132. Now with our extended definitions we can easily prove that all the rules and formulas given are true when the letters denote any numbers *whole* or *fractional*. Take, for example, the formula $\frac{a}{b} = \frac{ac}{bc}$, and suppose we wish to show that this is true when

$$a = \frac{m}{n},\ b = \frac{p}{q},\ \text{and}\ c = \frac{r}{s}.$$

Here $\quad \dfrac{a}{b} = \dfrac{m}{n} \div \dfrac{p}{q} = \dfrac{m}{n} \times \dfrac{q}{p} = \dfrac{mq}{np}.$

Also $\quad ac = \dfrac{mr}{ns},\ \text{and}\ bc = \dfrac{pr}{qs}.$

Then $\dfrac{ac}{bc} = \dfrac{mr}{ns} \div \dfrac{pr}{qs} = \dfrac{mr}{ns} \times \dfrac{qs}{pr} = \dfrac{mrqs}{nspr} = \dfrac{mq}{np}.$

Thus the formula is proved to be true.

133. Complex fractional expressions may be simplified by the aid of rules respecting fractions which have now been given.

Ex. 1. $\dfrac{1-\dfrac{x}{2}}{4x} = \dfrac{\dfrac{2-x}{2}}{\dfrac{4x}{1}} = \dfrac{2-x}{2} \times \dfrac{1}{4x} = \dfrac{2-x}{8x}.$

Hence observe that, when a complex fraction is put into the form of a $\dfrac{\text{fraction}}{\text{fraction}}$, the simple expression for it will be found by taking the product of the upper and lower quantities, or *extremes*, for the numerator, and that of the two middle ones, or *means*, for the denominator; and that any factor may be struck out from one of the extremes, if it be struck out also from one of the means.

Ex. 2. $\dfrac{2x}{x-\dfrac{1}{3}} = \dfrac{\dfrac{2x}{1}}{\dfrac{3x-1}{3}} = \dfrac{6x}{3x-1}.$

Ex. 3. $\dfrac{5-\tfrac{1}{4}x}{x+1\tfrac{1}{3}} = \dfrac{\dfrac{20-x}{4}}{\dfrac{3x+4}{3}} = \dfrac{60-3x}{4(3x+4)}.$

Ex. 4. $\dfrac{\dfrac{a+b}{a-b}+\dfrac{a-b}{a+b}}{\dfrac{a+b}{a-b}-\dfrac{a-b}{a+b}} = \dfrac{\dfrac{(a+b)^2+(a-b)^2}{a^2-b^2}}{\dfrac{(a+b)^2-(a-b)^2}{a^2-b^2}} = \dfrac{\dfrac{2a^2+2b^2}{a^2-b^2}}{\dfrac{4ab}{a^2-b^2}} = \dfrac{a^2+b^2}{2ab}.$

Ex. 5. Simplify $\dfrac{1}{a+\dfrac{1}{1+\dfrac{a+1}{3-a}}}$

COMPLEX FRACTIONS.

$$1+\frac{a+1}{3-a}=\frac{3-a}{3-a}+\frac{a+1}{3-a}=\frac{3-a+a+1}{3-a}=\frac{4}{3-a}.$$

$$1\div\frac{4}{3-a}=\frac{1}{1}\times\frac{3-a}{4}=\frac{3-a}{4},$$

$$a+\frac{3-a}{4}=\frac{4a}{4}+\frac{3-a}{4}=\frac{3+3a}{4}.$$

$$1\div\frac{3+3a}{4}=\frac{1}{1}\times\frac{4}{3+3a}=\frac{4}{3+3a}.$$

Ex. 6. Find the value of $\dfrac{a-x}{b-x}$ when $x=\dfrac{ab}{a+b}$.

Here $a-x=a-\dfrac{ab}{a+b}=\dfrac{a^2+ab-ab}{a+b}=\dfrac{a^2}{a+b},$

and $b-x=b-\dfrac{ab}{a+b}=ab+b^2-ab=\dfrac{b^2}{a+b}.$

Hence, $\dfrac{a-x}{b-x}=\dfrac{\dfrac{a^2}{a+b}}{\dfrac{b^2}{a+b}}=\dfrac{a^2}{b^2}.$

Examples—25.

Simplify

1. $\dfrac{\dfrac{1}{1+x}}{1-\dfrac{1}{1+x}}.$

2. $\dfrac{\dfrac{1}{1+x}+\dfrac{x}{1-x}}{\dfrac{1}{1-x}-\dfrac{x}{1+x}}.$

3. $\dfrac{1-\dfrac{1}{1+\dfrac{1}{x}}}{}.$

4. $\dfrac{1}{1-\dfrac{1}{1+\dfrac{1}{x}}}.$

5. $\dfrac{\dfrac{3x}{2}+\dfrac{x-1}{3}}{\dfrac{13}{6}(x+1)-\dfrac{x}{3}-2\tfrac{1}{2}}.$

6. $\dfrac{x-1+\dfrac{6}{x-6}}{x-2+\dfrac{3}{x-6}}.$

Find the value of

7. $\dfrac{x-a}{b} - \dfrac{x-b}{a}$ when $x = \dfrac{a^2}{a-b}$.

8. $\dfrac{x}{a} + \dfrac{x}{b-a} - \dfrac{a}{a+b}$ when $x = \dfrac{a^2(b-a)}{b(b+a)}$.

9. $\dfrac{a^2x + b^2y}{x+y}$ when $a = \dfrac{2}{3}$ and $b = \dfrac{2}{3}$.

10. $\dfrac{x}{x+y} + \dfrac{y}{x-y} - \dfrac{y^2}{x^2-y^2}$ when $y = \dfrac{3x}{4}$.

11. $\dfrac{x+2a}{2b-x} + \dfrac{x-2a}{2b+x} - \dfrac{4ab}{4b^2-x^2}$ when $x = \dfrac{ab}{a+b}$.

12. $\left(\dfrac{x-a}{x-b}\right)^2 - \dfrac{x-2a+b}{x+a-2b}$ when $x = \dfrac{a+b}{2}$.

13. $\dfrac{x+y-1}{x-y+1}$ when $x = \dfrac{a+1}{ab+1}$, and $y = \dfrac{ab+a}{ab+1}$.

134. The following results should be noticed.

If $\dfrac{a}{b} = \dfrac{c}{d}$, then

$1 \div \dfrac{a}{b} = 1 \div \dfrac{c}{d}$, or $\dfrac{b}{a} = \dfrac{d}{c}$ (i); $\dfrac{a}{b} \times \dfrac{b}{c} = \dfrac{b}{c} \times \dfrac{c}{d}$, or $\dfrac{a}{c} = \dfrac{b}{d}$ (ii);

$\dfrac{a}{b} + 1 = \dfrac{c}{d} + 1$, or $\dfrac{a+b}{b} = \dfrac{c+d}{d}$ (iii),

$\dfrac{a}{b} - 1 = \dfrac{c}{d} - 1$, or $\dfrac{a-b}{b} = \dfrac{c-d}{d}$ (iv).

hence $\dfrac{a \pm b}{b} \times \dfrac{b}{a} = \dfrac{c \pm d}{d} \times \dfrac{d}{c}$, or $\dfrac{a \pm b}{a} = \dfrac{c \pm d}{c}$

and $\quad \dfrac{a+b}{b} \times \dfrac{b}{a-b} = \dfrac{c+d}{d} \times \dfrac{d}{c-d}$, or $\dfrac{a+b}{a-b} = \dfrac{c+d}{c-d}$ (vi):

and any of these last may be *inverted* by (i), or *alternated* by (ii); thus, $\dfrac{a}{a\pm b} = \dfrac{c}{c\pm d}$, $\dfrac{a}{c} = \dfrac{a\pm b}{c\pm d}$, $\dfrac{a+b}{c+d} = \dfrac{a-b}{c-d}$, &c.

So that, *If any two fractions are equal, we may combine by addition or subtraction, in any way, the numerator and denominator of the one, provided that we do the same with the other.*

XX. Involution.

135. The process of obtaining the *powers* of quantities is called *Involution*. A *power* has been defined to be the *product* of two or more *equal factors*. All cases of Involution, then, are merely examples of multiplication, where all the factors are the *same;* and the rules given in the present chapter follow immediately from the laws of Multiplication.

136. *Any even power of a negative quantity is positive. Any odd power of a negative quantity is negative.*

This is a simple consequence of the Rule of Signs.

Thus, $-a \times -a = +a^2$; $-a \times -a \times -a = +a^2 \times -a = -a^3$; $-a \times -a \times -a \times -a = -a^3 \times -a = +a^4$; and so on.

Let the student notice: 1. That any *even* power of a quantity is the same whether that quantity be negative or positive. Thus $(+a)^2$ and $(-a)^2$ are each $= +a^2$; and $(-(a+b))^4$ and $(+(a+b))^4$ are each $= +(a+b)^4$. 2. No *even* power of *any* quantity can be *negative*. 3. Any *odd* power of a quantity will have the same sign as the quantity itself.

137. *The exponent of any power of a power is equal to the product of the exponents of the two powers.*

Thus, the cube of a^2, that is, $(a^2)^3 = a^6$; for, $(a^2)^3 = a^2 \times a^2 \times a^2 = a^{2+2+2} = a^{2\times 3} = a^6$.

Similarly, $(a^4)^3 = a^{12}$; $(-a^4)^3 = -a^{12}$; $(-a^4)^2 = -a^8$; $(a^m)^n = a^{mn}$; $[(a-b)^2]^3 = (a-b)^6$; $[(x+y)^4]^3 = (x+y)^{12}$.

138. Rule for obtaining any power of a monomial expression:

Multiply the exponent of every factor in the expression by the index of the required power, and give the proper sign to the result.

Thus, for example,

$(a^2b^3)^2 = a^4b^6$; $(-a^2b^3)^3 = -a^6b^9$; $(ab^2c^3)^4 = a^4b^8c^{12}$;

$(-a^2b^3c^4)^5 = -a^{10}b^{15}c^{20}$; $(2ab^2c^3)^6 = 2^6a^6b^{12}c^{18} = 64a^6b^{12}c^{18}$.

It is usual to raise the numerical coefficient at once to the required power, instead of first writing it with an exponent. Thus, $(-2xy^2z^3)^3 = -8x^3y^6z^9$.

139. Rule for obtaining any power of a fraction: *Raise both the numerator and denominator to that power, and give the proper sign to the result.* This follows from Art. 122.

For example,

$\left(\dfrac{a^2}{b^3}\right)^2 = \dfrac{a^4}{b^6}$; $\left(-\dfrac{a^2}{b^3}\right)^3 = -\dfrac{a^6}{b^9}$; $\left(\dfrac{2a^2}{3b}\right)^4 = \dfrac{2^4a^8}{3^4b^4} = \dfrac{16a^8}{81b^4}$.

140. Some examples of Involution of *binomial expressions* have already been given. Thus,

$(a+b)^2 = a^2 + 2ab + b^2.$

$(a-b)^2 = a^2 - 2ab + b^2.$

By (137) we may shorten the operation, finding the 4th power of a quantity by squaring its square; and similarly, to find the 6th, 8th, &c. powers, we may square the 3d, 4th, &c. powers.

Rule for obtaining any power of a monomial expression;—of a fraction. Involution of binomial expressions.

So also to find the cube or 3d power, we may take the product of the quantity itself and its square; to find the 5th, we may take that of the square and cube, &c.

Thus we shall have,

$(a+b)^3 = (a^2+2ab+b^2)(a+b) = a^3+3a^2b+3ab^2+b^3;$

$(a-b)^3 = (a^2-2ab+b^2)(a-b) = a^3-3a^2b+3ab^2-b^3;$

$(a+b)^4 = (a^2+2ab+b^2)(a^2+2ab+b^2) = a^4+4a^3b+6a^2b^2 +4ab^3+b^4;$

$(a-b)^4 = (a^2-2ab+b^2)(a^2-2ab+b^2) = a^4-4a^3b+6a^2b^2 -4ab^3+b^4;$

$(a+b)^5 = (a+b)^3(a+b)^2 = a^5+5a^4b+10a^3b^2+10a^2b^3+5ab^4 +b^5;$

$(a-b)^5 = (a-b)^3(a-b)^2 = a^5-5a^4b+10a^3b^2-10a^2b^3+5ab^4 -b^5.$

The student should remember the above results, though the higher powers of binomial expressions are best obtained by the Binomial Theorem, which we shall give subsequently.

It will be noticed in the above examples that any power of $a-b$ can be immediately obtained from the same power of $a+b$ by changing the signs of the terms which involve the odd powers of b.

141. The results of Art. 140, can readily be applied to *trinomial expressions*.

Ex. 1. $(a+b+c)^2 = a^2+2a(b+c)+(b+c)^2$

$= a^2+2ab+2ac+b^2+2bc+c^2.$

Involution of trinomial expressions.

Ex. 2. $(a+b+c)^3 = \{a+(b+c)\}^3$

$= a^3 + 3a^2(b+c) + 3a(b+c)^2 + (b+c)^3$

$= a^3 + 3a^2b + 3a^2c + 3ab^2 + 6abc + 3ac^2 + b^3$

$\quad + 3b^2c + 3bc^2 + c^3.$

Ex. 3. $(a-b-c)^3 = \{a-(b+c)\}^3$

$= a^3 - 3a^2(b+c) + 3a(b+c)^2 - (b+c)^3$

$= a^3 - 3a^2b - 3a^2c + 3ab^2 + 6abc + 3ac^2 - b^3 - 3b^2c$

$\quad - 3bc^2 - c^3.$

Or thus:

$(a-b-c)^3 = \{(a-b)-c\}^3 = (a-b)^3 - 3(a-b)^2c + 3(a-b)c^2 - c^3,$

which, of course, when expanded, would give the same result as before.

Ex. 4. $(2x-3)^4 = (2x)^4 - 4.3.(2x)^3 + 6.3^2.(2x)^2 - 4.3^3.(2x) + 3^4$

$= 16x^4 - 96x^3 + 216x^2 - 216x + 81.$

Examples—26.

1. Find the values of $(2ab^2)^3$, $(-3a^2b^2c^4)^3$, $\left(-\dfrac{3ab^2}{4c^3}\right)^3$, $\left(-\dfrac{x^2y^2z^4}{2}\right)^5.$

Write down the expansions of

2. $(x+2)^3.$ 3. $(x-2)^4.$ 4. $(x+3)^5.$ 5. $(1+2x)^5.$

6. $(2m-1)^3.$ 7. $(3x+1)^4.$ 8. $(2x-a)^4.$ 9. $(3x+2a)^3.$

10. $(4a-3b)^3.$ 11. $(ax-y^2)^3.$ 12. $(ax+x^2)^4.$

13. $(2am-m^2)^5.$ 14. $(a-b+c)^3.$ 15. $(1-x+x^2)^3.$

142. The square of any *polynomial* expression may be obtained by either of two rules. Take for example,

$$(a+b+c+d)^2.$$

We will find,

$$(a+b+c+d)^2 = a^2+b^2+c^2+d^2+2ab+2ac+2ad+2bc+2bd+2cd.$$

We see from this—the square of any polynomial may be found by setting down *the square of each term*, and then *the double products of all the terms, taken two and two*.

Again, we may put the result in this form,

$$(a+b+c+d)^2 = a^2+2a(b+c+d)+b^2+2b(c+d)+c^2+2cd+d^2,$$

and this may be obtained by the following rule:

The square of any multinomial expression consists of the square of each term, together with twice the product of each term by the sum of all the terms which follow it.

Ex. 1. $(1+2x+3x^2)^2 = 1+2(2x+3x^2)+4x^2+4x(3x^2)+9x^4$

$$= 1+4x+10x^2+12x^3+9x^4.$$

Ex. 2. $(1-2x)^6 = \{(1-2x)^3\}^2 = (1-6x+12x^2-8x^3)^2$

$$= 1-12x+24x^2-16x^3$$
$$+36x^2-144x^3+96x^4$$
$$+144x^4-192x^5+64x^6$$
$$= 1-12x+60x^2-160x^3+240x^4-192x^5+64x^6.$$

Examples—27.

Find

1. $(a+b+c+d)^2-(a-b+c-d)^2$.
2. $(a+b+c+d)^2+(a-b+c-d)^2$.
3. $(1+x+x^2)^2$.   4. $(1-x+x^2)^2$.   5. $(1+x-x^2)^2$.
6. $(1+3x+2x^2)^2$.   7. $(1-3x+3x^2)^2$.
8. $(2+3x+4x^2)^2+(2-3x+4x^2)^2$.
9. $(1-x+x^2+x^3)^2$.   10. $(1+2x+3x^2+4x^3)^2$.

XXI. Evolution.

143. *Evolution* is the inverse of Involution. Evolution is, then, the method of finding the *roots* of quantities. It is usual in this connection to use the word *extract* in the same sense as *find*. Thus to *extract the square root* is to *find the square root*.

144. It follows from (136) that—

1. *Any even root of a positive quantity will have the double sign* $\pm$.

Thus the square root of a^2 is $\pm a$, the fourth root of a^4 is $\pm a$.

2. *Any odd root of a quantity has the same sign as the quantity itself.*

Thus, for example, the cube root of a^3 is a, and the cube root of $-a^3$ is $-a$.

3. *There can be no even root of a negative quantity.*

Hence the indicated even root of a negative quantity is called an *impossible quantity* or *imaginary quantity*. $\sqrt{-a^2}$, $\sqrt{-a}$, $\sqrt{-1}$, are *imaginary quantities*.

145. Rule for finding any root of a monomial integral expression. *Extract the required root of the numerical coefficient, divide the exponent of each literal factor by the index of the root, and give the proper sign to the result.*

Since the cube *power* of a^2 is a^6, therefore the cube root of a^6 is a^2, and so on.

Thus, for example, $\sqrt{(16a^2b^4)} = \sqrt{(4^2a^2b^4)} = \pm 4ab^2$.
$\sqrt[3]{(-8a^6b^9c^{12})} = \sqrt[3]{(-2^3a^6b^9c^{12})} = -2a^2b^3c^4$.
$\sqrt{(256x^4y^8)} = \sqrt{(4^2x^4y^8)} = \pm 4xy^4$.

146. To obtain any root of a fraction: *Find the root of the numerator and denominator, and give the proper sign to the result.*

For example, $\sqrt{\left(\dfrac{4a^2}{9b^4}\right)} = \sqrt{\left(\dfrac{2^2a^2}{3^2b^4}\right)} = \pm\dfrac{2a}{3b^2}$.

$\sqrt[3]{\left(-\dfrac{27a^6}{64b^3}\right)} = \sqrt[3]{\left(-\dfrac{3^3a^6}{4^3b^3}\right)} = -\dfrac{3a^2}{4b}$.

147. Suppose we require the cube root of a^2. In this case the exponent 2 of the quantity is not divisible by the index 3 of the root; then we cannot find the root of it, but can only *indicate* that the root *is to be* extracted by writing it thus, $\sqrt[3]{a^2}$. Similarly, $\sqrt{a}$, $\sqrt{a^3}$, $\sqrt[4]{a^5}$, indicate roots which we cannot extract. Such quantities are called *surds*, or *irrational quantities;* the difference between surds and imaginary quantities being that surds have real values, though we cannot find them exactly, while there *cannot* be a quantity, positive or negative, an even power of which would produce a negative quantity.

Examples—28.

1. Find the square roots of $4a^2b^4c^6$, $49x^4y^6z^2$, $100a^6b^{12}c^{16}$.

2. Find the square roots of $\dfrac{9a^2x^4y^6}{25z^2}$, $\dfrac{49x^2y^4}{64a^2}$, $\dfrac{25x^8y^{10}}{16a^2b^4}$.

3. Find $\sqrt{\dfrac{a^4x^4y^2}{4}}$, $\sqrt[3]{-\dfrac{8a^3y^6}{27x^9}}$, $\sqrt[3]{\dfrac{64b^6c^9}{125a^{12}}}$, $\sqrt[3]{-\dfrac{216a^3b^3c^{15}}{343}}$.

4. Find $\sqrt[4]{\left(\dfrac{81a^4}{b^4c^4}\right)}$, $\sqrt[5]{\left(\dfrac{a^5}{32b^{10}}\right)}$, $\sqrt[6]{\left(\dfrac{64\,a^6b^{12}}{c^{24}}\right)}$.

148. To find the square root of a polynomial: We *know* that the square of $a+b$ is $a^2+2ab+b^2$. Let us observe, then, how from $a^2+2ab+b^2$ we may deduce its square root $a+b$. This will lead us to a general method of finding the square root of polynomial expressions.

$$\begin{array}{r} a^2+2ab+b^2\,(a+b \\ \underline{a^2} \\ 2a+b)\;2ab+b^2 \\ \underline{2ab+b^2} \end{array}$$

Arrange the terms according to the powers of one letter, a; then the first term is a^2, and its square root is a. Subtract the square of a, that is, a^2, from the whole expression, and bring down the remainder $2ab+b^2$. Divide $2ab$ by $2a$ and the quotient is b, which is the other term of the root; lastly, if we add this b to the $2a$, multiply the $2a+b$ thus formed by b, and subtract the product from $2ab+b^2$, there is no remainder.

Now we may follow this plan in any other case, and, if we find no remainder, we may conclude that the root is exactly obtained.

Ex. 1.

$$\begin{array}{r} 9x^2+6xy+y^2\,(3x+y \\ \underline{9x^2} \\ 6x+y)\;6xy+y^2 \\ \underline{6xy+y^2} \end{array}$$

Ex. 2.

$$\begin{array}{r} 16a^2-56ab+49b^2\,(4a-7b \\ \underline{16a^2} \\ 8a-7b)-56ab+49b^2 \\ \underline{-56ab+49b^2} \end{array}$$

To find the square root of a polynomial.

Ex. 3. $4a^2-4ab-b^2(2a-b$
$4a^2$
$\overline{4a-b)-4ab-b^2}$
$-4ab+b^2$
$\overline{-2b^2.}$

Here we find a remainder $-2b^2$; we conclude, therefore, that $2a-b$ is *not* the exact root of $4a^2-4ab-b^2$, which is a surd, and can only be written $\sqrt{4a^2-4ab-b^2}$.

149. If the root consist of more than two terms, a similar process will enable us to find it, as in the following example, where it will be seen that the divisor at any step is obtained *by doubling the quantity already found in the root*, or (which amounts to the same thing and is more convenient in practice) *by doubling the last term of the preceding divisor, and then annexing the new term of the root.*

Ex. $16x^6-24x^5+25x^4-20x^3+10x^2-4x+1(4x^3-3x^2+2x-1$
$16x^6$
$8x^3-3x^2)\overline{-24x^5+25x^4}$
$-24x^5+9x^4$
$8x^3-6x^2+2x)\overline{16x^4-20x^3+10x^2}$
$16x^4-12x^3+4x^2$
$8x^3-6x^2+4x-1)-\overline{8x^3+6x^2-4x+1}$
$-8x^3+6x^2-4x+1$

150. It has already been remarked that all even roots have *double* signs. Thus, the square root of $a^2+2ab+b^2$ may be $-(a+b)$, that is, $-a-b$, as well as $a+b$; and, in fact, the first term in the root, which we found by taking the square root of a^2, might have been $-a$ as well as a, and by using this we should have obtained, also, $-b$.

So in (148) Ex. 1, the root may also be $-3x-y$; in Ex. in (149), $-4x^3+3x^2-2x+1$; and in all such cases, we should get the two roots by giving a double sign to the first term in the root.

When the root consists of more than two terms. Double Signs.

151. As the 4th *power* of a quantity is the square of its square, so the 4th root of a quantity is the square root of its square root, and may therefore be found by the preceding rule. Similarly, the 8th root may be found by extracting the square root of the 4th root.

Thus, if it be required to find the 4th root of

$$a^4 + 4a^3x + 6a^2x^2 + 4ax^3 + x^4,$$

the square root will be found to be $a^2 + 2ax + x^2$, and the square root of this to be $a + x$, which is therefore the 4th root of the given quantity.

Examples—29.

Extract the square root of

1. $x^4 + 2x^3 + 3x^2 + 2x + 1.$
2. $1 - 2x + 5x^2 - 4x^3 + 4x^4$.
3. $x^4 + 6x^3 + 25x^2 + 48x + 64.$
4. $x^4 - 4x^2 + 8x + 4.$
5. $1 - 4x + 10x^2 - 12x^3 + 9x^4.$
6. $4x^6 - 4x^5 - 7x^4 + 4x^2 + 4.$
7. $x^4 - 2ax^3 + 5a^2x^2 - 4a^3x + 4a^4.$
8. $x^4 - 2ax^3 + (a^2 + 2b^2)x^2 - 2ab^2x + b^4.$
9. $x^6 - 12x^5 + 60x^4 - 160x^3 + 240x^2 - 192x + 64.$
10. $x^6 + 4ax^5 - 10a^2x^2 + 4a^3x + a^4.$
11. $1 - 2x + 3x^2 - 4x^3 + 5x^4 - 4x^5 + 3x^6 - 2x^7 + x^8.$
12. $\dfrac{4x^2}{9y^2} - \dfrac{x}{z} - \dfrac{16x^2}{15yz} + \dfrac{9y^2}{16z^2} + \dfrac{6xy}{5z^2} + \dfrac{16x^2}{25z^2}.$

Extract the 4th root

13. Of $1-4x+6x^2-4x^3+x^4$ and of $a^4-8a^3+24a^2-32a+16$.

14. Of $16a^4-96a^3b+216a^2b^2-216ab^3+81b^4$.

Find the 8th root

15. Of $\{x^4-2x^3y+3x^2y^2-2xy^3+y^4\}^4$.

152. The observation of the square roots of *trinomial expressions* enables us to find the square root of complete (*i. e.*), exact squares of these terms very easily, without going through the entire process of Art. 148.

RULE.—*Arrange the terms according to the powers of some one letter. Find separately the square roots of the extreme terms, and take their sum or difference accordingly as the sign of the middle term is $+$ or $-$.*

Thus, $a^2+2ax+x^2$ is a complete square arranged according to powers of a, and its square root is $\sqrt{a^2}+\sqrt{x^2}$, or $a+x$, $\therefore a+x$ squared produces $a^2+2ax+x^2$. The square root of $a^2-2ax+x^2$ is $a-x$, for the same reason.

Ex. 1. $\sqrt{a^2+1+2a}=\sqrt{a^2+2a+1}=\sqrt{a^2}+\sqrt{1}=a+1$.

Ex. 2. $\sqrt{x^2+9-6x}=\sqrt{x^2-6x+9}=\sqrt{x^2}-\sqrt{9}=x-3$.

Ex. 3. $\sqrt{4+y^2-4y}=\sqrt{y^2-4y+4}=\sqrt{y^2}-\sqrt{4}=y-2$.

Ex. 4. $\sqrt{x^2-px+\dfrac{p^2}{4}}=\sqrt{x^2}-\sqrt{\dfrac{p^2}{4}}=x-\dfrac{p}{2}$.

Ex. 5. $\sqrt{x^2+3x+\dfrac{9}{4}}=\sqrt{x^2}+\sqrt{\dfrac{9}{4}}=x+\dfrac{3}{2}$.

To find the square root of complete trinomial squares.

Ex. 6. $\sqrt{m^2x^2+2mnx+n^2} = \sqrt{m^2x^2} + \sqrt{n^2} = mx+n.$

Ex. 7. $\sqrt{9x^2y^2-6axy+a^2} = \sqrt{9x^2y^2} - \sqrt{a^2} = 3xy-a.$

Ex. 8. $\sqrt{\tfrac{1}{4}a^2b^2+abc+c^2} = \sqrt{\tfrac{1}{4}a^2b^2} + \sqrt{c^2} = \tfrac{1}{2}ab+c.$

Find the square roots of the following expressions:

Ex. 9. $16a^2+40ab+25b^2.$ 10. $49a^4-84a^2b+36b^2.$

Ex. 11. $36x^4+12x^2+1.$ 12. $64a^2+48abc+9b^2c^2.$

Ex. 13. $\dfrac{25a^2+20ab+4b^2}{25a^2+20ac+4c^2}$ 14. $\dfrac{9x^4-24x^2+16}{4x^2-12x+9}.$

153. By observing the terms of a complete trinomial square arranged according to one letter, we see that the middle term is twice the product of the square roots of the two extreme terms. Hence, the quantity which must be added to an expression of the form, x^2+2px, in order to form a complete trinomial square, is *the square of one-half* of the *co-factor*, or *coefficient*, $2p$ of x; that is, p^2. Observe that x represents the square root of the first term.

Thus, m^2x^2+2mnx requires the square of the half of $2n$, or n^2, to complete it, giving $m^2x^2+2mnx+n^2.$

$9x^2y^2-6axy$ requires the square of the half of $2a$, giving $9x^2y^2-6axy+a^2.$

Complete the squares in each of the following cases:

(1.) $x^2-12x+\underline{\quad}.$ (2.) $x^2-\dfrac{2x}{7}+\underline{\quad}.$

(3.) $x^2+11x+\underline{\quad}.$ (4.) $x^2-x+\underline{\quad}.$

(5.) $x^2-\tfrac{1}{4}x+\underline{\quad}.$ (6.) $36x^2+24x+\underline{\quad}.$

(7.) $x^2+px+\underline{\quad}.$ (8.) $16x^2-56x+\underline{\quad}.$

(9.) $x^2-\dfrac{7x}{10}+\underline{\quad}.$ (10.) $4a^2x^2+4abx+\underline{\quad}.$

To complete the square of expressions of the form of $x^2+2px.$

154. The method of finding the square root of numbers is derived from the methods of Arts. 148 and 149. (See Venable's Arithmetic—Square Root.)

The square root of 100 is 10; the square root of 10000 is 100; the square root of 1000000 is 1000, and so on. Hence, it follows that the square root of any number between 1 and 100, lies between 1 and 10, that is, the square root of any number having *one* or *two* figures is a number of *one* figure; so, also, the square root of any number between 100 and 1000, that is, having *three* or *four* figures, lies between 10 and 100, that is, is a number of *two* figures, and so on.

Hence, if we set a dot over every other figure of any given square number, *beginning with the units figure*, the number of dots will exactly indicate the number of figures in its square root. Thus, for example, the square roots of $2\dot{5}\dot{6}$ and $4\dot{0}9\dot{6}$ consist of two figures each, and the square roots of $1\dot{6}3\dot{8}4$ and $6\dot{1}15\dot{2}4$, of three figures each.

155. Find the square root of 3249. Set the dots according to the rule. The root must consist of two figures. Let $a+b$ denote the root, where a is the *value*

$$\begin{array}{r} 3\dot{2}4\dot{9}(50+7 \\ 2500 \\ \hline 100+7)\overline{749} \\ 749 \\ \hline \end{array}$$

of the figure in the tens place, and b of the figure in the units place. Then a must be the greatest multiple of ten, whose square is less than 3200, that is, a must be the square root of the greatest exact square contained in 3200. Now, as 25 is the greatest square in 32, 2500 must be the greatest in 3200; hence, a is 50. Subtract a^2—that is, the square of 50—from the given number, and the remainder is 749. Divide the remainder by $2a$—that is, by 100—and the quotient is 7, which is the value of b. Then $(2a+b)b$—that is, $(100+7)7$, or $107 \times 7 = 749$—is the number to be subtracted; and as there is no remainder, we conclude that $50+7$, or 57, is the required square root. If the number be such that its root consists of three places of figures, let a represent the *value* of the hundreds figure, and *b* of the tens figure; then having obtained *a* and *b* as before, let the hundreds and tens together be a new value of *a*, and then as before find a new value of *b* for the units.

Example.

$$186624\ (400+30+2$$
$$160000$$

$800+30 = 830)\ \overline{26624}$
24900

$800+60+2=862)\ \overline{1724}$
1724

Here the number of dots is three, and therefore the number of figures in the root will be three. Now the greatest square-number contained in 18, the first *period* (as it is called), is 16, and the number evidently lies between 160000 and 250000, that is, between the squares of 400 and 500. We take therefore 400 for the first term in the root, and proceeding just as before, we obtain the whole root, $400+30+2=432$.

$186624(432$
16
$83)\overline{266}$
249
$862)\overline{1724}$
1724

The ciphers are usually omitted in practice, and it will be seen that we need only, at any step, take down the next period, instead of the whole remainder.

156. Rule for finding the square root of any given number:

Set a dot over every other figure, beginning with that in the units' place, and thus divide the whole number into periods. Find the greatest number whose square is contained in the first period; this is the first figure in the root; subtract its square from the first period, and to the remainder bring down the next period. Divide this quantity, omitting the last figure, by twice the part of the root

Ex. 1.

$3249\ (57$
25
$107)\ \overline{749}$
749

already found, and annex the result to the root and also to the divisor; then multiply the divisor as it now stands by the part of the root last obtained for the subtrahend. If there be more periods to be brought down, the operation must be repeated.

Ex. 2.

$7\dot{7}8\dot{4}\dot{1}$ (279
4
47) 378
329
549) 4941
   4941

Ex. 3.

$1\dot{0}2\dot{9}1\dot{2}6\dot{4}$ (3208
9
62) 129
   124
6408) 51264
      51264

In Ex. 2, notice (i) that the second remainder, 49, is greater than the divisor 47; this may sometimes happen, but no difficulty can arise from it, as it would be found that, if instead of 7 we took 8 for the second figure, the subtrahend would be 384, which is too large. And (ii) that the last figure, 7, of the first divisor, being doubled in order to make the second divisor, and thus becoming 14, causes 1 to be added to the preceding figure, 4, which now becomes 5. In fact, the first divisor is 400+70, which, when its second term is doubled, becomes 400+140, or 540.

In Ex. 3, we have an instance of a cipher occurring in the root.

157. If the root have any number of decimal places, it is plain (by the rule for the multiplication of decimals) that the square will have *twice* as many, and therefore the number of decimal places in the root will be half that number. Hence, if the given square number be a decimal, and one of an *even* number of places, we set, as before, *the dot over the units' figure, and then over every other figure on both sides of it. The number of dots on the left of the decimal point will indicate the number of integers in the root, and the number of dots to the right, the number of decimal places in the root.*

For example:

The square root of 32.49, is one-tenth of the square root of 100×32.49; that is, of 3249. So, also, the square root of ·003249 is one thousandth of the square root of 1000000×·003249, that is, of 3249.

If the number have decimal places, how do we proceed?

Thus 10.291264 would be dotted 1̇0.2̇91̇26̇4, the dot being first placed on the units-figure 0; and the root will have one integral and three decimal places, that is, would be (Ex. 3 above) 3.208.

If, however, the given number be a decimal of an *odd* number of places, or if in any case of finding the square root there be a remainder, then there is no exact square root; but we may approximate to it as far as we please, by dotting, as before (*remembering always to set the dot first over the units figure*), and then annexing ciphers (which by the nature of decimals will not alter the value of the number itself), and taking them down as they are wanted until we have got as many decimal places in the root as we desire.

Ex. Find the square root of 2 and of 259.351, to three decimal places.

```
      2̇ (1.414 &c.              25̇9.3̇51̇0̇ (16.104 &c.
      1                         1
  24)100                    26)159
     96                        156
 281)400                   321)335
     281                       321
2824)11900               32204)141000
     11296                     128816
```

EXAMPLES—30.

Find the square roots

1. Of 177241, 120409, 4816.36, 543169, 1094116, 18671041.
2. Of 4334724, 437.6464, 1022121, 408.8484, 16803.9369.
3. Extract to five figures the square roots of 2.5, 2000, .3, .03, 111, .00111, .004, .005.

158. To find the *cube root* of a polynomial expression: We know that the cube root of $a^3+3a^2b+3ab^2+b^3$, is $a+b$; and we shall be led to a general rule for the extraction of the cube root of any polynomial by observing the manner in which $a+b$ may be derived from $a^3+3a^2b+3ab^2+b^3$.

Arrange the terms according to the dimensions of one letter, a; then the first term is a^3, and its cube root is a, which is the first term of the required root. Subtract its cube, that is, a^3, from the

$$\begin{array}{l} a^3+3a^2b+3ab^2+b^3\,(\,a+b \\ a^3 \\ \hline 3a^2\,)\quad 3a^2b+3ab^2+b^3 \\ 3a^2b+3ab^2+b^3 \end{array}$$

whole expression, and bring down the remainder, $3a^2b+3ab^2+b^3$. Divide $3a^2b$ by $3a^2$, and the quotient is b, which is the other term of the required root; then form $(3a^2+3ab+b^2)b$, (i. e.) $3a^2b+3ab^2+b^3$, and subtract it from the remainder, and the whole cube of $a+b$ has been subtracted. This finishes the operation in the present case.

If any quantity be left, proceed with $a+b$ as a new a; its cube, that is, $a^3+3a^2b+3ab^2+b^3$, has already been subtracted from the proposed expression, so we should divide the remainder by $3(a+b)^2$ for a new term in the root; and so on.

That the rule may be thus extended will be obvious from comparing the form of the cubes of $a+b+c$, $a+b+c+d$, &c., with that of $a+b$, from which the rule was deduced.

For,
$$(a+b+c)^3 = (a+b)^3 + 3(a+b)^2c + 3(a+b)c^2 + c^3,$$
$$= a^3 + (3a^2+3ab+b^2)b + [3(a+b)^2 + 3(a+b)c + c^2]c.$$

Similarly,
$$(a+b+c+d)^3 = a^3 + (3a^2+3ab+b^2)b + [3(a+b)^2 + 3(a+b)c + c^2]c$$
$$+ [3(a+b+c)^2 + 3(a+b+c)d + d^2]d;$$
and so on.

Pursuing the same course as above in any other case, if there be no remainder, we conclude that we have obtained the exact cube root.

$$\begin{array}{l} 8x^3+12x^2y+6xy^2+y^3\,(\,2x+y \\ 8x^3 \\ \hline 12x^2\,)\;12x^2y+6xy^2+y^3 \\ 12x^2y+6xy^2+y^3 \end{array}$$

Here the quantity corresponding to the *trial-divisor* $3a^2$ is $3(2x)^2=12x^2$, that to $3a^2b$ is $12x^2y$, that to $3ab^2$ is $6xy^2$, and that to b^3 is y^3; so that the whole subtrahend is $12x^2y+6xy^2+y^3$.

By attending, however, to the following hint, the subtrahend may be more easily constructed.

$$a^3 + 3a^2b + 3ab^2 + b^3 \, (a+b$$

$$\begin{array}{r|l} & a^3 \\ 3a+b \quad 3a^2 & \overline{} \, 3a^2b + 3ab^2 + b^3 \\ \underline{(3a+b)b} & \\ 3a^2 + 3ab + b^2 & 3a^2b + 3ab^2 + b^3 \end{array}$$

Set down first $3a$, some little way to the left of the first remainder, and then, multiplying this by a, obtain $3a^2$ as before; by means of this trial-divisor find b, and annex it to the $3a$, so making $3a+b$; multiply this by b, and set the product $(3a+b)b$ or $3ab+b^2$ under the $3a^2$, and add them up, making $3a^2 + 3ab + b^2$; then, multiplying this by b, we have $3a^2b + 3ab^2 + b^3$, the quantity required.

The value of the above method, in saving labor, will be more fully seen when the root has more than two terms, or, if numerical, more than two figures.

Ex.
$$8x^3 + 12x^2y + 6xy^2 + y^3 \, (2x + y$$

$$\begin{array}{r|l} & 8x^3 \\ 6x+y \quad 12x^2 & \overline{} \, 12x^2y + 6xy^2 + y^3 \\ \underline{+6xy+y^2} & \\ 12x^2 + 6xy + y^2 & 12x^2y + 6xy^2 + y^3 \end{array}$$

EXAMPLES—31.

Find the cube roots

1. Of $x^3 + 6x^2y + 12xy^2 + 8y^3$.
2. Of $a^3 - 9a^2 + 27a - 27$.
3. Of $x^3 + 12x^2 + 48x + 64$.
4. Of $8a^3 - 36a^2b + 54ab^2 - 27b^3$.
5. Of $a^3 + 24a^2b + 192ab^2 + 512b^3$.
6. Of $8x^3 - 84x^2y + 294xy^2 - 343y^3$.
7. Of $m^3 - 12m^2nx + 48mn^2x^2 - 64n^3x^3$.
8. Of $a^3x^3 - 15a^2bx^3 + 75ab^2x^3 - 125b^3x^3$.
9. Of $a^6 + 6a^5 + 15a^4 + 20a^3 + 15a^2 + 6a + 1$.
10. Of $x^6 - 12x^5 + 54x^4 - 112x^3 + 108x^2 - 48x + 8$.
11. Of $a^6 - 3a^5b + 6a^4b^2 - 7a^3b^3 + 6a^2b^4 - 3ab^5 + b^6$.
12. Of $a^3 - b^3 + c^3 - 3(a^2b - a^2c - ab^2 - ac^2 - b^2c + bc^2) - 6abc$.

159. The method of finding the cube root of an algebraic expression suggests a method for the extraction of the cube root of any number.

The cube root of 1000 is 10; the cube root of 1000000 is 100, and so on; hence, it follows that the cube root of a number less than 1000 must consist of only one figure; the cube root of a number between 1000 and 1000000, of two places of figures, and so on.

If, then, a point be placed over every third figure in any number, beginning with the figure in the units' place, the number of points will show the number of figures in the cube root. Thus, for example, the cube root of $40\dot{5}22\dot{4}$ consists of two figures, and the cube root of $1\dot{2}81\dot{2}90\dot{4}$ consists of three figures.

Suppose the cube root of 274625 required.

$$
\begin{array}{lll}
180+5 & 10800 & 27\dot{4}62\dot{5}(60+5 \\
       & 925 & 216000 \\ \cline{2-2}\cline{3-3}
       & 11725 & 58625 \\
       &   & 58625 \\
\end{array}
$$

Point the number according to the rule; thus it appears that the root must consist of two places of figures. Let $a+b$ denote the root, where a is the value of the figure in the tens' place, and b of that in the units' place. Then a must be the greatest multiple of ten which has its cube less than 274000; this is found to be 60. Place the cube of 60, that is 216000, in the third column under the given number and subtract. Place three times 60, that is 180, in the first column, and three times the square of 60, that is 10800, in the second column. Divide the remainder in the third column by the number in the second column, that is, divide 58625 by 10800; we thus obtain 5, which is the value of b. Add 5 to the first column, and multiply the sum thus formed by 5, that is, multiply 185 by 5; we thus obtain 925, which we place in the second column and add to the number already there. Thus we obtain 11725; multiply this by 5, place the product in the third column, and subtract. The remainder is zero, and therefore 65 is the required cube root.

The ciphers may be omitted for brevity, and the process will stand thus:

$$185 \qquad\qquad \begin{array}{r}108\\925\\\hline 11725\end{array} \qquad\qquad \begin{array}{r}274625(65\\216\\\hline 58625\\58625\end{array}$$

It will be seen by the following example, where the root has more than two figures, how the numerical process corresponds to the algebraical. The ciphers are omitted, except that in the numbers corresponding to $3a^2$, $3a'^2$, &c., it is better to express two at the end: thus a is really 4000, and therefore $3a^2$ is 48000000; but, as in the first remainder, we only need the figures of the first and second periods, corresponding to 43 in the root, we may treat the a as 40, and thus $3a^2$ will be 4800, and $3a$ will be 120, so that $3a+b$ will become 123.

Ex.

$$\begin{array}{ll}
 & 80677568161\ (4321 \\
 & 64 \\
\hline
\end{array}$$

$$\begin{array}{ll}
3a+b=123 \quad 3a^2=4800 & 16677 \qquad\qquad a'\ =\ 43\\
\qquad\quad (3a+b)b=\ \ 369 & \qquad\qquad\qquad\quad a''=432\\
\quad 3a^2+3ab+b^2=5169 & 15507\\
3a'+b=1292 \quad 3a'^2=554700 & 1170568\\
\qquad\quad (3a'+b)b=\ \ 2584 & \\
\quad 3a'^2+3a'b+b^2=557284 & 1114568\\
\qquad\qquad 12961 \qquad\quad 55987200 & 56000161\\
\qquad\qquad\qquad\qquad\qquad\quad 12961 & \\
\qquad\qquad\qquad\qquad\quad 56000161 & 56000161
\end{array}$$

EVOLUTION. 125

Note.—Our trial-divisors may frequently give figures too large for the next figure of the root. In such case try the *next less* figure, and if necessary, the next less, until we get the right one.

160. If the root have any number of decimal places, it is plain by the rule for the multiplication of decimals, that the cube will have *thrice* as many; and therefore the number of decimal places in every cube decimal will be necessarily a *multiple of three*, and the number of decimal places in the root will be a third of that number. Hence, if the given cube number be a decimal, and consequently have its number of decimal places a multiple of three, by setting as before the dot upon the *units-figure*, and then over every third figure on *both* sides of it, the number of dots to the left will still indicate the number of *integral* figures in the root, and the number of dots to the right the number of *decimal* places.

If the given number be not a perfect cube, we may dot as before (always *setting the dot first upon the units-figure*), and annex ciphers as in the case of the square root, so as to approximate to the cube root required, to as many decimal places as we please.

Example. Extract the cube root of 14102.327296.

$$
\begin{array}{lll}
\left.\begin{array}{r}64\\8\end{array}\right\} & \left.\begin{array}{r}1200\\256\end{array}\right\} & 14102.327296(24.16\\
& & 8\\
\left.\begin{array}{r}721\\2\end{array}\right\} & \left.\begin{array}{r}1456\\16\end{array}\right\} & \overline{6102}\\
& & 5824\\
\overline{7236} & 172800 & \overline{278327}\\
& \left.\begin{array}{r}721\\ \\173521\\1\end{array}\right\} & 173521\\
& & \overline{104806296}\\
& & 104806296\\
& \overline{17424300} & \overline{}\\
& 43416 & \\
& \overline{17467716} &
\end{array}
$$

NOTE.—A careful examination of the two columns of figures on the left will disclose a much abbreviated process of finding the divisors. In the left-hand column, adding to 64, 721, etc., twice the units-figure gives the same result as multiplying the root already found by 3. In the second column, adding the three numbers enclosed by a brace (*i. e.*, the last true divisor, the number above it, and the square of the last root figure), and annexing two ciphers, gives the next trial-divisor.

The examples and explanations above furnish us the following rule, given also in the Arithmetic:

I. *Place a dot over the units-figure of the number, and over every third figure to the left, and also to the right when the number contains decimals (always taking care in this latter case to make the number of decimal figures a multiple of* 3).

II. *Find the greatest cube in the number which forms the first period on the left, and place its root after the manner of a quotient in division. This root is the first figure of the required root. Subtract its cube from the first period, and to the remainder bring down the figures of the second period for a* First Dividend.

III. *Multiply the square of this first figure by* 3, *annex two ciphers, and find how often this* Trial-Divisor *is contained in the first dividend; place the quotient as the second (trial) figure of the root. Then to three times the first figure of the root annex this second figure, and multiply the result by the second figure; add the product to the Trial-Divisor, and call the sum the* First Divisor.

IV. *Multiply the First Divisor by the second figure of the root; if the product be greater than the First Dividend, use a lower figure for the second figure of the root, and thus repeat the process* III. *until the product be less than the First Dividend; subtract this product from this dividend, and to the remainder bring down the figures of the third period for a* Second Dividend.

Rule for extracting the cube root of any number.

EVOLUTION.

V. *Multiply the square of the two figures of the root by 3; annex two ciphers, and proceed as in* III. *and* IV. *Proceed in this manner until all the periods have been brought down.*

NOTE.—In extracting either the square or cube root of any number, when a certain number of figures in the root have been obtained by the common rule, that number *may be nearly doubled by division only*.

1. In the extraction of the *square* root, when $n+1$ figures are found in the root, n more *may be found by merely dividing the last remainder by the trial-divisor*. For, let N be the number whose square root is to be found, consisting of $2n+1$ figures.

Let $a=$ the part already found (consisting of $n+1$ figures, and n ciphers after them, that is, altogether of $2n+1$ figures).

Let $x=$ required remaining part of the root, consisting of n figures.

So that $\sqrt{N}=a+x;$

Then $N=a^2+2ax+x^2;$

$$\therefore \frac{N-a^2}{2a}=x+\frac{x^2}{2a}.$$

Now $N-a^2$ is the remainder, after $n+1$ figures of the root are found, and $2a$ the trial-divisor; if, then, we can show that $\frac{x^2}{2a}$ is a *proper fraction*, it will follow that the *integer* obtained by dividing $N-a^2$ by $2a$ will be x, the remaining part of the root.

But as x contains n figures, it must be $<10^n$, which has $n+1$ figures, and $x^2 < 10^{2n}$; and since a contains $2n+1$ figures, it cannot be $<10^{2n}$ (which is the smallest number of $2n+1$ figures).

Hence, $\frac{x^2}{2a} < \frac{10^{2n}}{2 \cdot 10^{2n}} < \frac{1}{2}$, and is therefore a proper fraction. That is, if the quotient of $\frac{N-a^2}{2a}$ be taken for the n remaining figures of the root, the sum is less than 1.

2. In the extraction of the cube root, when $n+2$ figures are found in the root, n more *may be found by dividing the last remainder by the trial-divisor*.

For let $N=$ the number;

$a=$ the part of root found (consisting of $n+2$ figures followed by n ciphers, that is, of $2n+2$ figures altogether);

$x=$ the required part of root (consisting of n figures).

Then $N=a^3+3a^2x+3ax^2+x^3$, and $\frac{N-a^3}{3a^2}=x+\frac{x^2}{a}+\frac{x^3}{3a^2};$ and here

$x < 10^n$; and a, since it contains $2n+2$ figures, cannot be $< 10^{2n+1}$; $\therefore \frac{x^2}{a} < \frac{10^{2n}}{10^{2n+1}}$ or $< \frac{1}{10}$, and $\frac{x^3}{3a^2} < \frac{10^{3n}}{3.10^{4n+2}}$ or $\frac{x^3}{3a^2} < \frac{1}{3.10^{n+2}}$. Hence, $\frac{x^2}{a} + \frac{x^3}{3a^2} < 1$. That is, if the quotient of $\frac{N-a^3}{3a^2}$ be taken for the n remaining figures of the root, the error is less than 1. Now $N-a^3=$ remainder after $n+2$ figures of root are found, and $3a^2$ is the Trial-Divisor for the next figure. Hence the rule as above.

Examples—32.

Find the cube roots of

1. 9261, 12167, 15625, 32768, 103.823, 110592, 262144, 884.736.
2. 1481544, 1601.613, 1953125, 1259712, 2.803221, 7077888.
3. Extract to 4 figures the cube roots of 2.5, .2, .01, 4.

XXII. Simple Equations.

161. The statement of the *equality* of two algebraical quantities which differ only in form, is called an "*Identity.*" An Identity is true for *any value whatever* of the letters which enter it.

Thus, $2x + 5x = 7x$; $2(a+x) = 2a + 2x$;

$(x+a)^2 = x^2 + 2ax + a^2$; $(x+a)(x-a) = x^2 - a^2$, are Identities. Up to this point we have been using Identities—especially to express general facts—by means of letters. Our formulas heretofore given are Identities.

162. An *equation*, however, is the statement of the equality of two *different* algebraical expressions; in which case the equality does not exist for *all* values, but only for some particular values, of one or more of the letters contained in it.

Thus the equation $x - 5 = 4$, will be found true only when

SIMPLE EQUATIONS.

we give x the value 9; and $x^2=3x-2$, true only when we give x the value 1 or 2.

In equations, the question always is, what value of the letter or letters not already known will *verify* or *satisfy*, (i.e.) *make true*, the expressed equality. The finding of such value or values is called *solving* the *equation*.

163. The two expressions connected by the symbol $=$ are called *sides* of the equation, or *members* of the equation. The expression to the left of the sign of equality, is called the *first* side; and the expression to the right is called the *second* side.

164. Those quantities to which particular values are to be given in order to satisfy the equation, are called the *unknown quantities*. The last letters of the alphabet, x, y, z, &c., are usually employed to denote these quantities.

165. An equation is said to be *satisfied* by any value of the unknown quantity which makes the values of the two sides of the equation the same, (*i.e.*) which makes the *Equation* an *Identity*.

This includes the case where all the terms of an equation lie on one side and 0 on the other, as in $x^2-3x+2=0$, which is satisfied by 1 or 2, either of which being put for x makes the first side also 0.

Those values of the unknown quantities by which the equation is satisfied, are called the *roots* of the equation.

Thus, 7 is the root of $x-3=4$; 1 and 2 are the roots of $x^2-3x+2=0$.

166. An equation of one unknown quantity, when cleared of surds and fractions, is said to be of as many *dimensions* as there are units in the index of the *highest power* of the unknown quantity.

Thus, $x-5=4$ is an equation of *one dimension*, or, of

Solving the Equation. Sides or Members of the Equation. Unknown Quantities. Satisfying an Equation.

the *first degree*, or a *simple* equation; $x^2=3x-2$, is of *two* dimensions, or, of the *second degree*, or *a quadratic equation*; $x^3-5=6x^2$ is of three dimensions, or of the *third degree*, or a *cubic equation*; $x^4-4x=13$, is of *four* dimensions, or the *fourth* degree, or a *biquadratic* equation, &c., &c.

167. In the present chapter we shall show how to solve simple equations. We have first to indicate some operations which we may perform on any equation without destroying the equality which it expresses.

168. *If every term of each side of an equation be multiplied by the same quantity, the two sides will still be equal.*

For, if equals be multiplied by the same quantity, the results are equal.

This principle is chiefly used for *clearing an equation of fractions*, if they stand in the way of solving it.

Thus, taking the equation $7x-6=\dfrac{5x}{3}$, multiplying every term by 3, the denominator of the fractional term, we have $21x-18=3\times\dfrac{5x}{3}$, or $21x-18=5x$, in which no fraction appears.

An equation of several fractional terms may be *cleared of fractions* by multiplying every term by any common multiple of all the denominators. If the L.C.M. of the denominators be employed, the equation will be expressed in its simplest terms.

Take, for example, $\dfrac{x}{3}+\dfrac{x}{4}+\dfrac{x}{6}=9$.

Multiply every term by $3\times 4\times 6$, or, 72; thus,

$$\dfrac{72x}{3}+\dfrac{72x}{4}+\dfrac{72x}{6}=648;$$

that is, $24x+18x+12x=648$, cleared of fractions.

Instead of multiplying every term by 72, we may multiply every term by 12, the L.C.M. of 3, 4, and 6. We would thus have $\frac{12x}{3}+\frac{12x}{4}+\frac{12x}{6}=108$; that is, $4x+3x+2x=108$, expressed in simple terms.

Ex. Clear the equation $\frac{5x+4}{2}-\frac{7x+5}{10}=\frac{28}{5}-\frac{x-1}{2}$, of fractions.

The L.C.M. of the denominators is 10. Multiply by 10.

Thus, $\quad 5(5x+4)-(7x+5)=56-5(x-1)$;
that is, $\quad 25x+20-7x-5=56-5x+5.$

The beginner should write the operations out in full, as above, using brackets, in order that he may attend to the signs of such expressions as $-\frac{7x+5}{10}$, and $-\frac{x-1}{2}$.

169. *Any term may be transferred from one side of an equation to the other side without destroying the equality, provided we change the sign of the term.*

This transference is called *transposing*.

Suppose, for example, $x-a=b-y.$

Add a to each side (which of course will not destroy the equality);

then, $\quad\quad x-a+a=b-y+a$;
that is, $\quad\quad x=b-y+a.$

Now subtract b from each side; thus,

$$x-b=b+a-y-b;$$

that is, $\quad\quad x-b=a-y.$

Here we see that $-a$ has been removed from one side of the equation, and appears as $+a$ on the other side; and $+b$ has been removed from one side and appears as $-b$ on the other side.

Transposition of Terms.

170. *If the sign of every term of an equation be changed the equality still holds.*

This follows from Art. 169, by transposing every term. Thus, suppose, for example, that $x-a=b-y$.

By transposition, $\quad y-b=a-x$;
that is, $\quad\quad\quad\quad\quad a-x=y-b$.

And this result is what we shall obtain if we change the sign of every term in the original equation.

It is also clear that if the same quantity occur with the same sign on both sides of the equation, *it may be erased from both sides.* For, by the erasure we either subtract equals from equals or add equals to equals, according as the sign of the term erased is $+$ or $-$.

171. *Every term of each side of an equation may be divided by the same quantity without destroying the equality expressed by it.*

For, if equals be divided by the same quantity, the quotients are equal.

Thus, the equation $12x+5x=136$, or $17x=136$, gives

$$\frac{17x}{17}=\frac{136}{17}, \text{ or } x=\frac{136}{17}=8.$$

Also, if $ax=b$, $\quad \dfrac{ax}{a}=\dfrac{b}{a}$, or $x=\dfrac{b}{a}$.

Again: if $24x+18x+12x=648$ be divided by 6, we get

$$4x+3x+2x=108, \text{ or } 9x=108.$$

Hence, $\quad\dfrac{9x}{9}=\dfrac{108}{9}$, or $x=\dfrac{108}{9}=12$.

Again: if $ax+bx-cx=d$, or $(a+b-c)x=d$;

then $\quad \dfrac{(a+b-c)x}{a+b-c}=\dfrac{d}{a+b-c}$, or $x=\dfrac{d}{a+b-c}$.

172. The operations indicated in the preceding articles may be performed upon equations of any degree, and containing any number of unknowns; for they depend on principles true of every equation. Of course all these operations can be performed on Identities, or *identical equations*, as they are sometimes called.

173. To solve a simple equation of one unknown quantity:

Rule. *Clear the equation of fractions, if necessary. Collect all the terms involving the unknown quantity on one side of the equation and the known quantities on the other side, transposing them, when necessary, with change of sign. Add together the terms of each side, and divide both sides by the coefficient or sum of the coefficients of the unknown quantity; and thus the root required will be found.*

NOTE I.—Erase terms by Art. 170, or simplify the equation by division, Art. 171, at any stage of the process.

NOTE II.—It is usual to collect all the unknown quantities on the first side, and the known on the second side of the equation.

174. We shall now give some examples.

Ex. 1. Solve $7x+25=35+5x$.

Here there are no fractions; by transposing we have

$$7x-5x=35-25;$$

that is, $\quad 2x=10;$

dividing by 2, $\quad x=\dfrac{10}{2}=5.$

We may verify this result by putting 5 for x in the original equation; then each side is equal to 60.

Ex. 2. $4x+5=10x-16$.

Here $10x-4x=5+16$; $\therefore$ $6x=21$, and $x=\tfrac{21}{6}=3\tfrac{3}{6}=3\tfrac{1}{2}$.

Ex. 3. $5(x+1)-2=3(x-5)$.

Here, removing the brackets, $5x+5-2=3x-15$;
$\therefore 5x-3x=-15-5+2$, or $2x=-18$, and $\therefore x=-9$.

Ex. 4. Solve $4(3x-2)-2(4x-3)-3(4-x)=0$.
Performing the multiplications indicated,
$$12x-8-(8x-6)-(12-3x)=0.$$
Removing the brackets,
$$12x-8-8x+6-12+3x=0;$$
collecting the terms, $\qquad 7x-14=0;$
transposing, $\qquad 7x=14;$
dividing by 7, $\qquad x=\dfrac{14}{7}=2.$

The student will find it a useful exercise to verify the correctness of his solutions. Thus, in the above example, if we put 2 for x in the original equation, we shall obtain $16-10-6$, that is 0, as it should be.

Ex. 5. $\qquad bx+2x-a=3x+2c.$
Transposing, $\qquad bx+2x-3x=a+2c;$
or, $\qquad bx-x=a+2c;$
collecting the coefficients, $(b-1)x=a+2c;$
dividing by $b-1$, $\qquad x=\dfrac{a+2c}{b-1}.$

Examples—33.

1. $4x-2=3x+3.$ 2. $3x+7=9x-5.$ 3. $4x+9=8x-3.$
4. $3+2x=7-5x.$ 5. $x=7+15x.$ 6. $mx+a=nx+d.$
7. $3(x-2)+4=4(3-x).$ 8. $5-3(4-x)+4(3-2x)=0.$
9. $13x-21(x-3)=10-21(3-x).$
10. $5(a+x)-2x=3(a-5x).$

SIMPLE EQUATIONS. 135

11. $3(x-3)-2(x-2)+x-1=x+3+2(x+2)+3(x+1)$.

12. $2x-1-2(3x-2)+3(4x-3)-4(5x-4)=0$.

13. $(2+x)(a-3)=-4-2ax$.

14. $(m+n)(m-x)=m(n-x)$.

15. $5x-[8x-3\{16-6x-(4-5x)\}]=6$.

175. The following examples will illustrate the solution of equations containing fractions.

Ex. 1. If $\dfrac{x}{2}-\dfrac{5x}{3}-\dfrac{4}{3}=\dfrac{4x}{3}-3$, find x.

Multiplying by 2×3, or 6,

$$3x-10x-8=8x-18;$$

transposing, $\quad 3x-10x-8x=8-18;$

combining, $\quad -15x=-10;$

dividing by -15, $\quad x=\dfrac{-10}{-15}=\dfrac{2}{3}.$

Ex. 2. $\tfrac{1}{2}x-\tfrac{2}{3}x+\tfrac{3}{4}x=11+\tfrac{1}{8}x$.

Here we first clear the equation of fractions, by multiplying every term by 24, the L.C.M. of the denominators, and (observing that in the first fraction $\tfrac{24}{2}=12$, in the second $\tfrac{24}{3}=8$, and so in the others) thus we get $12x-8\times 2x+6\times 3x=264+3x$, or

$$12x-16x+18x=264+3x;$$

$\therefore 12x-16x+18x-3x=264;\ \therefore 11x=264,$ and $x=\tfrac{264}{11}=24$.

Ex. 3. If $x+\dfrac{3x-5}{2}=12-\dfrac{2x-4}{3}$, find x.

To clear of fractions, multiply by 2×3, or 6, and we have

$$6x+3(3x-5)=72-2(2x-4);$$

or $\quad 6x+(9x-15)=72-(4x-8);$

$\therefore\ 6x+9x-15=72-4x+8.$

Transposing, $6x+9x+4x=72+8+15$;

combining, $19x=95$;

dividing, $x=\dfrac{95}{19}=5.$

Ex. 4. Solve $\dfrac{1}{3}(5x+3)-\dfrac{1}{7}(16-5x)=37-4x.$

This is the same as
$$\dfrac{5x+3}{3}-\dfrac{16-5x}{7}=37-4x.$$

Multiplying by 21, $7(5x+3)-3(16-5x)=21(37-4x)$

that is, $35x+21-48+15x=777-84x$;

transposing, $35x+15x+84x=777-21+48$;

that is, $134x=804$;

therefore, $x=\dfrac{804}{134}=6.$

Ex. 5. $\frac{1}{2}(x+1)+\frac{1}{3}(x+2)=16-\frac{1}{4}(x+3).$

Multiplying by 12, we have
$$6(x+1)+4(x+2)=192-3(x+3),$$
$$\text{or } 6x+6+4x+8=192-3x-9;$$

$\therefore 6x+4x+3x=192-9-6-8$; $\therefore 13x=169$, and $x=\dfrac{169}{13}=13.$

Examples—34.

1. $\frac{1}{2}x+\frac{1}{3}x=x-7.$

2. $\frac{1}{2}x-\frac{1}{3}x=\frac{1}{4}x-1.$

3. $\frac{1}{2}x-\frac{1}{3}x+\frac{1}{4}x=2-\frac{1}{6}x+\frac{5}{12}x.$

4. $\dfrac{2x}{5}+\dfrac{x-2}{3}=2x-7.$

5. $\dfrac{2x}{7}+\dfrac{x-2}{5}=x-4.$

6. $\frac{1}{2}(9-2x)=\frac{3}{5}-\frac{1}{10}(7x-18).$

7. $x+\frac{1}{3}(14-x)=\frac{1}{2}(21-x).$

8. $2x-\frac{1}{3}=\frac{2}{3}(3-2x)+\frac{1}{2}x.$

9. $\frac{1}{4}(2x+7)-\frac{1}{11}(9x-8)=\frac{1}{2}(x-11).$

10. $\dfrac{x-a}{3} - \dfrac{2x-3b}{5} - \dfrac{a-x}{2} = 0.$ 11. $\dfrac{5x-7}{2} - \dfrac{2x+7}{3} = 3x - 14.$

12. $x - 1 - \dfrac{x-2}{2} + \dfrac{x-3}{3} = 0.$ 13. $\dfrac{x+3}{2} + \dfrac{x+4}{3} + \dfrac{x+5}{4} = 16.$

14. $\dfrac{7x+9}{4} = 7 + x - \dfrac{2x-1}{9}.$ 15. $\dfrac{3x-4}{2} - \dfrac{6x-5}{8} = \dfrac{3x-1}{16}.$

16. $\dfrac{2x-5}{3} - \dfrac{5x-3}{4} + 2\tfrac{2}{3} = 0.$ 17. $\dfrac{7x-4}{8} + 2\tfrac{2}{3} + \dfrac{4-7x}{4} = x - \dfrac{7}{12}.$

18. $\dfrac{2-x}{3} + \dfrac{3-x}{4} + \dfrac{4-x}{5} + \dfrac{5-x}{6} + \dfrac{3}{4} = 0.$

19. $\dfrac{5x-3}{7} - \dfrac{9-x}{3} = \dfrac{5x}{2} + \dfrac{19}{6}(x-4).$

XXIII. Simple Equations Continued.

176. We shall now give some examples which are a little more difficult than those in the preceding chapter. In many of these examples the common multiple of all the denominators is too large to be conveniently employed. In such a case we may see whether two or three of the denominators have a simple common multiple, and get rid of these fractions first, observing to collect the terms and simplify as much as possible after each step.

Ex. 1. $\dfrac{2x+3}{11} - \dfrac{x-12}{3} + \dfrac{3x+1}{4} = 5\tfrac{1}{3} + \dfrac{4x+3}{12}.$

Here the L.C.M. of all the denominators would be 132; but as 12 will include three of them, multiplying by it (having first changed $5\tfrac{1}{3}$ to $\tfrac{16}{3}$), we get

$$\dfrac{12(2x+3)}{11} - 4(x-12) + 3(3x+1) = 64 + 4x + 3;$$

$$\therefore \tfrac{12}{11}(2x+3) - 4x + 48 + 9x + 3 = 64 + 4x + 3;$$

When the Common Multiple of all the denominators is too large for convenience, what course may you pursue?

hence, collecting terms and simplifying, we have

$$\tfrac{12}{11}(2x+3) - 4x + 9x - 4x = 64 + 3 - 48 - 3,$$

or $\tfrac{12}{11}(2x+3) + x = 16;$

$\therefore 12(2x+3) + 11x = 176,$ or $24x + 11x = 176 - 36;$

$\therefore 35x = 140,$ and $x = \tfrac{140}{35} = 4.$

177. It will often happen that *the unknown quantity is found in the denominator* of one or more of the fractions.

Ex. 2. Solve $\dfrac{2}{x} + \dfrac{4}{x} = \dfrac{3}{x} + \dfrac{5}{x} - \dfrac{2}{17}.$

Since the first four fractions have a common denominator,

by addition, $\dfrac{6}{x} = \dfrac{8}{x} - \dfrac{2}{17};$

transposing, $\dfrac{8}{x} - \dfrac{6}{x} = \dfrac{2}{17};$

combining, $\dfrac{2}{x} = \dfrac{2}{17};$

$\therefore x = 17.$

Ex. 3. $\dfrac{3}{x} - \dfrac{2}{3x} = \dfrac{5}{3x} + \dfrac{1}{3},$ to find $x.$

Multiplying by $3x,$ $9 - 2 = 5 + x;$ $\therefore x = 2.$

If any of the denominators which contain the unknown quantity *consists of two or more terms*, it will generally be advisable to follow the method of Art. 176, and clear the equation of the simplest denominators *first*, leaving the others to be dealt with afterward, when, by transposing, collecting the terms, &c., the equation has been reduced to *fewer terms*. Or, if all the denominators consist of two or more terms, then they may be cleared off *singly, one by one*, till all have disappeared.

How may you proceed when the unknown quantity is found in the denominator? When any of the denominators consists of more than two terms?

Ex. 4. Solve $\dfrac{6x+13}{15}-\dfrac{3x+5}{5x-25}=\dfrac{2x}{5}$.

Multiply by 15 to clear away the *simple* denominators first, and we have

$$6x+13-\dfrac{15(3x+5)}{5x-25}=6x;$$

erasing, and transposing, $13=\dfrac{15(3x+5)}{5x-25}$;

or, dividing numerator and denominator of the fraction by 5,

$$13=\dfrac{3(3x+5)}{x-5}.$$

Multiplying by $x-5$, $13x-65=9x+15$;
transposing, $\qquad 13x-9x=65+15$;
combining, $\qquad 4x=80$;
dividing, $\qquad x=\dfrac{80}{4}=20.$

Ex. 5. Solve $\dfrac{10x+17}{18}-\dfrac{12x+2}{11x-8}=\dfrac{5x-4}{9}$.

To remove first the denominators 18 and 9, multiply the whole by 18, and we have

$$10x+17-\dfrac{216x+36}{11x-8}=10x-8;$$

erasing, and transposing,

$$17+8=\dfrac{216x+36}{11x-8};$$

combining, $\qquad 25=\dfrac{216x+36}{11x-8};$

multiplying by $11x-8$, $25(11x-8)=216x+36$;
or, $\qquad 275x-200=216x+36$;
transposing, $\qquad 275x-216x=200+36$;
combining, $\qquad 59x=236$;
dividing, $\qquad x=\dfrac{236}{59}=4.$

Ex. 6. Solve $\dfrac{2x+3}{x+1}=\dfrac{4x+5}{4x+4}+\dfrac{3x+3}{3x+1}$.

Here it is convenient to multiply by $4x+4$, that is by $4(x+1)$;

thus $\qquad 4(2x+3)=4x+5+\dfrac{4(x+1)\,3(x+1)}{3x+1}$;

therefore, $\qquad 8x+12-4x-5=\dfrac{12(x+1)^2}{3x+1}$;

that is, $\qquad 4x+7=\dfrac{12(x+1)^2}{3x+1}$.

Multiplying by $3x+1$, $(3x+1)(4x+7)=12(x+1)^2$;

that is, $\qquad 12x^2+25x+7=12x^2+24x+12$.

Here $12x^2$ is found on both sides of the equation. Remove it by subtraction, and the equation becomes a *simple equation*; that is,

$$25x+7=24x+12;$$
or, $\qquad 25x-24x=12-7$;

$$\therefore x=5.$$

Ex. 7. Solve $\dfrac{x-1}{x-2}-\dfrac{x-2}{x-3}=\dfrac{x-4}{x-5}-\dfrac{x-5}{x-6}$.

Reducing the terms on the *first side* to a common denominator, we get $\dfrac{x^2-4x+3-(x^2-4x+4)}{(x-2)(x-3)}$, or $-\dfrac{1}{(x-2)(x-3)}$.

Reducing the terms of the *second side* to a common denominator, we have for this side

$$\dfrac{x^2-10x+24-(x^2-10x+25)}{(x-5)(x-6)}, \text{ or } -\dfrac{1}{(x-5)(x-6)}.$$

Thus the proposed equation becomes

$$-\dfrac{1}{(x-2)(x-3)}=-\dfrac{1}{(x-5)(x-6)};$$

changing the signs, $\dfrac{1}{(x-2)(x-3)} = \dfrac{1}{(x-5)(x-6)}$;

clearing of fractions, $(x-5)(x-6) = (x-2)(x-3)$;

that is, $x^2 - 11x + 30 = x^2 - 5x + 6$;

whence, $-11x + 5x = 6 - 30$;

that is, $-6x = -24$;

therefore, $x = 4$.

Ex. 8. Solve $.5x + \dfrac{.45x - .75}{.6} = \dfrac{1.2}{.2} - \dfrac{.3x - .6}{.9}$.

To insure accuracy, it is advisable to express all the decimals as common fractions; thus

$$\dfrac{5x}{10} + \dfrac{10}{6}\left(\dfrac{45x}{100} - \dfrac{75}{100}\right) = \dfrac{10}{2} \times \dfrac{12}{10} - \dfrac{10}{9}\left(\dfrac{3x}{10} - \dfrac{6}{10}\right).$$

Simplifying, $\dfrac{x}{2} + \dfrac{5}{3}\left(\dfrac{9x}{20} - \dfrac{3}{4}\right) = 6 - \left(\dfrac{x}{3} - \dfrac{2}{3}\right)$;

that is, $\dfrac{x}{2} + \dfrac{3x}{4} - \dfrac{5}{4} = 6 - \dfrac{x}{3} + \dfrac{2}{3}$.

Multiplying by 12, $6x + 9x - 15 = 72 - 4x + 8$;

transposing, $19x = 72 + 8 + 15 = 95$;

therefore, $x = \dfrac{95}{19} = 5$.

178. Complex fractions in an equation should first be reduced to simple ones, by the known rules.

Ex. 9. $\dfrac{25 - \tfrac{1}{3}x}{x+1} + \dfrac{16x + 4\tfrac{1}{5}}{3x+2} = 5 + \dfrac{23}{x+1}$.

Here, first simplifying the complex fractions, we get

$$\dfrac{75 - x}{3(x+1)} + \dfrac{80x + 21}{5(3x+2)} = 5 + \dfrac{23}{x+1};$$

then, multiplying by 15, $\dfrac{375-5x}{x+1}+\dfrac{240x+63}{3x+2}=75+\dfrac{345}{x+1}$;
whence, multiplying by $x+1$,
$$375-5x+\dfrac{240x^2+303x+63}{3x+2}=75x+75+345;$$
or, simplifying,
$$\dfrac{240x^2+303x+63}{3x+2}=75x+5x+75+345-375=80x+45;$$
$\therefore 240x^2+303x+63=240x^2+295x+90$, and $8x=27$, or $x=3\tfrac{3}{8}$.

179. We will now solve three more equations, in which letters are used to represent known quantities.

Ex. 10. Solve $\dfrac{x}{a}+\dfrac{x}{b}=c$.

Multiplying by ab, $bx+ax=abc$;
that is, $(a+b)x=abc$;
$$\therefore x=\dfrac{abc}{a+b}.$$

Ex. 11. Solve $a\dfrac{x-a}{b}+b\dfrac{x-b}{a}=x$.

Multiplying by ab, $a^2(x-a)+b^2(x-b)=abx$;
that is, $a^2x-a^3+b^2x-b^3=abx$;
transposing and collecting, $a^2x+b^2x-abx=a^3+b^3$;
that is, $(a^2-ab+b^2)x=a^3+b^3$;
dividing by a^2+ab+b^2, $x=\dfrac{a^3+b^3}{a^2-ab+b^2}$;
$$\therefore x=a+b.$$

Ex. 12. Solve $\dfrac{x-a}{x-b}=\dfrac{(2x-a)^2}{(2x-b)^2}$.

Clearing of fractions,
$$(x-a)(2x-b)^2=(x-b)(2x-a)^2;$$
that is, $(x-a)(4x^2-4bx+b^2)=(x-b)(4x^2-4ax+a^2)$,

multiplying, we obtain
$$4x^3-4x^2(a+b)+x(4ab+b^2)-ab^2$$
$$=4x^3-4x^2(a+b)+x(4ab+a^2)-a^2b;$$
whence, $\qquad b^2x-ab^2=a^2x-a^2b;$

$\therefore (a^2-b^2)x=a^2b-ab^2=ab(a-b);$

$\therefore x=\dfrac{ab(a-b)}{a^2-b^2}=\dfrac{ab}{a+b}.$

Examples—35.

1. $\dfrac{12}{x}+\dfrac{1}{12x}=\dfrac{29}{24}.$
2. $\dfrac{42}{x-2}=\dfrac{35}{x-3}.$
3. $\dfrac{128}{3x-4}=\dfrac{216}{5x-6},$

4. $\dfrac{45}{2x+3}=\dfrac{57}{4x-5}.$
5. $\dfrac{3x-1}{2}-\dfrac{2x-5}{3}+\dfrac{x-3}{4}-\dfrac{x}{6}=x+1.$

6. $\dfrac{\frac{1}{2}x-3}{5}+\dfrac{\frac{3}{4}x-10}{2}+\dfrac{4-x}{4}=\dfrac{10-x}{6}.$

7. $\dfrac{5}{6}\left(x-\dfrac{1}{3}\right)+\dfrac{7}{6}\left(\dfrac{x}{5}-\dfrac{1}{7}\right)=4\frac{8}{9}.$
8. $x+\dfrac{5x-8}{3}=6-\dfrac{3x-8}{5}.$

9. $\dfrac{x-2}{4}+\dfrac{1}{3}=x-\dfrac{2x-1}{3}.$
10. $x+1-\dfrac{x^2+3}{x+2}=2.$

11. $\dfrac{x-1}{x-2}=\dfrac{7x-21}{7x-26}.$
12. $\dfrac{7x-4}{x-1}=\dfrac{7x-26}{x-3}.$

13. $\dfrac{x}{7}-\dfrac{3x}{2}+\dfrac{71}{7}=\dfrac{3x+1}{2}+1\frac{1}{14}.$
14. $\dfrac{2x-6}{3x-8}=\dfrac{2x-5}{3x-7}.$

15. $x-3-(3-x)(x+1)=x(x-3)+8.$

16. $3-x-2(x-1)(x+2)=(x-3)(5-2x).$

17. $\dfrac{7+9x}{4}-1+\dfrac{2-x}{9}=7x.$
18. $(x+7)(x+1)=(x+3)^2.$

19. $\frac{1}{3}(2x-10)-\frac{1}{11}(3x-40)=15-\frac{1}{5}(57-x)$.

20. $\frac{6x+8}{2x+1}-\frac{2x+38}{x+12}=1$.

21. $\frac{1}{12}(2x-3)-\frac{1}{6}(3x-2)=\frac{1}{8}(4x-3)-3\frac{5}{24}$.

22. $\frac{4}{7}(x-9)+\frac{3}{5}(x-5)=\frac{8}{5}(x-7)+1\frac{2}{3}$.

23. $\frac{1}{15}(2x-1)-\frac{1}{18}(3x-2)=\frac{1}{18}(x-12)-\frac{1}{24}(x+12)$.

24. $\frac{1}{8}(7x+20)-\frac{3}{16}(3x+4)=\frac{1}{10}(3x+1)-\frac{1}{20}(29-8x)$.

25. $\frac{3x-1}{2x-1}-\frac{4x-2}{3x-2}=\frac{1}{6}$.   26. $\frac{2}{2x-3}+\frac{1}{x-2}=\frac{6}{3x+2}$.

27. $\frac{x-4}{x-5}-\frac{x-5}{x-6}=\frac{x-7}{x-8}-\frac{x-8}{x-9}$.

28. $\frac{x}{x-2}+\frac{x-9}{x-7}=\frac{x+1}{x-1}+\frac{x-8}{x-6}$.

29. $\frac{3+x}{3-x}-\frac{2+x}{2-x}-\frac{1-x}{1+x}=1$.   30. $.5x-2=.25x+.2x-1$.

31. $.5x+.6x-.8=.75x+.25$.

32. $.15x+\frac{.135x-.225}{.6}=\frac{.36}{.2}-\frac{.09x-.18}{.9}$.

33. $a\frac{a-x}{b}-b\frac{b+x}{a}=x$.   34. $\frac{x^2-a^2}{bx}-\frac{a-x}{b}=\frac{2x}{b}-\frac{a}{x}$.

35. $x(x-a)+x(x-b)=2(x-a)(x-b)$.

36. $(x-a)(x-b)=(x-a-b)^2$.   37. $\frac{a}{x-a}-\frac{b}{x-b}=\frac{a-b}{x-c}$.

38. $\frac{1}{x-a}-\frac{1}{x-b}=\frac{a-b}{x^2-ab}$.

39. $\dfrac{1}{x-a} - \dfrac{1}{x-a+c} = \dfrac{1}{x-b-c} - \dfrac{1}{x-b}.$

40. $\dfrac{mx-a-b}{nx-c-d} = \dfrac{mx-a-c}{nx-b-d}.$

41. $(a-b)(x-c) - (b-c)(x-a) - (c-a)(x-b) = 0.$

42. $\dfrac{x-a}{a-b} - \dfrac{x+a}{a+b} = \dfrac{2ax}{a^2-b^2}.$

43. $\dfrac{x-a}{x-a-1} - \dfrac{x-a-1}{x-a-2} = \dfrac{x-b}{x-b-1} - \dfrac{x-b-1}{x-b-2}.$ (See Ex. 6, Art. 177.)

XXIV. Problems solved by Simple Equations.

180. We shall now see the practical application of the above methods in the solution of many arithmetical problems. In these problems certain quantities are given, and another quantity, which has certain given relations to these, has to be found: the quantity which has to be found is called the *unknown quantity*. The relations between the given quantities and this *unknown* are expressed in the enunciation of the problem in ordinary language, and these are to be *translated* into *algebraical expressions*, to be used in the solution of the problem. The method of solving the problem may be given in general terms, as follows:

Put x to represent the unknown quantity. Set down, in algebraical language, the statements made in the problem, and the relations between the unknown quantity and given quantities derived from these statements, using x whenever the unknown quantity occurs. We shall thus arrive at an equation from which the value of x may be found.

Solution of problems by means of Simple Equations. State in general terms the steps to be taken.

Ex. 1. What number is that, to which if 8 be added, one-fourth of the sum is equal to 29?

Let x represent the number required.
Adding 8 to it, we have $x+8$, and one-fourth of this is $\frac{1}{4}(x+8)$;
we have, therefore, the equation $\frac{1}{4}(x+8)=29$; whence $x=108$.

Ex. 2. What number is that, the double of which exceeds its half by 6?

Let $x=$ the number; then the double of x is $2x$, and the half of x is $\frac{1}{2}x$; hence, $2x-\frac{1}{2}x=6$; whence $x=4$.

Ex. 3. The ages of 3 children together amount to 24 years, and they were born two years apart: what is the age of each?

Here we have

Known quantities.	*Unknown and required.*
1. The sum of the ages of all three, 24 years.	1. Age of youngest.
2. The difference between the ages of any two of them.	2. Age of next.
	3. Age of the oldest.

But, in reality, we have only *one* unknown quantity to *find*, because, when we know the age of one of the children, the ages of the two others immediately follow. So that we say,

let x be the age of the youngest;
then $x+2=$ .... next;
and $x+4=$ .... oldest.

Thus far we have expressed, algebraically, *one* of the two known conditions of the problem. There still remains to notice, that the sum of the ages is 24 years. Now this sum is $3x+6$, adding together x, $x+2$, and $x+4$;

$\therefore 3x+6=24$, an *equation* from which to find x.

Transposing, $3x=24-6$, or 18;
dividing, $x=\frac{18}{3}$, or 6.

$\therefore$ the age of the youngest is 6 years,
next .. 8
oldest .. 10

SIMPLE EQUATIONS.

Ex. 4. A cask, which held 270 gallons, was filled with a mixture of brandy, wine, and water. There were 30 gallons of wine in it more than of brandy, and 30 of water more than there were of wine and brandy together. How many were there of each?

Let $x=$ number of gals. of brandy;

$\therefore x+30=$ . . . . wine;

and $2x+30=$ . . . . wine and brandy together;

$\therefore 2x+30+30$ or $2x+60=$gals. of water;

but the whole number of gallons was 270;

$\therefore x+(x+30)+(2x+60)=270$;

whence $x=$ 45, the number of gals. of brandy,

$x+30=$ 75, ... wine,

$2x+60=150$, ... water.

Ex. 5. A sum of £50 is to be divided among A, B, and C, so that A may have 13 guineas more than B, and C £5 more than A: determine their shares.

Let $x=B$'s share in *shillings:*

$\therefore x+273=A$'s, and $(x+273)+100$ or $x+373=C$'s;

$\therefore$, since £50 $=1000s.$, $(x+273)+x+(x+373)=3x+646=1000$;

$\therefore 3x=354$, and $x=118$, $x+273=391$, $x+373=491$,

and the shares are 391$s.$, 118$s.$, 491$s.$, or £19 11$s.$, £5 18$s.$, £24 11$s.$, respectively.

Ex. 6. A, B, C divide among themselves 620 cartridges, A taking 4 to B's 3, and 6 to C's 5: how many did each take?

Let $x=A$'s share; then $\frac{3}{4}x=B$'s, $\frac{5}{6}x=C$'s;

$\therefore x+\frac{3}{4}x+\frac{5}{6}x=620$; whence $x=240$, $\frac{3}{4}x=180$, $\frac{5}{6}x=200$.

We might have avoided fractions by assuming $12x$ for A's share, when we should have had $9x=B$'s, and $10x=C$'s;

$\therefore 12x+9x+10x=620$; whence $x=20$;

and the shares are 240, 180, 200, as before.

Ex. 7. A line is 2 feet 4 inches long; it is required to divide it into two parts, such that one part may be three-fourths of the other part.

Let x denote the number of inches in the larger part; then $\dfrac{3x}{4}$ will denote the number of inches in the other part.

The number of inches in the whole line is 28; therefore

$$x + \frac{3x}{4} = 28;$$

whence, $\qquad\qquad 4x + 3x = 112;$

that is, $\qquad\qquad 7x = 112;$

and, $\qquad\qquad x = 16.$

Thus one part is 16 inches long, and the other part 12 inches long.

Ex. 8. A grocer has some tea worth half-a-dollar a lb., and some worth $87\frac{1}{2}$ cents a lb.; how many lbs. must he take of each sort to produce 100 lbs. of a mixture worth $62\frac{1}{2}$ cents a lb.?

Let $x =$ the number of pounds of the first sort; then $100-x$ will denote the number of lbs. of the second sort. The value of the x lbs. is $\frac{1}{2}x$ dollars, and the value of the $(100-x)$ lbs. is $\frac{7}{8}(100-x)$ dollars; and the whole value is to be $\frac{5}{8} \times 100$ dollars.

Therefore, $\qquad \frac{5}{8} \times 100 = \frac{1}{2}x + \frac{7}{8}(100-x);$

multiplying by 8, $\qquad 500 = 4x + 700 - 7x;$

whence, $\qquad\qquad 3x = 200;$

$\qquad\qquad\therefore x = \dfrac{200}{3} = 66\frac{2}{3}.$

Thus there must be $66\frac{2}{3}$ lbs. of the first sort, and $33\frac{1}{3}$ lbs. of the second sort.

Ex. 9. A person had $5000, part of which he lent at 4 per cent., and the rest at 5 per cent.; the whole annual interest received was $220: how much was lent at 4 per cent.?

Let $x =$ the number of dollars lent at 4 per cent.;

then $\qquad 5000 - x =$ the number of dollars lent at 5 per cent.;

and $\quad \dfrac{4x}{100} =$ the annual interest from the former;

and $\quad \dfrac{5(5000-x)}{100} =$ the annual interest from the latter;

therefore, $\quad \dfrac{4x}{100} + \dfrac{5(5000-x)}{100} = 220;$

whence, $\quad 4x + 5(5000-x) = 22000;$

that is, $\quad 4x + 25000 - 5x = 22000;$

$\therefore -x = -3000,$ or $x = 3000.$

Thus $3000 was lent at 4 per cent.

Ex. 10. Divide 42 into 4 parts which shall be 4 consecutive numbers.

Let x be one part;

then $\quad x+1, x+2, x+3,$ are the other parts;

and $\quad x + (x+1) + (x+2) + (x+3) = 42,$ by the question;

combining, $\quad 4x + 6 = 42,$

or, $\quad 4x = 36;$

$\therefore x = 9,$ and $x+1 = 10, x+2 = 11, x+3 = 12;$

$\therefore 9, 10, 11, 12,$ are the required parts.

181. The great difficulty which the beginner finds in solving these problems is in translating the statements of the enunciation into algebraical language. In this, practice alone can give readiness and accuracy. The teacher will find it advantageous to train the student orally in such translations, by means of examples like those given in Art. 40.

182. The student should always read carefully and consider well the meaning of the question proposed; and in order to avoid error, he should observe that x represents an *unknown number of dollars, pounds, feet, miles, hours,* or in general, *an unknown number of things* or *units,* and both the *kind* and *denomination* of the units of x should be distinctly noticed in the statement.

What caution is given to the student in Art. 181?

183. Many of the problems given below may be solved readily by Arithmetic, but the student will soon perceive the superiority of the method of solution by Algebra, in power and generality and easy application.

Examples—36.

1. What number is that which exceeds its sixth part by 10?

2. What number is that, to which if 7 be added, twice the sum will be equal to 32?

3. Find a number, such that its half, third, and fourth parts shall be together greater than its fifth part by 106.

4. A bookseller sold 10 books at a certain price, and afterward 15 more at the same rate, and at the latter time received $8.75 more than at the former: what was the price per book?

5. What two numbers are those, whose sum is 48 and difference 22?

6. At an election where 979 votes were given, the successful candidate had a majority of 47: what were the numbers for each?

7. A spent $62\frac{1}{2}$ cents in oranges, and says, that 3 of them cost as much under 25 cts., as 9 of them cost over 25 cts.: how many did he buy?

8. The sum of the ages of two brothers is 49, and one of them is 13 years older than the other: find their ages.

9. Find a number such that if increased by 10 it will become five times as great as the third part of the original number.

10. Divide 150 into two parts, so that one of them shall be two-thirds of the other.

11. A child is born in November, and on the tenth day of December he is as many days old as the month was on the day of his birth: when was he born?

12. There is a number such that, if 8 be added to its double, the sum will be five times its half. Find it.

13. Divide 87 into three parts, such that the first may exceed the second by 7, and the third by 17.

14. Find a number such that, if 10 be taken from its double, and 20 from the double of the remainder, there may be 40 left.

15. A market-woman being asked how many eggs she had, replied: If I had as many more, half as many more, and one egg and a half, I should have 104 eggs: how many had she?

16. A is twice as old as B; twenty-two years ago he was three times as old. Required A's present age.

17. Divide $64 among three persons, so that the first may have three times as much as the second, and the third, one-third as much as the first and second together.

18. A workman is engaged for 28 days at $62\frac{1}{2}$ cts. a day, but is to pay 25 cts. a day, instead of receiving anything, on all days upon which he is idle. He receives altogether 13.12\frac{1}{2}$: for how many idle days did he pay?

19. A person buys 4 horses, for the second of which he gives £12 more than for the first, for the third £6 more than for the second, and for the fourth £2 more than for the third. The sum paid for all was £230. How much did each cost?

20. A person bought 20 yards of cloth for 10 guineas, for part of which he gave 11s. 6d. a yard, and for the rest 7s. 6d. a yard: how many yards of each did he buy?

21. Two coaches start at the same time from A and B, a distance of 200 miles, travelling one at $9\frac{1}{2}$ miles an hour, the other at $9\frac{1}{4}$: where will they meet, and in what time from starting?

22. A father has six sons, each of whom is four years older than his next younger brother; and the eldest is three times as old as the youngest: find their respective ages.

23. A is twice as old as B, and seven years ago their united ages amounted to as many years as now represent the age of A: find the ages of A and B.

24. Two persons, A and B, are travelling together; A has £100 and B has £48: they are met by robbers, who take twice as much from A as from B, and leave to A three times as much as to B: how much was taken from each?

25. Find two consecutive numbers, such that one-half and one-fifth of the first, taken together, shall be equal to one-third and one-fourth of the second, taken together.

26. A cistern is filled in 20 minutes by 3 pipes, the first of which conveys 10 gallons more, and the second 5 gallons less, than the third, per minute. The cistern holds 820 gallons. How much flows through each pipe in a minute?

27. A garrison of 1000 men was victualled for 30 days; after 10 days it was re-enforced, and then the provisions were exhausted in 5 days: find the number of men in the re-enforcement.

28. In a certain weight of gunpowder, the saltpetre composed 6 lbs. more than a half of the weight, the sulphur 5 lbs. less than one-third, and the charcoal 3 lbs. less than one-fourth: how many pounds were there of each of the three ingredients?

29. A general, after having lost a battle, found that he had left, fit for action, 3600 men more than half of his army; 600 men more than one-eighth of his army were wounded;

and the remainder, forming one-fifth of his army, were slain, taken prisoners, or missing: what was the number of the army?

30. A tradesman starts with a certain sum of money: at the end of the first year he had doubled his original stock, all but £100; also, at the end of the second year he had doubled the stock at the beginning of that year, all but £100; also in like manner at the end of the third year; and at the end of the third year he found himself three times as rich as at first: what was his original stock?

XXV. Problems—Continued.

184. We shall now give some examples rather more difficult than the examples of the preceding chapter.

Ex. 1. Find a number, such that if $\frac{3}{8}$ of it be subtracted from 20, and $\frac{5}{11}$ of the remainder from $\frac{1}{4}$ of the original number, 12 times the second remainder shall be half the original number.

Let $x =$ the number;

$\therefore 20 - \frac{3}{8}x =$ 1st remainder, and $\frac{1}{4}x - \frac{5}{11}(20 - \frac{3}{8}x) =$ 2d remainder;

$\therefore 12[\frac{1}{4}x - \frac{5}{11}(20 - \frac{3}{8}x)] = \frac{1}{2}x$, by the question; whence $x = 24$.

Ex. 2. A certain number consists of two digits whose difference is 3; and, if the digits be inverted, the number so formed will be $\frac{4}{7}$ of the former: find the original number.

Let $x =$ lesser digit, and $\therefore x+3 =$ the greater: then, since the value of a number of two digits $=$ ten times the first digit $+$ the second digit, (thus $67 = 10 \times 6 + 7$), the number in question $= 10(x+3) + x$; similarly, the number formed by the same digits inverted $= 10x + (x+3)$; hence, by question, $10x + (x+3) = \frac{4}{7}[10(x+3) + x]$, whence $x = 3$, $x+3 = 6$, and the number required is 63.

Ex. 3. *A* can do a piece of work in 10 days; but, after he has been upon it 4 days, *B* is sent to help him, and they finish it together in 2 days. In what time would B have done the whole?

Let $x=$ number of days B would have taken, and W denote the work:

$\therefore \frac{W}{10}, \frac{W}{x}$, are the portions of the work which A, B would do in *one* day; hence in 4 days, A does $\frac{4W}{10}$, and in 2 days, A and B together do $\frac{2W}{10}+\frac{2W}{x}$: $\therefore \frac{4W}{10}+\frac{2W}{10}+\frac{2W}{x}=W$; whence $x=5$.

It is plain that, in the above, we might have omitted W altogether, or taken *unity* to represent the work, as follows:

A, B do $\frac{1}{10}, \frac{1}{x}$ of the work, respectively, in *one* day, and therefore, reasoning just as before, $\frac{4}{10}+\frac{2}{10}+\frac{2}{x}=$ the whole work $=1$.

[In all such questions, the student should notice that, if a person does $\frac{m}{n}$ ths of any work in one day, he will do $\frac{1}{n}$ th of it in $\frac{1}{m}$ th of a day, and therefore the *whole* work in $\frac{n}{m}$ days.

Thus, if he does $\frac{3}{7}$ in one day, he will do $\frac{1}{7}$ in $\frac{1}{3}$ of a day, and therefore the *whole*, or $\frac{7}{7}$, in $\frac{7}{3}=2\frac{1}{3}$ days.]

Ex. 4. A alone can perform a piece of work in 9 days, and B alone can perform it in 12 days: in what time will they perform it if they work together?

Let x denote the required number of days. In one day A can perform $\frac{1}{9}$ th of the work; therefore, in x days he can perform $\frac{x}{9}$ ths of the work. In one day B can perform $\frac{1}{12}$ of the work; therefore, in x days he can perform $\frac{x}{12}$ ths of the work. And since in x days A and B together perform the *whole* work, the sum of the *fractions* of the work must be equal to *unity*; that is,

$$\frac{x}{9}+\frac{x}{12}=1.$$

Multiplying by 36, $\qquad 4x+3x=36,$

that is, $\qquad\qquad\qquad 7x=36;$

therefore, $\qquad\qquad\quad x=\frac{36}{7}=5\frac{1}{7}.$

Ex. 5. A cistern could be filled with water by means of one pipe alone in 6 hours, and by means of another pipe alone in 8 hours; and it could be emptied by a tap in 12 hours, if the two pipes were closed: in what time will the cistern be filled if the pipes and the tap are all open?

Let x denote the required number of hours. In one hour the first pipe fills $\frac{1}{6}$th of the cistern; therefore, in x hours it fills $\frac{x}{6}$ths of the cistern. In one hour the second pipe fills $\frac{1}{8}$th of the cistern; therefore, in x hours it fills $\frac{x}{8}$ths of the cistern. In one hour the tap empties $\frac{1}{12}$th of the cistern; therefore, in x hours it empties $\frac{x}{12}$ths of the cistern. And since in x hours the *whole* cistern is filled, we have

$$\frac{x}{6}+\frac{x}{8}-\frac{x}{12}=1.$$

Multiplying by 24, $\quad 4x+3x-2x=24,$

that is, $\quad 5x=24;$

therefore, $\quad x=\frac{24}{5}=4\frac{4}{5}.$

185. It is sometimes convenient to take x to represent not the quantity which is actually demanded in the question, but some other unknown quantity on which it depends. This we will illustrate by some examples. But experience is the only guide to the best selection of the unknown quantity.

Ex. 6. A colonel, on attempting to draw up his regiment in the form of a solid square, finds that he has 31 men over, and that he would require 24 men more in his regiment in order to increase the side of the square by one man: how many men were there in the regiment?

Let x denote the number of men in the side of the first square; then the number of men in the square is x^2, and the number of men in the regiment is x^2+31. If there were $x+1$ men in a side of the square, the number of men in the square would be $(x+1)^2$; thus the number of men in the regiment is $(x+1)^2-24.$

Therefore, $(x+1)^2 - 24 = x^2 + 31$;

that is, $x^2 + 2x + 1 - 24 = x^2 + 31$.

From these two equal expressions we can remove x^2, which occurs in both; thus,

$$2x + 1 - 24 = 31;$$

therefore, $2x = 31 - 1 + 24 = 54$;

or, $x = \dfrac{54}{2} = 27$.

Hence the number of men in the regiment is $(27)^2 + 31$; that is, $729 + 31$; that is, 760.

Ex. 7. A starts from a certain place and travels at the rate of 21 miles in 5 hours; B starts from the same place 8 hours after A, and travels in the same direction at the rate of 15 miles in 3 hours: how far will A travel before he is overtaken by B?

Let $x=$ the number of hours which A travels before he is overtaken; then $x-8=$ the number of hours B travels.

Now since A travels 21 miles in 5 hours, (i.e.) $\dfrac{21}{5}$ of a mile in one hour, therefore,

$\dfrac{21x}{5}=$ the number of miles which A travels in x hours;

and similarly, $\dfrac{15}{3}(x-8)=$ number of miles which B travels in x hours

Therefore, $\dfrac{15}{3}(x-8) = \dfrac{21x}{5}$;

$$25(x-8) = 21x;$$

$$25x - 21x = 200;$$

$$x = 50.$$

Therefore, $\dfrac{21x}{5} = \dfrac{21}{5} \times 50 = 210$; so that A travelled 210 miles before he was overtaken.

186. The principles of proportion, as taught in Arithmetic, are often used to form the equations.

Ex. 8. It is required to divide the number 60 into three parts, such that they may be to each other in the proportion of the numbers 3, 4, and 5.

Let the number x denote the first part. Then, since

1st part : 2d part :: 3 : 4, therefore $\dfrac{4x}{3}$ is the second part;

and since 1st part : 3d part :: 3 : 5, therefore $\dfrac{5x}{3}$ is the third part.

Therefore, the sum of the parts

$$x + \dfrac{4}{3}x + \dfrac{5}{3}x = 60;$$

$$3x + 4x + 5x = 180;$$

$$12x = 180;$$

$$x = 15, \text{ the first part.}$$

Hence the 2d part is $\dfrac{4}{3} \times 15$, or 20, and the 3d part is $\dfrac{5}{3} \times 15$, or 25.

The preceding mode of solution, and many similar solutions involving proportions, may be shortened after the following manner:

Let $3x$ denote the first part; then the second part must be $4x$, and the third part must be $5x$.

Therefore, $\qquad 3x + 4x + 5x = 60;$

$\qquad\qquad\qquad 12x = 60; \qquad x = 5.$

∴ $3 \times 5 = 15$, the first part; $4 \times 5 = 20$, the second part; $5 \times 5 = 25$, the third part.

Ex. 9. There are two bars of metal, the first containing 14 oz. of silver and 6 of tin, the second containing 8 of silver and 12 of tin: how much must be taken from each to form a bar of 20 oz., containing equal weights of silver and tin?

Let $x =$ number of oz., to be taken from first bar, $20 - x$ from second; now $\frac{14}{20}$ of the first bar, and therefore of *every* oz. of it, is silver; and, similarly, $\frac{8}{20}$ of every oz. of the second bar is silver; and there are to be, altogether, 10 oz. of silver in the compound;

∴ $\frac{14}{20}x + \frac{8}{20}(20 - x) = 10$, whence $x = 6\frac{2}{3}$, and $20 - x = 13\frac{1}{3}$.

Ex. 10. Find the time between two and three o'clock, when the minute-hand of a watch is exactly over the hour-hand. Find, also, the time between 2 and 3 o'clock, when the hands are exactly opposite each other.

1st Case.—Let x denote the required number of minutes after 2 o'clock. In x minutes the minute-hand moves over x divisions of the watch-face; and as the long hand moves 12 times as fast as the short hand, the latter will move over $\frac{x}{12}$ divisions in x minutes. At 2 o'clock the short hand is 10 divisions in advance of the long hand; so that in the x minutes the long hand must pass over 10 more divisions than the short hand.

Therefore,
$$x = \frac{x}{12} + 10;$$
$$12x = x + 120;$$
$$11x = 120;$$
$$x = \frac{120}{11} = 10\tfrac{10}{11} \text{ minutes.}$$

Or more briefly, thus: The minute-hand in every minute gains $\frac{11}{12}$ of one minute-division on the hour-hand. Hence, in x minutes, it gains $\frac{11x}{12}$ divisions. Therefore, $\frac{11x}{12} = 10$. $\therefore x = \frac{120}{11} = 10\tfrac{10}{11}$.

2d Case.—Here the minute-hand must not only overtake the hour-hand, but advance so as to leave it 30 minute-divisions behind. Then let $x =$ required number of minutes after 2 o'clock; then the gain of the minute-hand, or $\frac{11x}{12} = 10 + 30$.

$\therefore \frac{11x}{12} = 40$, $11x = 480$; $x = 43\tfrac{7}{11}$ minutes. Hence the hands are in the required position at $43\tfrac{7}{11}$ minutes past 2 o'clock.

Ex. 11. A hare takes four leaps to a greyhound's three, but two of the greyhound's leaps are equivalent to three of the hare's; the hare has a start of 50 leaps: how many leaps must the greyhound take to catch the hare?

Suppose that $3x$ denote the number of leaps taken by the greyhound; then $4x$ will denote the number of leaps taken by the hare in the same time. Let a denote the number of inches in one leap of the hare; then $3a$ denotes the number of inches in three leaps of the hare, and therefore also the number of inches in two leaps of the greyhound: therefore $\frac{3a}{2}$ denotes the number of inches in one leap of the greyhound. Then $3x$ leaps of the greyhound will contain $3x \times \frac{3a}{2}$ inches. And $50 + 4x$ leaps of the hare will contain $(50 + 4x)a$ inches; therefore,
$$\frac{9xa}{2} = (50 + 4x)a.$$

SIMPLE EQUATIONS.

Dividing by a, $\qquad \dfrac{9x}{2} = 50 + 4x;$

therefore, $\qquad 9x = 100 + 8x;$

or, $\qquad x = 100.$

Thus the greyhound must take 300 leaps.

Here an auxiliary symbol a has been introduced to enable us to form the equation more easily. Being in every term, it is removed by division when the equation is formed.

Ex. 12. If the specific gravity of pure milk be 1·03, and a certain mixture of milk and water be found (by means of an instrument for the purpose) to be of specific gravity 1·02625, how much water has been added?

[DEFINITION.—By the *specific gravity* of a substance is meant the number of times which its weight is of an equal bulk of *water*. Thus the *specific gravity* of silver is 10·5, or $10\frac{1}{2}$, which means that any quantity of silver is $10\frac{1}{2}$ times the weight of the same *bulk* of *water*. The specific gravity of milk being 1.03, signifies that milk is $1\frac{3}{100}$ times as heavy as *water;* and so on.]

Let 1 quart of water be added to x quarts of pure milk to form the mixture; then,

Since the weight of x quarts of pure milk

$\qquad = 1.03$ times the weight of x quarts of water,

$\qquad = 1.03 \times x \times$ weight of 1 quart of water;

∴ whole weight of water and milk

$\qquad = (1 + 1.03x) \times$ weight of 1 quart of water.

But there are $1 + x$ quarts of the mixture whose specific gravity is 1.02625; ∴ the whole weight of this

$\qquad = 1.02625(1 + x) \times$ weight of 1 quart of water;

∴ $1 + 1.03x = 1.02625(1 + x).$

Therefore, $\qquad (1.03 - 1.02625)x = 1.02625 - 1;$

that is, $\qquad .00375x = .02625;$

∴ $x = \dfrac{.02625}{.00375} = 7.$

Hence, 1 quart of water has been added to 7 quarts of milk; (i. e.) *one-eighth* of the mixture is water.

Examples—37.

1. Out of a cask of wine of which a fifteenth part had leaked away, 12 gallons were drawn, and then it was two-thirds full: how much did it hold?

2. In a garrison of 2744 men there are two cavalry soldiers to twenty-five infantry, and half as many artillery as cavalry: find the number of each.

3. The first digit of a certain number exceeds the second by 4, and when the number is divided by the sum of the digits, the quotient is 7: find it.

4. The length of a floor exceeds the breadth by 4 feet; if each had been increased by a foot, there would have been 27 more square feet in it: find its original dimensions.

5. In a mixture of copper, lead, and tin, the copper was 5 lbs. less than half the whole quantity, and the lead and tin each 5 lbs. more than a third of the remainder: find the respective quantities.

6. A horse was sold at a loss, for $210; but if it had been sold for $262.50, the gain would have been three-fourths of the former loss: find its real value.

7. A can do a piece of work in 10 days, which B can do in eight; after A has been at work upon it 3 days, B comes to help him: in what time will they finish it?

8. There is a number of two digits whose difference is 2, and, if it be diminished by half as much again as the sum of the digits, it will give a number expressed by the digits inverted: find it.

9. A number of troops being formed into a solid square, it was found that there were 60 over; but when formed into a column with five men more in front than before, and three less in depth, there was just one man wanting to complete it: what was the number of troops?

10. A person has travelled altogether 3036 miles, of which he has gone seven miles by water to four on foot, and five by water to two on horseback: how many did he travel each way?

11. A mass of copper and tin weighs 80 lbs., and for every 7 lbs. of copper there are 3 lbs. of tin: how much copper must be added to the mass, that there may be 4 lbs. of tin for every 11 lbs. of copper?

12. A does $\frac{4}{5}$ of a piece of work in 10 days, when B comes to help him, and they take three days more to finish it: in what time would they have done the whole, each separately, or both together?

13. A and B were employed together for 50 days, each at \$1.20 a day; during which time A, by spending 12 cents a day less than B, had saved three times as much as B, and $2\frac{1}{2}$ days' pay besides: what did each spend per day?

14. There are two silver cups, and one cover for both; the first weighs 12 oz., and with the cover weighs twice as much as the other cup without it; but the second with the cover weighs a third as much again as the first without it: find the weight of the cover.

15. Find a number of three digits, each greater by unity than that which follows it, so that its excess above one-fourth of the number formed by inverting the digits shall be 36 times the sum of the digits.

16. If 19 lbs. of gold weigh 18 lbs. in water, and 10 lbs. of silver weigh 9 lbs. in water, find the quantity of gold and silver respectively in a mass of gold and silver weighing 106 lbs. in air and 99 lbs. in water.

17. A and B can reap a field together in 12 hours, A and C in 16 hours, and A by himself in 20 hours: in what time could, 1st, B and C together, and, 2d, A, B, and C together, reap it?

18. Find two numbers whose difference is 4, and the difference of their squares 112.

19. Divide the number 88 into four parts, such that the first increased by 2, the second diminished by 3, the third multiplied by 4, and the fourth divided by 5, may all be equal.

20. Three persons whose powers for work are as the numbers 3, 4, 5, can together complete a piece of work in 60 days: in what time could each alone complete the work?

21. A and B are at present of the same age; if A's age be increased by 36 years, and B's by 52 years, their ages will be as 3 to 4: what is the present age of each?

22. Divide 100 into two parts, such that the square of their difference may exceed the square of twice the less part by 2000.

23. A cistern has two supply-pipes which will singly fill it in $4\frac{1}{2}$ hours, and 6 hours, respectively; and it has also a leak, by which it would be emptied in 5 hours: in how many hours will it be filled when all are working together?

24. A market-woman bought a certain number of eggs at the rate of 5 for 2 cents; she sold half of them at 2 for a cent, and half of them at 3 for a cent, and gained 4 cents by so doing: what was the number of eggs?

25. A and B shoot by turns at a target; A puts 7 bullets out of 12 into the bull's-eye, and B puts in 9 out of 12; between them they put in 32 bullets: how many shots did each fire?

26. Two casks, A and B, contain mixtures of wine and water; in A the quantity of wine is to the quantity of water as 4 to 3; in B the like proportion is that of 2 to 3. If A contains 84 gallons, what must B contain, so that when the two are put together the new mixture may be half wine and half water?

27. How many minutes does it want to 4 o'clock, if three-quarters of an hour ago it was twice as many minutes past two o'clock?

28. What is the time after 6 o'clock at which the hands of a watch are, 1st, directly opposite, and, 2d, at right angles to each other?

29. It is between 11 and 12 o'clock, and it is observed that the number of minute-spaces between the hands is two-thirds of what it was ten minutes previously: find the time.

30. The national debt of a country was increased by one-fourth in a time of war. During a long peace which followed, $125,000,000 was paid off, and at the end of that time the rate of interest was reduced from $4\frac{1}{2}$ to 4 per cent. It was then found that the amount of annual interest was the same as before the war: what was the amount of debt before the war?

31. Find three numbers, the sum of which is 70, and such that the second divided by the first gives 2 for quotient, and 1 for remainder; and the third divided by the second gives 3 for quotient, and 3 for remainder.

32. Shells are thrown from two mortars in a besieged city; the first mortar has thrown 36 shells before the second commences its fire, and it sends 8 shells for every 7 sent by the second; but the second expends as much powder in 3 discharges as the first does in 4: how many shells must the second mortar throw in order to expend the same amount of powder as the first?

187. We shall now give a few problems in which the known quantities are represented by the first letters of the alphabet, instead of numbers.

Examples—38.

1. Find a number, such that being divided successively by m and n, the sum of the quotients shall be equal to a.

2. Divide a number a into two such parts that the quotient of the one divided by m, and the other divided by n, may be equal to b.

3. Divide a number a into two parts proportional to the numbers m and n.

4. Divide a number a into three parts, such that the first may be to the second as m is to n, and the second to the third as p is to q.

5. Two numbers, a and b, being given, what number must be added to each one of them in order that the ratio of the two sums may be equal to $\dfrac{m}{n}$?

6. Three fountains will fill a certain reservoir, when each one runs alone, in the times a, b, and c, respectively. In what time will they fill it, all running together?

7. Two couriers, whose distance apart when they set out was d miles, travel toward each other, the one moving at the rate of b miles an hour, and the other at the rate of c miles an hour. In what time after starting will they meet?

8. A can do a piece of work in b days, and B can do the same work in c days. In what time can they together do the work?

XXVI. SIMULTANEOUS EQUATIONS OF THE FIRST DEGREE.

188. If *one* equation contain *two* unknown quantities, there are an infinite number of pairs of values of these by which it may be satisfied.

Thus in $x = 10 - 2y$, if we give *any value* to y, we shall get a corresponding value for x, by which pair of values the equation will of course be satisfied. If, for example, we take

---

When one equation contains two unknown quantities, what values may they have?

$y=1$, we shall get $x=10-2=8$; if $y=2$, $x=6$; if $y=3$, $x=4$, &c.

One equation then, containing *two* unknown quantities (or, as it is expressed, "between two unknown quantities"), admits of an infinite number of solutions; but if we have as many different equations as there are quantities, the number of solutions will be limited; for it will be seen that they can always be reduced to a single equation containing a single unknown quantity.

Thus, while each of the equations, $x=10-2y$, $4x=32-6y$, separately considered, is satisfied by an infinite number of pairs of values of x and y, we shall find there is only *one* value of x, and *one* value of y, which will satisfy *both* equations; for, multiplying the first equation by 3,

$$3x=30-6y;$$ now take this from

the second equation $4x=32-6y$, and we get $x=2$.

Thus $x=2$ is the only value of x common to both equations. Put this value of x in either of the two given equations—for example, in the first; and we obtain,

$$2=10-2y;$$
$$\therefore 2y=8; \quad \therefore y=4.$$

Thus, $x=2$, $y=4$, are the only pair of values which satisfy both equations.

189. Equations of this kind, which are to be satisfied by the *same* pair or pairs of values of x and y, are called *simultaneous equations*. In the present chapter we treat of simultaneous equations of the first degree, (i. e.) where each unknown quantity occurs only in the first power, and the product of the unknown quantities does not occur. If there be *three* unknown quantities there must be *three* equations, and so on.

190. These *simultaneous equations* must *all* express *different* relations between the unknown quantities.

Thus, if we had the equation $x=10-2y$, it would be of no use to join with it the equation $2x=20-4y$ (which is the double of the former), or any other derived like this from the former.

191. There are generally given three methods for solving simultaneous equations of two unknowns; but the object aimed at is the same in each, viz., to combine the two equations in such a manner as to expel, or *eliminate*, one unknown from the result, and so get an equation of *one* unknown only.

192. First Method.—*Multiply the equations by the least numbers which will make the coefficients of one of the unknown quantities the same in both resulting equations; then adding or subtracting the two equations thus obtained, according as the equal terms have different or the same signs, these terms will destroy each other, and the elimination will be effected.*

Ex. 1.
$$2x+3y= 4 \quad (1)$$
$$3x-2y=-7 \quad (2)$$

Multiply (1) by 3, $\quad 6x+9y= 12.$
Multiply (2) by 2, $\quad 6x-4y=-14.$
Subtracting, $\quad 13y=26 \quad$ and $\therefore y=2.$

Then put this value of y in either (1) or (2); for example, in (1). We have thus:

$$2x+6=4; \quad \therefore 2x=4-6=-2; \quad \therefore x=-1.$$

Ex. 2.
$$8x+7y=100 \quad (1)$$
$$12x-5y= 88 \quad (2)$$

What is said of the relations expressed by simultaneous equations? Of the object aimed at by each of the three methods of solving them? First method?

We might multiply (1) by 12 and (2) by 8, giving thus:

$$96x + 84y = 1200$$
$$96x - 40y = 704$$

Subtracting, $\quad 124y = 496 \quad \therefore y = 4.$

But the process is more simple if we multiply equation (1) by 3 and equation (2) by 2. Thus:

$$24x + 21y = 300$$
$$24x - 10y = 176$$

$31y = 124; \therefore y = 4;$ and, substituting in (1), $\quad 8x + 28 = 100; \therefore 8x = 72,$ and $x = 9.$

We see here the advantage of multiplying by the *least numbers* which will make the coefficients the same, though we may multiply by *any numbers* which will effect the same object.

It is sometimes possible to multiply *one* of the given equations by some number which will make the coefficient of x or y in it the same as in the other equation. The process is in this case much shortened.

Ex. 3.
$$4x + y = 34 \quad (1)$$
$$4y + x = 16 \quad (2)$$

Here multiplying (2) by 4, $16y + 4x = 64;$

but $\quad y + 4x = 34; \quad (1)$

$\therefore$ subtracting, $\quad 15y = 30,$ and $\therefore y = 2.$,

and (2) $x = 16 - 4y = 16 - 8 = 8.$

Ex. 4.
$$4x - y = 7 \quad (1)$$
$$3x + 4y = 29 \quad (2)$$

Here $\quad 3x + 4y = 29,$

and, multiplying (1) by 4, $16x - 4y = 28;$

$\therefore$ adding, $19x = 57,$ and $\therefore x = 3;$

and (1) $\quad y = 4x - 7 = 12 - 7 = 5.$

193. Second Method.—*Express one of the unknown quantities in terms of the other by means of one of the equations, and put this expression for it in the other equation.*

Thus, taking the example 1 in the preceding article,

$$2x+3y= 4 \quad (1)$$
$$3x-2y=-7 \quad (2)$$

From (1), $x=\dfrac{4-3y}{2}$; substituting this expression in (2), we obtain

$$3\left(\dfrac{4-3y}{2}\right)-2y=-7,$$

whence $\qquad 3(4-3y)-4y=-14;$

that is, $\quad 12-9y-4y=-14; \quad \therefore -13y=-26; \quad \therefore y=2.$

$\therefore x=\dfrac{4-3y}{2}=\dfrac{4-6}{2}=-1.$

Ex. 5. $\quad 7x+\frac{1}{5}(2y+4)=16 \quad$ or reducing, $35x+2y=76 \quad (1)$
$\qquad 3y-\frac{1}{4}(x+2)= 8 \qquad\qquad\qquad\qquad 12y- x=34 \quad (2)$

Here from (2), $x=12y-34$, and from (1), $35(12y-34)+2y=76$; whence $y=3$, and $\therefore x=2$.

194. Third Method.—*Express the same unknown quantity in terms of the other in both equations, and put these expressions equal.*

Thus, taking again Ex. 1, $\quad 2x+3y= 4 \quad (1)$
$\qquad\qquad\qquad\qquad\qquad\quad 3x-2y=-7 \quad (2).$

(1) gives $y=\dfrac{4-2x}{3}$; (2) gives $y=\dfrac{3x+7}{2}$;

therefore, $\qquad \dfrac{3x+7}{2}=\dfrac{4-2x}{3}.$

SIMULTANEOUS EQUATIONS.

Clearing of fractions,

$$9x+21=8-4x. \therefore 13x=-13. \quad x=-1.$$

$$\therefore y=\frac{4-2x}{3}=\frac{4+2}{3}=2.$$

Ex. 6. $5x-\frac{1}{4}(5y+2)=32$ } or reducing, $20x-5y=130$ } (1)
$3y+\frac{1}{3}(x+2)= 9$ } $\quad\quad\quad\quad\quad 9y+ x= 25$ } (2)

Here in (1), $y=\frac{1}{5}(20x-130)$, in (2), $y=\frac{1}{9}(25-x)$;

$\therefore \frac{1}{5}(20x-130)=\frac{1}{9}(25-x)$, whence $x=7, y=2.$

The *first method* is to be preferred generally; but the second may be used with advantage whenever either x or y has a coefficient *unity* in one of the equations.

NOTE.—It may be well to give, here, an abbreviation of the first method, which saves much trouble when the coefficients are large. Two examples will serve to illustrate it.

Ex. $\quad 54x-121y=15$ } (1) to find x and y.
$\quad\quad\quad 36x- 77y=21$ } (2)

Subtracting, $\quad 18x-44y=-6$;
multiplying by 2, $\quad 36x-88y=-12$; }
from 2d equation, $\quad 36x-77y= 21$; }
subtracting, $\quad\quad 11y=33$;

$\therefore y=3.$

And $18x=44y-6=132-6=126$; $\therefore x=7.$

Ex. $\quad 101x-24y=63$ } (1) to find x and y.
$\quad\quad\quad 103x-28y=29$ } (2)

Subtracting, $\quad 2x- 4y=-34$;
multiplying by 6, $\quad 12x-24y=-204$; }
but $\quad 101x-24y= 63$; }
subtracting, $\quad\quad 89x=267$;

$\therefore x=\frac{267}{89}=3.$

And $4y=2x+34=40$; $\therefore y=10.$

Which method is preferable?

195. Ex. 7. Solve
$$\left. \begin{array}{l} \dfrac{12}{x}+\dfrac{8}{y}=8 \\ \dfrac{27}{x}-\dfrac{12}{y}=3 \end{array} \right\} \begin{array}{l}(1)\\(2)\end{array}$$

If we cleared these equations of fractions they would contain xy, and could not then be solved by the methods of this chapter. But if we do not clear them of fractions, they may be solved readily by the methods given. Thus,

multiplying (1) by 3, $\quad \dfrac{36}{x}+\dfrac{24}{y}=24;$

multiplying (2) by 2, $\quad \dfrac{54}{x}-\dfrac{24}{y}=6;$

adding, $\quad \dfrac{90}{x}=30; \therefore 90=30x; \therefore x=3.$

$\therefore$ (1) gives $\quad \dfrac{12}{3}+\dfrac{8}{y}=8;$

therefore, $\quad \dfrac{8}{y}=8-4=4; \therefore 8=4y; \therefore y=2.$

Ex. 8. Solve $a^2x+b^2y=c^2$ (1), $ax+by=c$ (2).

Multiplying (2) by b, and subtracting it from (1),

$$a^2x+b^2y=c^2$$
$$abx+b^2y=bc$$
$$\overline{a^2x-abx=c^2-bc\,;}$$

that is, $\quad a(a-b)x=c(c-b);$

$$\therefore x=\frac{c(c-b)}{a(a-b)};$$

substituting this value of x in (2),

$$\frac{ac(c-b)}{a(a-b)}+by=c;$$

therefore, $$by = c - \frac{c(c-b)}{(a-b)} = \frac{c(a-c)}{a-b};$$

$$\therefore y = \frac{c(a-c)}{b(a-b)}.$$

Or this value of y might be found in the same way as that of x was found.

Examples—39.

Find the values of x and y in the following pairs of equations:

1. $3x - 4y = 2$, $7x - 9y = 7$.
2. $7x - 5y = 24$, $4x - 3y = 11$.
3. $3x + 2y = 32$, $20x - 3y = 1$.
4. $11x - 7y = 37$, $8x + 9y = 41$.
5. $7x + 5y = 60$, $13x - 11y = 10$.
6. $6x - 7y = 42$, $7x - 6y = 75$.
7. $\frac{3x}{19} + 5y = 13$, $2x + \frac{4 - 7y}{2} = 33$.
8. $\frac{x}{7} + \frac{y}{14} = 10\frac{1}{2}$, $2x - y = 7$.
9. $\frac{x+y}{3} + \frac{y-x}{2} = 9$, $\frac{x}{2} + \frac{x+y}{9} = 5$.
10. $\frac{3x}{4} - \frac{2y}{3} = 1$, $\frac{7x}{3} + \frac{5y}{6} = 6$.
11. $\frac{1-3x}{7} + \frac{3y-1}{5} = 2$, $\frac{3x+y}{11} + y = 9$.
12. $2(2x + 3y) = 3(2x - 3y) + 10$, $4x - 3y = 4(6y - 2x) + 3$.

13. $\begin{array}{l}x(y+7)=y(x+1) \\ 2x+20=3y+1\end{array}\Big\}$ 14. $\begin{array}{l}\frac{1}{2}x+\frac{1}{3}y=13 \\ \frac{1}{3}x+\frac{1}{2}y=5\end{array}\Big\}$

15. $\begin{array}{l}\frac{1}{4}x+\frac{1}{5}y=43 \\ \frac{1}{5}x+\frac{1}{4}y=42\end{array}\Big\}$

16. $3x+9y=2.4, \quad .21x-.06y=.03.$

17. $.3x+.125y=x-6, \quad 3x-.5y=28-.25y.$

18. $.08x-.21y=.33, \quad .12x+.7y=3.54.$

19. $\dfrac{9}{x}-\dfrac{4}{y}=1, \quad \dfrac{18}{x}+\dfrac{20}{y}=16.$

20. $\dfrac{x}{a}+\dfrac{y}{b}=2, \quad bx-ay=0.$

21. $x+y=a+b, \quad bx+ay=2ab.$

22. $\dfrac{x}{a}+\dfrac{y}{b}=1, \quad \dfrac{x}{b}+\dfrac{y}{a}=1.$

23. $(a+c)x-by=bc, \quad x+y=a+b.$

24. $\dfrac{x}{a}+\dfrac{y}{b}=c, \quad \dfrac{x}{b}-\dfrac{y}{a}=0.$

25. $x+y=c, \quad ax-by=c(a-b).$

26. $a(x+y)+b(x-y)=1, \quad a(x-y)+b(x+y)=1.$

27. $\dfrac{x-a}{b}+\dfrac{y-b}{a}=0, \quad \dfrac{x+y-b}{a}+\dfrac{x-y-a}{b}=0.$

196. Simultaneous equations of three unknown quantities are solved by eliminating one of the unknown quantities by means of any pair of the equations, and then the *same* unknown by means of another pair; we shall then have two equations involving only two unknown quantities, which we may solve by the preceding rules. The remaining unknown is found by substituting the values obtained for the other two in any of the given equations.

Similarly for simultaneous equations of more than three unknown quantities.

Ex. 1.
$$x - 2y + 3z = 2 \quad (1)$$
$$2x - 3y + z = 1 \quad (2)$$
$$3x - y + 2z = 9 \quad (3)$$

From (1) $\quad 2x - 4y + 6z = 4$
(2) $\quad\quad 2x - 3y + z = 1$
$\therefore \quad -y + 5z = 3 \quad (4)$

Again, from (1) $\quad 3x - 6y + 9z = 6$
(3) $\quad\quad 3x - y + 2z = 9$
$\therefore \quad -5y + 7z = -3 \quad (5)$

but from (4) $\quad -5y + 25z = 15$
$\therefore \quad -18z = -18, \text{ and } z = 1$

hence (4), $\quad y = 5z - 3 = 2$
and (1), $\quad x = 2 + 2y - 3z = 2 + 4 - 3 = 3.$

Ex. 2.
$$\frac{1}{x} + \frac{2}{y} - \frac{3}{z} = 1 \quad (1)$$

$$\frac{5}{x} + \frac{4}{y} + \frac{6}{z} = 24 \quad (2)$$

$$\frac{7}{x} - \frac{8}{y} + \frac{9}{z} = 14 \quad (3)$$

Multiplying (1) by 2, $\quad \dfrac{2}{x} + \dfrac{4}{y} - \dfrac{6}{z} = 2$

Adding (2) to this, $\quad \dfrac{5}{x} + \dfrac{4}{y} + \dfrac{6}{z} = 24$

$$\frac{7}{x} + \frac{8}{y} = 26 \quad (4)$$

Multiply (1) by 3, $\quad \dfrac{3}{x} + \dfrac{6}{y} - \dfrac{9}{z} = 3$

Add (3) to this, $\dfrac{7}{x}-\dfrac{8}{y}+\dfrac{9}{z}=14$

$\dfrac{10}{x}-\dfrac{2}{y}=17 \qquad (5)$

Now multiply (5) by 4, $\dfrac{40}{x}-\dfrac{8}{y}=68$

Add (4) to this, $\dfrac{7}{x}+\dfrac{8}{y}=26$

$\dfrac{47}{x}=94; \qquad \therefore 47=94x. \qquad \therefore x=\dfrac{47}{94}=\dfrac{1}{2}.$

Substitute the value of x in (5); thus,

$20-\dfrac{2}{y}=17; \qquad \therefore \dfrac{2}{y}=20-17=3; \qquad \therefore y=\dfrac{2}{3}.$

Substitute the values of x and y in (1); thus,

$2+3-\dfrac{3}{z}=1; \qquad \therefore \dfrac{3}{z}=4; \qquad \therefore z=\dfrac{3}{4}.$

Ex. 3. Solve $\dfrac{x}{a}+\dfrac{y}{b}=1 \quad (1)$

$\dfrac{x}{a}+\dfrac{z}{c}=1 \quad (2)$

$\dfrac{y}{b}+\dfrac{z}{c}=1 \quad (3)$

From (1) $\dfrac{x}{a}+\dfrac{y}{b}=1$

subtract (2) $\dfrac{x}{a}+\dfrac{z}{c}=1;$

to the result, $\dfrac{y}{b}-\dfrac{z}{c}=0$

add (3) $\dfrac{y}{b}+\dfrac{z}{c}=1$

$\dfrac{2y}{b}=1 \qquad y=\dfrac{b}{2}.$

Substitute this value in (1); thus,

$$\frac{x}{a}+\frac{1}{2}=1; \quad \therefore \frac{x}{a}=1-\frac{1}{2}; \quad \therefore x=\frac{a}{2}.$$

Substitute the same value in (3); thus,

$$\frac{1}{2}+\frac{z}{c}=1; \quad \therefore \frac{z}{c}=\frac{1}{2}; \quad \therefore z=\frac{c}{2}.$$

These values of z and x might have been written down at once from the *symmetry* of the equations, since it is obvious that the values of x and z will be of the same form as that of y, only interchanging a and c, respectively, with b.

Examples—40.

1. $\left.\begin{array}{l} 2x+3y+4z=20 \\ 3x+4y+5z=26 \\ 3x+5y+6z=31 \end{array}\right\}$

2. $\left.\begin{array}{l} 5x+3y=65 \\ 2y-z=11 \\ 3x+4z=57 \end{array}\right\}$

3. $\left.\begin{array}{l} 3x+2y-z=20 \\ 2x+3y+6z=70 \\ x-y+6z=41 \end{array}\right\}$

4. $\left.\begin{array}{l} x+y+z=5 \\ x+y=z-7 \\ x-3=y+z \end{array}\right\}$

5. $\left.\begin{array}{l} x+2y=7 \\ y+2z=2 \\ 3x+2y=z-1 \end{array}\right\}$

6. $\left.\begin{array}{l} xy=x+y \\ xz=2(x+z) \\ yz=3(y+z) \end{array}\right\}$

7. $\left.\begin{array}{l} 2(x-y)=3z-2 \\ x+1=3(y+z) \\ 2x+3z=4(1-y) \end{array}\right\}$

8. $\left.\begin{array}{l} \frac{1}{2}x+\frac{1}{3}y=12-\frac{1}{6}z \\ \frac{1}{2}y+\frac{1}{3}z=8+\frac{1}{6}x \\ \frac{1}{2}x+\frac{1}{3}z=10 \end{array}\right\}$

9. $\left.\begin{array}{l} y+\frac{1}{3}z=\frac{1}{2}x+5 \\ \frac{1}{4}(x-1)-\frac{1}{5}(y-2)=\frac{1}{10}(z+3) \\ x-\frac{1}{3}(2y-5)=1\frac{3}{4}-\frac{1}{12}z \end{array}\right\}$

10. $\dfrac{1}{x}-\dfrac{1}{y}=\dfrac{1}{6},\qquad \dfrac{1}{y}+\dfrac{1}{z}=3\tfrac{5}{8},\qquad \dfrac{4}{x}+\dfrac{3}{y}=\dfrac{4}{z}.$

11. $y+z=a,\qquad z+x=b,\qquad x+y=c.$

12. $x+y+z=a+b+c,\qquad x+a=y+b=z+c.$

13. $y+z-x=a,\qquad z+x-y=b,\qquad x+y-z=c.$

14. $\dfrac{x}{a}+\dfrac{y}{b}+\dfrac{z}{c}=1,\qquad \dfrac{x}{a}+\dfrac{y}{c}+\dfrac{z}{b}=1,\qquad \dfrac{x}{b}+\dfrac{y}{a}+\dfrac{z}{c}=1.$

NOTE.—In Ex. 6, divide the equations by xy, xz, and yz, respectively, and they will then be of the form of those given in Ex. 10.

XXVII. PROBLEMS SOLVED BY SIMULTANEOUS EQUATIONS OF THE FIRST DEGREE.

197. PROB. 1. There is a certain fraction which becomes equal to $\tfrac{1}{2}$ when both numerator and denominator are diminished by 1; but, if 2 be taken from the numerator and added to the denominator, the fraction becomes equal to $\tfrac{1}{3}$: find it.

Let x denote the numerator, and y the denominator of the required fraction; then the conditions of the problem give,

$$\dfrac{x-1}{y-1}=\dfrac{1}{2},\qquad \dfrac{x-2}{y+2}=\dfrac{1}{3}.$$

Clear the equations of fractions,—transpose, and reduce. We obtain thus,

$$2x-y=1 \quad (1)$$
$$3x-y=8 \quad (2)$$

Subtracting (1) from (2) we get $x=7$; $\therefore$ (1) gives $14-y=1$; $\therefore y=13$; therefore, the required fraction is $\tfrac{7}{13}$.

PROB. 2. There is a certain number composed of two figures or digits, which is equal to four times the sum of its digits; and if the digits exchange places, the number thus formed is less by 12 than twice the former number: what is the number?

SIMULTANEOUS EQUATIONS.

Let x be the digit in the *tens'* place,

y .... *units'* ....;

then $10x+y$ is the number (just as $23 = 10 \times 2 + 3$), ∴ by the conditions of the question,

$$10x + y = 4(x+y),$$

that is, $\qquad = 4x + 4y;$

transposing, $\qquad 10x - 4x = 4y - y;$

uniting, $\qquad 6x = 3y;$

or, $\qquad 2x = y \quad (1).$

Again, if the digits be reversed, $10y+x$ will be the number; ∴ by the question,

$$10y + x = 2(10x+y) - 12;$$

that is, $\qquad = 20x + 2y - 12;$

transposing, $\qquad 19x - 8y = 12;$

or, $[\because y=2x, (1)], \quad 19x - 16x = 12; \quad (2)$

uniting, $\qquad 3x = 12;$

∴ $x = 4$; and $y = 2x = 8$.

∴ the number required is 48.

PROB. 3. A railway train after travelling an hour is detained 24 minutes, after which it proceeds at six-fifths of its former rate, and arrives 15 minutes late. If the detention had taken place 5 miles further on, the train would have arrived 2 minutes later than it did. Find the original rate of the train, and the distance travelled.

Let $5x$ denote the number of miles per hour at which the train originally travelled, and let y denote the number of miles in the whole distance travelled. Then $y-5x$ will denote the number of miles which remain to be travelled after the detention. At the original rate of the train this distance would be travelled in $\dfrac{y-5x}{5x}$ hours; at the increased rate it will be travelled in $\dfrac{y-5x}{6x}$ hours. Since the train is detained 24 minutes, and yet is only 15 minutes late at its arrival, it follows

8*

that the remainder of the journey is performed in 9 minutes less than it would have been if the rate had not been increased; and 9 minutes is $\frac{9}{60}$ of an hour; therefore,

$$\frac{y-5x}{6x}=\frac{y-5x}{5x}-\frac{9}{60} \quad (1).$$

If the detention had taken place 5 miles further on, there would have been $y-5x-5$ miles left to be travelled. Thus we shall find that

$$\frac{y-5x-5}{6x}=\frac{y-5x-5}{5x}-\frac{7}{60} \quad (2).$$

Subtracting (2) from (1),

$$\frac{5}{6x}=\frac{5}{5x}-\frac{2}{60};$$

therefore, $50=60-2x;$

whence, $2x=10$; and $x=5$.

Substitute this value of x in (1), and it will be found by solving the equation that $y=47\frac{1}{2}$.

PROB. 4. A and B can together do a piece of work in a days; A and C can together do it in b days; B and C can together perform it in c days: find the number of days in which each alone could perform the work.

Let x denote the number of days in which A alone could perform it, y the number of days in which B alone could perform it, z the number of days in which C alone could perform it.

Then we have,

$$\frac{1}{x}+\frac{1}{y}=\frac{1}{a} \quad (1);$$

$$\frac{1}{x}+\frac{1}{z}=\frac{1}{b} \quad (2);$$

$$\frac{1}{y}+\frac{1}{z}=\frac{1}{c} \quad (3).$$

Subtracting (2) from (1) we obtain,

$$\frac{1}{y}-\frac{1}{z}=\frac{1}{a}-\frac{1}{b} \quad (4)$$

SIMULTANEOUS EQUATIONS. 179

adding (3),
$$\frac{1}{y}+\frac{1}{z}=\frac{1}{c};$$

$$\frac{2}{y}=\frac{1}{a}-\frac{1}{b}+\frac{1}{c}=\frac{bc+ab-ac}{abc}.$$

Therefore,
$$y=\frac{2abc}{bc+ab-ac};$$

$$\therefore\ z=\frac{2abc}{ab+ac-bc},\ \text{and}\ x=\frac{2abc}{ac+bc-ab};$$

these latter values being written out at once by the *symmetry* of the equations.

Or we might have solved the problem thus:

Let $x=$ the number of units of work performed by A in one day;
Let $y=$ " " " performed by B in one day;
Let $z=$ " " " performed by C in one day.

Then,
$$x+y=\frac{1}{a}\ \ (1);$$

$$x+z=\frac{1}{b}\ \ (2);$$

$$y+z=\frac{1}{c}\ \ (3).$$

These give by eliminating, as before,
$$y=\frac{bc+ab-ac}{2abc}.$$

Therefore B's time of performing the whole work, or $\frac{1}{y}=\frac{2abc}{bc+ab-ac}$ as before.

198. A problem may often be solved as readily by a single equation and one unknown quantity, as by simultaneous equations with two or more unknown quantities. The advantage to a beginner in taking several letters to denote the unknowns is that, though he has more equations and longer work, he can more easily follow the steps by which the equations are formed.

Thus Ex. 19, Chap. XXV., may be solved by four simultaneous equations, involving four unknown quantities.

Examples—41.

1. What fraction is that, to the numerator of which if 7 be added, its value will be $\frac{2}{3}$; but if 7 be taken from the denominator its value will be $\frac{2}{5}$?

2. There is a number of two digits which, when divided by their sum, gives the quotient 4; but if the digits change places, and the number thus formed be increased by 12, and then divided by their sum, the quotient is 8: find the number.

3. A rectangular bowling-green having been measured, it was observed that, if it were 5 feet broader and 4 feet longer, it would contain 116 feet more; but if it were 4 feet broader and 5 feet longer it would contain 113 feet more: find its present area.

4. A person rows on a uniformly flowing stream a distance of 20 miles and back again, in 10 hours; and he finds that he can row 2 miles against the stream in the same time that he rows 3 miles with it. Find the time of rowing down and the time of rowing up.

5. A and B can do a piece of work together in 12 days, which B, working for 15 days, and C for 30 days, would together complete. In 10 days, working all three together, they would finish the work: in what time could they separately do it?

6. Some smugglers found a cave which would just exactly hold the cargo of their boat, viz., 13 bales of silk and 33 casks of rum. While unloading, a revenue cutter came in sight, and they were obliged to sail away, having landed only 9 casks and 5 bales, and filled one-third of the cave. How many bales separately, or how many casks, would it hold?

7. Seven years ago, A was three times as old as B was; and seven years hence, A will be twice as old as B will be: find their present ages.

8. A certain fishing-rod consists of two parts: the length of the upper part is to the length of the lower as 5 to 7; and 9 times the upper part, together with 13 times the lower part, exceed 11 times the whole rod by 36 inches: find the lengths of the two parts.

9. If the numerator of a certain fraction be increased by 1, and the denominator be diminished by 1, the value will be 1; if the numerator be increased by the denominator, and the denominator diminished by the numerator, the value will be 4: find the fraction.

10. A number of posts are placed at equal distances in a straight line. If to twice the number of them we add the number of feet between two consecutive posts, the sum is 68. If from four times the number of feet between two consecutive posts we subtract half the number of posts, the remainder is 68. Find the distance between the extreme posts.

11. On the addition of 9 to a certain number of two digits, its digits change places; and the sum of the first number and the number thus formed is 33: find the digits.

12. A and B ran a race which lasted five minutes. B had a start of 20 yards; but A ran 3 yards while B was running 2, and won by 30 yards: find the length of the course, and the speed of each.

13. A person has two casks, with a certain quantity of wine in each. He draws out of the first into the second as much as there was in the second to begin with; then he draws out of the second into the first, as much as was left in the first; and then again out of the first into the second, as much as was left in the second. There are then exactly 8 gallons in each cask. How much was there in each at first?

14. The year of our Lord in which the '*change of style*' from the Julian to the Gregorian Calendar was made in England, may be thus expressed: The first digit being 1 for thousands, the second is the sum of the third and fourth, the third is the *third* part of the sum of all four, and the fourth is the *fourth* part of the sum of the first two. Determine the year.

15. A and B can together perform a certain work in 30 days: at the end of 18 days, however, B is called off, and A finishes it alone in 20 more days. Find the time in which each could perform the work alone.

16. A cistern holding 1200 gallons is filled by three pipes, A, B, C, together, in 24 minutes. The pipe A requires 30 minutes more than C to fill the cistern; and 10 gallons less run through C per minute than through A and B together: find the time in which each pipe alone would fill the cistern.

17. Find two numbers, the sum of which is equal to 3 times their difference, and their product equal to 4 times their difference. (See Note at the end of "Examples—40.")

18. The sum of two numbers is 13, and the difference of their squares is 39. What are these numbers?

    NOTE.—Here divide the second equation by the first.

19. A and B are two towns, situated 24 miles apart, on the same bank of a river: a gentleman goes from A to B in 7 hours by rowing the first half of the distance, and walking the second half. In returning, he walks the first half at three-fourths his former rate; but the stream being with him in returning, he rows at double his rate in going; and he accomplishes the whole distance in 6 hours: find his rates of walking and rowing.

20. Two trains, 92 feet long and 84 feet long, respectively, are moving with uniform velocities on parallel rails: when

they move in opposite directions, they are observed to pass each other in one second and a half; but when they move in the same direction, the faster train is observed to pass the other in six seconds: find the rate at which each train moves.

21. A railroad runs from A to C. A freight train starts from A at 12 o'clock, and a passenger train at 1 o'clock. After going two-thirds of the distance the freight train breaks down, and can only travel at three-fourths of its former rate. At 40 minutes past 2 o'clock a collision occurs, 10 miles from C. The rate of the passenger train is double the diminished rate of the freight train. Find the distance from A to C, and the rates of the trains.

22. A certain sum of money was divided between A, B, and C, so that A's share exceeded four-sevenths of the shares of B and C by \$30; also B's share exceeded three-eighths of the shares of A and C by \$30; and C's share exceeded two-ninths of the shares of A and B by \$30: find the share of each person.

23. A, B, and C can together perform a piece of work in 30 days; A and B can together perform it in 32 days, and B and C can together perform it in 120 days: find the number of days in which each alone could perform the work.

24. Express the two numbers whose sum is a, and their difference b.

25. Find two numbers, such that the product of the first increased by a, and the second increased by b, exceeds by c the product of the two numbers; and the product of the first increased by m, and the second increased by n, exceeds by h the product of the two numbers.

26. The sum of two numbers is a, and the difference of their squares is b: find the two numbers.

27. Find two numbers, whose sum is m times their difference, and their product is n times their difference.

XXVIII. Indices.

199. The indices or exponents which we have used hitherto are positive whole numbers, which express briefly the repetition of the same factor in any product. (See Art. 15.)

Under this definition we have proved (Art. 59),

$$a^m \times a^n = a^{m+n}.$$

Also (Art. 74), $\qquad a^m \div a^n = a^{m-n}.$

200. Hence it will follow that $(a^m)^n = a^{mn} = (a^n)^m.$

For $(a^m)^n = a^m \cdot a^m \cdot a^m$ &c. n factors $= a^{m+m+m+\text{&c. }n\text{ terms}} = a^{mn}$,

and $(a^n)^m = a^n \cdot a^n \cdot a^n$ &c. m factors $= a^{n+n+n+\text{&c. }m\text{ terms}} = a^{nm}$;

$\therefore$ since $a^{mn} = a^{nm}$, we have $(a^m)^n = a^{mn} = (a^n)^m$:

that is, *the* n^{th} *power of the* m^{th} *power of* a $=$ *the* m^{th} *power of the* n^{th} *power of* a; and either of them is found by multiplying the two indices.

201. Hence, also, it will follow that $\sqrt[n]{a^m} = (\sqrt[n]{a})^m.$

For let $\sqrt[n]{a^m} = x^m$; then $a^m = (x^m)^n = (x^n)^m$ by (199);

hence $a = x^n$, and $\therefore \sqrt[n]{a} = x$, and $(\sqrt[n]{a})^m = x^m$;

but also, by our first assumption, $\qquad \sqrt[n]{a^m} = x^m$;

hence, we have, $\sqrt[n]{a^m} = (\sqrt[n]{a})^m$;

that is, *the* n^{th} *root of the* m^{th} *power of* a $=$ *the* m^{th} *power of the* n^{th} *root of* a.

202. These results refer so far to positive integral indices. But now suppose we write down a quantity with a positive *fraction* for an index, and agree that the law of multiplication, $a^m \times a^n = a^{m+n}$, *shall hold true for* m *and* n *fractions as well as* m *and* n *positive whole numbers.* What would such a fractional index denote?

For example: *required the meaning of* $a^{\frac{1}{2}}$.

INDICES. 185

By supposition we are to have $a^{\frac{1}{2}} \times a^{\frac{1}{2}} = a^1 = a$. Thus $a^{\frac{1}{2}}$ must be such a number that if it be multiplied by itself the result is a; and the *square root* of a is by definition such a number; therefore $a^{\frac{1}{2}}$ must be equivalent to the square root of a, that is, $a^{\frac{1}{2}} = \sqrt{a}$.

Again; *required the meaning of* $a^{\frac{1}{3}}$.

By supposition we are to have,

$$a^{\frac{1}{3}} \times a^{\frac{1}{3}} \times a^{\frac{1}{3}} = a^{\frac{1}{3}+\frac{1}{3}+\frac{1}{3}} = a^1 = a.$$

Hence, as before, $a^{\frac{1}{3}}$ must be equivalent to the cube root of a; that is, $a^{\frac{1}{3}} = \sqrt[3]{a}$.

Again; *required the meaning of* $a^{\frac{3}{4}}$.

By supposition, $\quad a^{\frac{3}{4}} \times a^{\frac{3}{4}} \times a^{\frac{3}{4}} \times a^{\frac{3}{4}} = a^3;$

therefore, $\quad\quad\quad\quad\quad a^{\frac{3}{4}} = \sqrt[4]{a^3}.$

To give the definition in general symbols:

1. *Required the meaning of* $a^{\frac{1}{n}}$ *where* n *is any positive whole number.*

By supposition,

$$a^{\frac{1}{n}} \times a^{\frac{1}{n}} \times a^{\frac{1}{n}} \times \ldots \text{ to } n \text{ factors} = a^{\frac{1}{n}+\frac{1}{n}+\frac{1}{n}+\ldots \text{to } n \text{ terms}} = a^1 = a;$$

therefore $a^{\frac{1}{n}}$ must be equivalent to the nth root of a,

that is, $\quad\quad\quad\quad\quad a^{\frac{1}{n}} = \sqrt[n]{a}.$

2. *Required the meaning of* $a^{\frac{m}{n}}$ *where* m *and* n *are any positive whole numbers.*

By supposition,

$$a^{\frac{m}{n}} \times a^{\frac{m}{n}} \times a^{\frac{m}{n}} \times \ldots \text{ to } n \text{ factors} = a^{\frac{m}{n}+\frac{m}{n}+\frac{m}{n}+\ldots \text{to } n \text{ terms}} = a^m;$$

therefore $a^{\frac{m}{n}}$ must be equivalent to the nth root of a^m;

that is, $\quad\quad\quad\quad\quad a^{\frac{m}{n}} = \sqrt[n]{a^m}.$

Hence, $a^{\frac{m}{n}}$ means the nth root of the mth power of a; that is, in a fractional index the numerator denotes a power, and the denominator a root.

203. Again; if we write down a quantity with a negative index, as a^{-p} (where p is either an integer or a fraction), and agree that this symbol shall be treated by the same law of multiplication as a positive index; what would this symbol denote?

By this law of multiplication, $a^{m+p} \times a^{-p} = a^{m+p-p} = a^m$; but we have also, $a^{m+p} \div a^p = \dfrac{a^{m+p}}{a^p} = \dfrac{a^m \cdot a^p}{a^p} = a^m$;

so that to *multiply* by a^{-p} is the same as to *divide* by a^p; and therefore,

$$1 \times a^{-p} = 1 \div a^p, \text{ or } a^{-p} = \dfrac{1}{a^p}.$$

Hence, any quantity with a *negative* index denotes the *reciprocal* of the same quantity with the same *positive* index.

Thus $a^{-1} = \dfrac{1}{a}$, $a^{-3} = \dfrac{1}{a^3}$, $a^{-\frac{1}{2}} = \dfrac{1}{a^{\frac{1}{2}}} = \dfrac{1}{\sqrt{a}}$, or $= \sqrt{a^{-1}} = \sqrt{\dfrac{1}{a}}$;

$a^{-\frac{2}{3}} = \dfrac{1}{a^{\frac{2}{3}}} = \dfrac{1}{\sqrt[3]{a^2}}$, or $= \sqrt[3]{a^{-2}} = \sqrt[3]{\dfrac{1}{a^2}}$.

Hence, also, any power in the numerator of a quantity may be removed into the denominator, and *vice versâ*, by merely changing the sign of its index.

Thus $a^{-3}b^2c^{-1} = \dfrac{a^{-3}b^2}{c} = \dfrac{a^{-3}}{b^{-2}c} = \dfrac{b^2c^{-1}}{a^3} = \&c.$

204. Lastly, if we write down a quantity with *zero* for an index, as a^0, and agree that this symbol shall be treated as if the index were an actual number—what then would it denote?

Since, by this law, $a^0 \times a^m = a^{0+m} = a^m$, it follows that a^0 is only equivalent to 1, whatever be the value of a.

In actual practice, such a quantity as a^0 would only occur in certain cases, where we wish to keep in mind from what a certain number may have arisen: thus $(a^3 + 2a^2 + 3a + \&c.) \div a^2 = a + 2 + 3a^{-1} + \&c.$, where the 2 has lost all sign of its having been originally a coefficient of some power of a; if, however, we write the quotient $a + 2a^0 + 3a^{-1} + \&c.$, we preserve an indication of this, and have, as it were, a connecting link between the positive and negative powers of a.

The quantity $a^{\frac{p}{q}}$ is still called *a to the power of* $\frac{p}{q}$, and similarly in the case of a^{-m}, a^0; but the word *power* has here lost its original meaning, and denotes merely *a quantity with an index*, whatever that index may be, subject, in all cases, to the Law, $a^m \cdot a^n = a^{m+n}$.

Examples—42.

Express, with *fractional* indices,

1. $\sqrt{x^3} + \sqrt[3]{x^4} + (\sqrt{x})^5 + (\sqrt[3]{x})^2$; $\sqrt[3]{(a^3b^2)} + \sqrt[4]{(a^2b^4)} + \sqrt[5]{(ab^6)}$
$+ \sqrt[3]{(a^5b^4)}$.

2. $a^2\sqrt{b^3} + (\sqrt{a})^5 + \sqrt[3]{(a^5b)} + \sqrt[4]{(a^3b^4)}$; $\sqrt[5]{(a^2b^6)} + a(\sqrt[3]{b})^5$
$+ \sqrt[4]{(a^3b^{10})} + \sqrt{(a^3b^4)}$.

Express, with *negative* indices, so as to remove all powers, 1st, into the numerators, and 2d, into the denominators.

3. $\dfrac{1}{a} + \dfrac{2}{b^2} + \dfrac{3}{c^3} + \dfrac{4a}{b} + \dfrac{5b}{a}$; $\dfrac{a^3}{b^3} + \dfrac{3a^2}{b} + \dfrac{5a}{b^2} + \dfrac{4b}{a^2} + \dfrac{2b^2}{a^3}$.

4. $\dfrac{a^3}{3b^3c^2} + \dfrac{4c^2}{a^2b} + \dfrac{2bc}{a} + \dfrac{1}{3abc}$; $\dfrac{ab}{2\sqrt{c}} + \dfrac{2b^2c^2}{3\sqrt{a^3}} + \dfrac{3}{4\sqrt[3]{(a^2bc^3)}} + \dfrac{5c}{d\sqrt{b^5}}$.

Express, with *signs of Evolution*,

5. $a^{\frac{1}{2}} + 2a^{\frac{2}{3}} + 3a^{\frac{3}{4}} + 4a^{\frac{4}{5}} + a^{\frac{3}{4}}$; $\dfrac{a^{\frac{1}{4}}}{b^{\frac{3}{4}}} + \dfrac{a^{\frac{3}{5}}b^{\frac{1}{3}}}{2c^{\frac{1}{2}}} + \dfrac{2a^{\frac{1}{4}}c^{\frac{2}{3}}}{3b^{\frac{1}{2}}}$
$+ \dfrac{b^{\frac{2}{3}}c^{\frac{3}{4}}}{4a^{\frac{1}{5}}} + \dfrac{b^{\frac{1}{6}}c^{\frac{4}{5}}}{5a^{\frac{3}{4}}}$.

Express, with *positive* indices, and with the sign of Evolution,

6. $a^{-1}bc + ab^{-2}c + a^{-1}b^{-1}c^{-1} + a^{-1}b^{-2}c^2$; $a^{-\frac{2}{3}} + a^{\frac{1}{2}}b^{-\frac{1}{3}} + a^{-\frac{1}{2}}b^{\frac{2}{3}} + b^{-\frac{4}{3}}$.

7. $\dfrac{a^{-2}b^{-2}}{c^{-1}} + \dfrac{2a}{b^{-1}c^{-1}} + \dfrac{3b^{-1}c^{-2}}{a^{-3}} + \dfrac{1}{a^{-1}b^{-2}c^{-3}}$; $\dfrac{a^{-2}}{b^{-\frac{1}{3}}} + \dfrac{b^{-\frac{2}{3}}}{a^{-\frac{1}{2}}} + \dfrac{b^{-\frac{1}{3}}}{a^{-\frac{2}{3}}} + \dfrac{a^{-\frac{1}{2}}}{b^{-2}}$.

205. From our definitions, $(a^{\frac{1}{2}})^3 = a^{\frac{3}{2}}$ and $(a^3)^{\frac{1}{2}} = a^{\frac{3}{2}}$; and in general, $(a^{\frac{1}{n}})^m = (a^m)^{\frac{1}{n}}$; then, also, $(a^{\frac{2}{3}})^{\frac{2}{5}} = a^{\frac{4}{15}}$; also, $a^{\frac{1}{n}} \cdot b^{\frac{1}{n}} \cdot c^{\frac{1}{n}} \ldots = (abc \ldots)^{\frac{1}{n}}$, since each, raised to the nth power, gives abc.

It follows, then, that *whatever be the indices*,

$$a^m \times a^n = a^{m+n}; \quad \dfrac{a^m}{a^n} = a^m \times \dfrac{1}{a^n} = a^m \times a^{-n}; \quad (a^m)^n = a^{mn}.$$

It will be observed, also, that since a fraction may take different forms without changing its value, the form of a fractional index may be changed without altering the value of the quantity.

Thus $a^{\frac{1}{3}} = a^{\frac{2}{6}}$; for either raised to the sixth power gives a^2; and in general, $a^{\frac{m}{n}} = a^{\frac{mp}{np}}$, for either raised to the np power gives a^{mp}. Hence we can reduce the indices of two quantities to a common denominator without changing the value of the expressions.

206. Hence, (1) to *multiply* together any powers of the same quantity we must *add the indices;* (2), to divide any one power of a quantity by another power of the same quantity, *subtract the index of the divisor from that of the dividend;* and, (3), to obtain any *power of a power* of a quantity, we must *multiply together the two indices.*

The signs of the indices must of course be carefully observed.

Ex. 1. Multiply $a^{\frac{2}{3}}b^{\frac{3}{4}}c^{\frac{1}{3}}$ by $a^{\frac{1}{2}}b^{\frac{1}{3}}c^{\frac{2}{3}}$.

Reduction of the indices of two quantities to a common denominator. Rule for (1) multiplying together powers of the same quantity; (2) for dividing one power of a quantity by another power of the same quantity; (3) for obtaining any power of a power of a quantity.

$$\frac{2}{3}+\frac{1}{2}=\frac{7}{6}, \qquad \frac{3}{4}+\frac{1}{3}=\frac{13}{12}, \qquad \frac{1}{3}+\frac{2}{3}=1;$$

therefore, $\quad a^{\frac{2}{3}} b^{\frac{3}{4}} c^{\frac{1}{3}} \times a^{\frac{1}{2}} b^{\frac{1}{3}} c^{\frac{2}{3}} = a^{\frac{7}{6}} b^{\frac{13}{12}} c.$

Ex. 2. Divide $x^{\frac{3}{4}} y^{\frac{2}{3}}$ by $x^{\frac{1}{2}} y^{\frac{1}{6}}$.

$$\frac{3}{4}-\frac{1}{2}=\frac{1}{4}, \qquad \frac{2}{3}-\frac{1}{6}=\frac{1}{2};$$

therefore, $\quad x^{\frac{3}{4}} y^{\frac{2}{3}} \div x^{\frac{1}{2}} y^{\frac{1}{6}} = x^{\frac{1}{4}} y^{\frac{1}{2}}.$

Also,

$a^3 \times a^{-2} = a^{3-2} = a; \; a^3 \div a^{-\frac{1}{2}} = a^{3+\frac{1}{2}} = a^{\frac{7}{2}}; \; a^{-\frac{1}{2}} \div a^{-\frac{3}{5}} = a^{-\frac{1}{2}+\frac{3}{5}} = a^{\frac{1}{10}};$

$(a^3)^{-2} = a^{-6}; \; (a^{-3})^{-\frac{1}{2}} = a^{\frac{3}{2}}; \; \{(a^{-\frac{1}{2}})^{\frac{2}{3}}\}^{-12} = a^4;$

$[\sqrt{\{ab^{-2}\sqrt{(ab)}\}}]^4 = \{a^{\frac{1}{2}} b^{-1} \cdot a^{\frac{1}{4}} b^{\frac{1}{4}}\}^4 = (a^{\frac{3}{4}} b^{-\frac{3}{4}})^4 = a^3 b^{-3}.$

Ex. 3. Multiply $x + x^{\frac{1}{3}} + x^{-\frac{1}{3}}$ by $x^{\frac{1}{3}} + x^{-\frac{1}{3}} - x^{-\frac{2}{3}}.$

$$\begin{array}{l}
x \;\; + x^{\frac{1}{3}} \;\; + x^{-\frac{1}{3}} \\
x^{\frac{1}{3}} + x^{-\frac{1}{3}} - x^{-1} \\
\hline
x^{\frac{4}{3}} + x^{\frac{2}{3}} + 1 \\
\qquad x^{\frac{2}{3}} + 1 + x^{-\frac{2}{3}} \\
\qquad\qquad - 1 - x^{-\frac{2}{3}} - x^{-\frac{4}{3}} \\
\hline
x^{\frac{4}{3}} + 2x^{\frac{2}{3}} + 1 \qquad - x^{-\frac{4}{3}}
\end{array}$$

Here in the first line, $x^{\frac{1}{3}} \times x = x^{\frac{1}{3}+1} = x^{\frac{4}{3}}$; $x^{\frac{1}{3}} \times x^{\frac{1}{3}} = x^{\frac{2}{3}}$; $x^{\frac{1}{3}} \times x^{-\frac{1}{3}} = x^0 = 1$; and so on.

Ex. 4. Divide

$x^{\frac{5}{2}} - a^{\frac{1}{2}} x^2 - 4ax^{\frac{3}{2}} + 6a^{\frac{3}{2}} x - 2a^2 x^{\frac{1}{2}}$ by $x^{\frac{3}{2}} - 4ax^{\frac{1}{2}} + 2a^{\frac{3}{2}}.$

$$\begin{array}{l}
x^{\frac{3}{2}} - 4ax^{\frac{1}{2}} + 2a^{\frac{3}{2}}) \; x^{\frac{5}{2}} - a^{\frac{1}{2}} x^2 - 4ax^{\frac{3}{2}} + 6a^{\frac{3}{2}} x - 2a^2 x^{\frac{1}{2}} \; (x - a^{\frac{1}{2}} x^{\frac{1}{2}} \\
\qquad\qquad\qquad x^{\frac{5}{2}} \qquad\qquad - 4ax^{\frac{3}{2}} + 2a^{\frac{3}{2}} x \\
\qquad\qquad\qquad\overline{\qquad\qquad\qquad\qquad\qquad\qquad\qquad\qquad} \\
\qquad\qquad\qquad - a^{\frac{1}{2}} x^2 \qquad\qquad + 4a^{\frac{3}{2}} x - 2a^2 x^{\frac{1}{2}} \\
\qquad\qquad\qquad - a^{\frac{1}{2}} x^2 \qquad\qquad + 4a^{\frac{3}{2}} x - 2a^2 x^{\frac{1}{2}}
\end{array}$$

Examples—43

Find the value of

1. $9^{-\frac{1}{2}}$.　　2. $4^{-\frac{3}{2}}$.　　3. $(100)^{-\frac{1}{2}}$.　　4. $(1000)^{\frac{1}{3}}$.　　5. $81^{-\frac{3}{4}}$.

Simplify

6. $(a^2)^{-3}$.　　7. $(a^{-2})^{-3}$.　　8. $\sqrt{a^{-4}}$.　　9. $\sqrt[3]{a^{-2}}$.

10. $a^{\frac{1}{2}} \times a^{\frac{1}{3}} \times a^{-\frac{1}{4}}$.

Multiply

11. $x^{\frac{3}{4}} + y^{\frac{1}{4}}$ by $x^{\frac{3}{4}} - y^{\frac{1}{4}}$.
12. $a^{\frac{2}{3}} + a^{\frac{1}{3}} b^{\frac{1}{3}} + b^{\frac{2}{3}}$ by $a^{\frac{1}{3}} - b^{\frac{1}{3}}$.
13. $x + x^{\frac{1}{2}} + 2$ by $x + x^{\frac{1}{2}} - 2$.
14. $x^4 + x^2 + 1$ by $x^{-4} - x^{-2} + 1$.
15. $a^{-\frac{2}{3}} + a^{-\frac{1}{3}} + 1$ by $a^{-\frac{1}{3}} - 1$.
16. $a^{\frac{1}{3}} - 2 + a^{-\frac{1}{3}}$ by $a^{\frac{1}{3}} - a^{-\frac{1}{3}}$.
17. $a + a^{\frac{1}{2}} b^{\frac{1}{2}} - x^{\frac{1}{3}} y^{\frac{2}{3}}$ by $a + a^{\frac{1}{2}} b^{\frac{1}{2}} + x^{\frac{1}{3}} y^{\frac{2}{3}}$.

Divide

18. $x^{\frac{1}{3}} - y^{\frac{2}{3}}$ by $x^{\frac{1}{6}} - y^{\frac{1}{6}}$.　　19. $a - b$ by $a^{\frac{1}{3}} - b^{\frac{1}{3}}$.
20. $64x^{-1} + 27y^{-2}$ by $4x^{-\frac{1}{3}} + 3y^{-\frac{2}{3}}$.
21. $x^{\frac{3}{2}} - xy^{\frac{1}{2}} + x^{\frac{1}{2}}y - y^{\frac{3}{2}}$ by $x^{\frac{1}{2}} - y^{\frac{1}{2}}$.
22. $a^{\frac{2}{3}} + a^{\frac{1}{3}} b^{\frac{1}{3}} + b^{\frac{2}{3}}$ by $a^{\frac{1}{3}} + a^{\frac{1}{6}} b^{\frac{1}{6}} + b^{\frac{1}{3}}$.
23. $a^{\frac{2}{3}} + b^{\frac{2}{3}} - c^{\frac{2}{3}} + 2a^{\frac{1}{3}} b^{\frac{1}{3}}$ by $a^{\frac{1}{3}} + b^{\frac{1}{3}} + c^{\frac{1}{3}}$.
24. $x^{\frac{3}{4}} - 2a^{\frac{1}{2}} x^{\frac{1}{2}} + a^2$ by $x^{\frac{1}{4}} - 2a^{\frac{1}{2}} x^{\frac{1}{4}} + a$.

Find the square roots of the following expressions.

25. $x^{\frac{1}{2}} - 4 + 4x^{-\frac{1}{2}}$.　　26. $(x + x^{-1})^2 - 4(x - x^{-1})$.
27. $a^2 b^{-2} + 2ab^{-1} + 3 + 2a^{-1} b + a^{-2} b^2$.

XXIX. Surds.

207. It was stated (Art. 147) that when any root of a quantity cannot be exactly obtained it is expressed by the use of the sign of Evolution, as $\sqrt{5}$, $\sqrt[3]{(3ab)}$, $\sqrt[3]{(a^2+c^2)}$; and such quantities are called *Irrational quantities*, or *Surds*.

It is also stated in (147) that there cannot be any *even* root of a *negative* quantity, but that such roots may be expressed in the form of surds, as $\sqrt{-3}$, $\sqrt{-b^2}$, $\sqrt{-(a^2+b^2)}$, and are then called *impossible*, or *imaginary*, quantities.

208. Since every fractional index indicates by its denominator a root to be extracted, all quantities having such indices are expressed as Surds.

When a *negative* quantity has the denominator of its index (reduced to its lowest terms) *even*, the expression will be imaginary.

Thus, $(-3)^{\frac{1}{2}}$, $(-9)^{\frac{1}{4}}$, are imaginary quantities; but $(-4)^{\frac{4}{6}}$ is not so, since it is the same as $(-4)^{\frac{2}{3}}$, where the root to be taken is *odd*.

209. The operations of the preceding chapter are operations on *surds*, but we may apply the rules which are demonstrated in that chapter by the use of fractional indices, also to surds expressed by the sign of Evolution, or *Radical Sign*.

210. In the case of a *numerical* surd expressed with a fractional index, should the numerator be any other than unity, we may take at once the required power, and so have unity only for the numerator, and simply a root to be extracted.

Thus, $2^{\frac{2}{3}} = (2^2)^{\frac{1}{3}} = 4^{\frac{1}{3}} = \sqrt[3]{4}$; $3^{-\frac{2}{3}} = (3^{-2})^{\frac{1}{3}} = (\frac{1}{27})^{\frac{1}{3}} = \sqrt[3]{\frac{1}{27}}$.

Surds. Surds expressed by the radical sign.

211. Quantities are often expressed in the *form* of surds, which are not really so—*i.e.*, when we *can*, if we please, extract the roots indicated.

Thus, $\sqrt{a}$, $\sqrt[3]{7}$, $(a^2+ab+b^2)^{\frac{1}{3}}$ are *actually* surds, whose roots we cannot obtain; but $\sqrt{a^2}$, $\sqrt[3]{27}$, $(4a^2+4ab+b^2)^{\frac{1}{2}}$, are only *apparently* so, and are respectively equivalent to a, 3, $2a+b$.

Conversely, any rational quantity may be expressed in the form of a surd, by raising it to the power indicated by the root-index of the surd.

For example, $3 = \sqrt{3^2} = \sqrt{9}$; $4 = \sqrt[3]{4^3} = \sqrt[3]{64}$;

$$a = \sqrt[n]{a^n}; \quad a+b = \sqrt[n]{(a+b)^n}.$$

212. In like manner a *mixed* surd, *i.e.* a product partly rational and partly surd, or a surd with a rational coefficient, may be expressed as an entire, *i.e.*, complete surd, by raising the rational factor to the power indicated by the root-index of the surd, and placing beneath the sign of Evolution the product of this power and the surd factor. An *entire* or *complete* surd is one in which the whole expression is under the sign of Evolution.

Thus,

$2\sqrt{3} = \sqrt{4} \times \sqrt{3} = \sqrt{12}$; $3.2^{\frac{1}{3}} = 3\sqrt[3]{4} = \sqrt[3]{27} \times \sqrt[3]{4} = \sqrt[3]{108}$;

$$2a\sqrt{b} = \sqrt{(4a^2b)}; \quad 4a\sqrt[3]{\frac{c}{2a}} = \sqrt[3]{\frac{64a^3c}{2a}} = \sqrt[3]{(32a^2c)}.$$

Conversely, a surd may often be reduced to a mixed form, by separating the quantity beneath the sign of Evolution into factors, of one of which the root required may be obtained, and set outside the sign.

Thus, $\sqrt{20} = \sqrt{(4\times5)} = 2\sqrt{5}$; $\sqrt[3]{24} = \sqrt[3]{(8\times3)} = 2\sqrt[3]{3}$;

$$\sqrt{(\tfrac{4.8}{9}a^2b)} = \tfrac{2}{3}a\sqrt{(3ab)}; \quad \sqrt[3]{(\tfrac{3.2}{8.1}a^3b^4c^3)} = \tfrac{2}{3}ab\sqrt[3]{(2ac^3)}.$$

Rational quantities in the form of a surd. Mixed surds and entire surds.

213. A surd is reduced to its simplest form, when the quantity beneath the root, or *surd-factor*, is made as *small* as possible, but so as still to remain *integral*.

Hence, if the surd-factor be a *fraction*, its numerator and denominator should both be multiplied by such a number as will allow us to take the latter from under the root.

Thus,

$$\sqrt{\frac{2}{3}}=\sqrt{\frac{2.3}{3^2}}=\frac{1}{3}\sqrt{6}\,;\quad \frac{5}{2}\sqrt[3]{\frac{24}{5}}=5\sqrt[3]{\frac{3}{5}}=5\sqrt[3]{\frac{3.5^2}{5^3}}=\sqrt[3]{75}\,;$$

$$\sqrt{\frac{3}{8}}=\sqrt{\frac{3\times 2}{8\times 2}}=\sqrt{\frac{6}{16}}=\frac{\sqrt{6}}{4}\,;$$

$$\sqrt[3]{\frac{2}{3}}=\sqrt[3]{\frac{2\times 9}{3\times 9}}=\sqrt[3]{\frac{18}{27}}=\frac{\sqrt[3]{18}}{3}.$$

214. Surds which have not the same index may be transformed into equivalent surds which have. (See Art. 204.)

For example, take $\sqrt{5}$ and $\sqrt[3]{11}$;

$$\sqrt{5}=5^{\frac{1}{2}},\ \sqrt[3]{11}=(11)^{\frac{1}{3}}\,;$$

$$5^{\frac{1}{2}}=5^{\frac{3}{6}}=\sqrt[6]{5^3}=\sqrt[6]{125},\ (11)^{\frac{1}{3}}=11^{\frac{2}{6}}=\sqrt[6]{(11)^2}=\sqrt[6]{121}.$$

215. *Similar* surds are those which have, or may be made to have, the *same* surd-factors.

• Thus $3\sqrt{a}$ and $\sqrt{a}$, $2a\sqrt{c}$ and $3b\sqrt{c}$, are pairs of similar surds; $5\sqrt[3]{a}$ and $2\sqrt[3]{a^2}$ are similar surds, because $2\sqrt[3]{a^2}$ may be written $2\sqrt[3]{a}$; and $\sqrt{8}$, $\sqrt{50}$, $\sqrt{18}$ are also similar, because they may be written $2\sqrt{2}$, $5\sqrt{2}$, $3\sqrt{2}$.

Examples—44.

1. Express $4^{\frac{3}{4}}$, $9^{\frac{2}{3}}$, $3^{-\frac{2}{3}}$, $2^{-\frac{3}{4}}$, $(\frac{2}{3})^{-\frac{1}{2}}$, $(\frac{1}{4})^{-\frac{2}{3}}$, with indices, whose numerator is in each case unity.

Reduction of surds to their simplest form,—to equivalent surds having a given index. Similar surds.

2. Express 5, $2\frac{1}{2}$, $\frac{2}{3}a$, $\frac{3}{4}a^2$, $\frac{1}{2}(a+b)$, as surds, with indices $\frac{1}{2}$ and $\frac{1}{3}$.

3. Express 3^{-2}, $(3\frac{1}{3})^{-1}$, a^{-2}, $ab^{-1}c^{-2}$, with indices $\frac{1}{3}$ and $-\frac{1}{4}$.

Reduce to complete or entire surds,

4. $5\sqrt{5}$, $2\sqrt{\frac{3}{4}}$, $\frac{2}{3}\cdot 3^{\frac{3}{2}}$, $\frac{3}{4}\sqrt{1\frac{2}{3}}$, $\frac{1}{4}(\frac{3}{4})^{-\frac{1}{2}}$, $25(1\frac{1}{4})^{-\frac{3}{2}}$.

5. $3\sqrt[3]{2}$, $8\times 2^{-\frac{1}{3}}$, $4\times 2^{\frac{2}{3}}$, $3\times 3^{-\frac{3}{4}}$, $\frac{2}{3}(\frac{2}{3})^{-\frac{2}{3}}$, $\frac{1}{2}(\frac{3}{4})^{-\frac{2}{3}}$.

6. $2\sqrt{a}$, $7a\sqrt{(2x)}$, $(a+b)(a^2-b^2)^{-\frac{1}{2}}$.

7. $a\sqrt{\dfrac{2b}{a}}$, $3ax\sqrt{\dfrac{2a}{3x}}$, $\dfrac{2a}{3b}\sqrt[3]{\dfrac{3b}{2a}}$, $\dfrac{2a}{3}\sqrt[3]{\dfrac{9}{4a^2}}$, $(a+x)\sqrt{\dfrac{a-x}{a+x}}$.

Reduce to their simplest form,

8. $\sqrt{45}$, $\sqrt{125}$, $3\sqrt{432}$, $\sqrt[3]{135}$, $3\sqrt[3]{432}$, $\sqrt{\frac{3}{2}}$, $2\sqrt[3]{\frac{2}{3}}$, $3\sqrt[3]{\frac{2}{3}}$, $4\sqrt[3]{3\frac{3}{4}}$.

9. $8^{\frac{2}{3}}$, $32^{\frac{3}{5}}$, $72^{\frac{2}{3}}$, $(1\frac{1}{8})^{-\frac{1}{3}}$, $(20\frac{1}{4})^{-\frac{3}{2}}$, $(30\frac{3}{8})^{-\frac{2}{3}}$, $\frac{3}{4}\sqrt{1\frac{7}{9}}$, $5\sqrt[3]{4\frac{1}{20}}$, $\frac{4}{5}\sqrt[3]{9\frac{3}{8}}$.

10. Show that $\sqrt{12}$, $3\sqrt{75}$, $\frac{1}{2}\sqrt{147}$, $\frac{3}{3}\sqrt{\frac{4}{75}}$, $\sqrt{\frac{9}{16}}$, and $(144)^{-\frac{1}{4}}$ are similar surds.

216. To compare surds with one another in magnitude, *express them as entire surds, and then reduce them, if necessary, to a common surd-index, and simplify as in* Art. 213. Their relative values will then be apparent.

Thus, $3\sqrt{2}$ and $2\sqrt{3}$, expressed as entire surds, are $\sqrt{18}$ and $\sqrt{12}$, and it is at once plain which is the greater.

To compare $\sqrt{5}$ and $\sqrt[3]{11}$:

$$\sqrt{5} = 5^{\frac{1}{2}} = 5^{\frac{3}{6}} = \sqrt[6]{125};$$
$$\sqrt[3]{11} = 11^{\frac{1}{3}} = 11^{\frac{2}{6}} = \sqrt[6]{121}.$$

We see now that $\sqrt{5}$ is greater than $\sqrt[3]{11}$.

217. To *add* or *subtract* similar surds, *reduce them, when necessary, to the same surd-factor, then add or subtract their rational factors or coefficients, and affix to the result the common surd-factor.*

SURDS. 195

Thus, $\sqrt{8}+\sqrt{50}-\sqrt{18}=2\sqrt{2}+5\sqrt{2}-3\sqrt{2}=4\sqrt{2}$;

$4a\sqrt[3]{(a^2b^4)}+b\sqrt[3]{(8a^5b)}-\sqrt[3]{(125a^5b^4)}=4a^2b\sqrt[3]{b}+2a^2b\sqrt[3]{b}-5a^2b\sqrt[3]{b}=a^2b\sqrt[3]{b}$.

$$\frac{2}{3}\sqrt[3]{\frac{3}{2}}+\frac{1}{4}\sqrt[3]{\frac{256}{9}}=\frac{2}{3}\sqrt[3]{\frac{12}{8}}+\frac{1}{4}\sqrt[3]{\frac{64\times12}{27}}$$

$$=\frac{2}{3}\frac{\sqrt[3]{12}}{2}+\frac{1}{4}\frac{4\sqrt[3]{12}}{3}=\frac{2\sqrt[3]{12}}{3}.$$

Dissimilar surds can be added or subtracted only by connecting them with their proper signs.

218. To *multiply* simple surds which have the same surd-index, *multiply separately the rational factors and the surd factors, retaining the same surd-index for the product of the latter.*

Thus, $3\sqrt{2}\times\sqrt{3}=3\sqrt{6}$; $4\sqrt{5}\times7\sqrt{6}=28\sqrt{30}$;

$2\sqrt[3]{4}\times3\sqrt[3]{2}=6\sqrt[3]{8}=6\times2=12$;

$2\sqrt{3}\times3\sqrt{10}\times4\sqrt{6}=24\sqrt{180}=144\sqrt{5}$.

219. To multiply simple surds which have *not* the same surd-index, *reduce them to the same surd-index and proceed as before.*

Thus,

$4\sqrt{5}\times2\sqrt[3]{11}=4\sqrt[6]{125}\times2\sqrt[6]{121}=8\sqrt[6]{(125\times121)}=8\sqrt[6]{15125}$;

$2\sqrt{3}\times3\sqrt[3]{2}=2\sqrt[6]{27}\times3\sqrt[6]{4}=6\sqrt[6]{108}$.

Compound surd-expressions are multiplied according to the method of compound rational expressions.

Ex. 1. $(2\pm\sqrt{3})^2=4\pm4\sqrt{3}+3=7\pm4\sqrt{3}$.

Ex. 2. $(2+\sqrt{3})(2-\sqrt{3})=4-3=1$.

Ex. 3. $(2+\sqrt{3})(3-\sqrt{2})=6+3\sqrt{2}-2\sqrt{2}-\sqrt{6}$.

220. To divide one simple surd by another, *reduce both surds to the same surd-index, when necessary; then divide the coefficients and surd-factors separately, retaining the common surd-index over the quotient of the latter.*

The result may be simplified by Art. 212.

Ex. 1. $3\sqrt{2} \div 4\sqrt{3} = \dfrac{3\sqrt{2}}{4\sqrt{3}} = \dfrac{3}{4}\sqrt{\dfrac{2}{3}} = \dfrac{3}{4}\sqrt{\dfrac{6}{9}} = \dfrac{\sqrt{6}}{4}.$

Ex. 2. $4\sqrt{5} \div 2\sqrt[3]{11} = \dfrac{4\sqrt{5}}{2\sqrt[3]{11}} = \dfrac{4\sqrt[6]{125}}{3\sqrt[6]{121}} = \dfrac{4}{3}\sqrt[6]{\dfrac{125}{121}}$

$= \dfrac{4}{3}\sqrt[6]{\dfrac{125 \times 121 \times 121}{121 \times 121 \times 121}} = \dfrac{4\sqrt[6]{1830125}}{3 \times 11}.$

Ex. 3. $(8\sqrt{2} - 12\sqrt{3} + 3\sqrt{6} - 4) \div 2\sqrt{6}$

$= 4\sqrt{\tfrac{2}{6}} - 6\sqrt{\tfrac{3}{6}} + \tfrac{3}{2} - \dfrac{2}{\sqrt{6}} = \dfrac{4}{3}\sqrt{3} - 3\sqrt{2} + \tfrac{3}{2} - \tfrac{1}{3}\sqrt{6}.$

Ex. 4. $(2\sqrt{3} - 6\sqrt[3]{2}) \div \sqrt{6} = 2\sqrt{\tfrac{3}{6}} - 6\sqrt[6]{\tfrac{4}{216}} = \sqrt{2} - \sqrt[6]{864}.$

221. But, if the divisor be not monomial, the division is not so easily performed. The form, however, in which compound surds usually occur, is that of a *binomial quadratic surd*, *i.e.* a binomial, one or both of whose terms are surds, in which the *square* root is to be taken, such as $3 + 2\sqrt{5}$, $2\sqrt{3} - 3\sqrt{5}$, or, generally, $\sqrt{a} \pm \sqrt{b}$, where one or both terms may be irrational; and it will be easy, in such a case, to convert the operation of division into one of multiplication, *by putting the dividend and divisor in the form of a fraction, and multiplying both numerator and denominator by that quantity which is obtained by changing the sign between the two terms of the denominator.* By this means the denominator will be made *rational*: thus, if it be originally of the form $\sqrt{a} \pm \sqrt{b}$, it will become a rational quantity, $a - b$, when both numerator and denominator are multiplied by $\sqrt{a} \mp \sqrt{b}$.

SURDS.

Ex. 1. $\dfrac{2+\sqrt{3}}{3+\sqrt{3}} = \dfrac{(2+\sqrt{3})(3-\sqrt{3})}{(3+\sqrt{3})(3-\sqrt{3})} = \dfrac{6+3\sqrt{3}-2\sqrt{3}-3}{9-3}$

$= \dfrac{3+\sqrt{3}}{6}$

Ex. 2. $\dfrac{1}{2\sqrt{2}-\sqrt{3}} = \dfrac{2\sqrt{2}+\sqrt{3}}{8-3} = \dfrac{2\sqrt{2}+\sqrt{3}}{5}$.

This process is called *rationalizing the denominators of the fractions*, and the fractions thus modified are considered to be reduced to their simplest form.

EXAMPLES—45.

1. Compare $6\sqrt{3}$ and $4\sqrt{7}$; $3\sqrt[3]{3}$ and $2\sqrt[3]{10}$; $2\sqrt[3]{15}$, $4\sqrt[3]{2}$, and $3\sqrt[3]{5}$.

Simplify

2. $3\sqrt{2}+4\sqrt{8}-\sqrt{32}$.   3. $2\sqrt[3]{4}+5\sqrt[3]{32}-\sqrt[3]{108}$

4. $2\sqrt{3}+3\sqrt{(1\tfrac{1}{3})}-\sqrt{(5\tfrac{1}{3})}$.   5. $\dfrac{1}{\sqrt{2}} - \dfrac{1}{\sqrt{16}}$.

Multiply

6. $\sqrt{5}+\sqrt{(1\tfrac{1}{4})}-\dfrac{1}{\sqrt{5}}$ by $\sqrt{3}$.   7. $\sqrt[3]{4}-\dfrac{1}{\sqrt[3]{16}}+\dfrac{1}{\sqrt[3]{2}}$ by $\sqrt[3]{4}$.

8. $1+\sqrt{3}-\sqrt{2}$ by $\sqrt{6}-\sqrt{2}$.   9. $\sqrt{3}+\sqrt{2}$ by $\dfrac{1}{\sqrt{3}}+\dfrac{1}{\sqrt{2}}$.

10. Divide

$2\sqrt{3}+3\sqrt{2}+\sqrt{30}$ by $3\sqrt{6}$, and $2\sqrt{3}+3\sqrt[3]{2}+\sqrt[3]{30}$ by $3\sqrt{2}$

11. Rationalize the denominators of

$\dfrac{1}{2\sqrt{2}-\sqrt{3}}$, $\dfrac{4}{\sqrt{5}-1}$, $\dfrac{3}{\sqrt{5}+\sqrt{2}}$, $\dfrac{8-5\sqrt{2}}{3-2\sqrt{2}}$, $\dfrac{3+\sqrt{5}}{3-\sqrt{5}}$.

12. Rationalize the denominator of $\dfrac{\sqrt{(a+x)}+\sqrt{(a-x)}}{\sqrt{(a+x)}-\sqrt{(a-x)}}$.

222. The square root of a binomial, one of whose terms is a quadratic surd and the other rational, may sometimes be expressed by a binomial, one or both of whose terms are

---

Rationalizing the denominators of fractions. To express the square root of a binomial, one of whose terms is a quadratic surd and the other rational.

quadratic surds. (A quadratic surd is one whose indicated root is the square root.)

Since $(\sqrt{x} \pm \sqrt{y})^2 = x \pm 2\sqrt{xy} + y$, therefore $\sqrt{x \pm 2\sqrt{xy} + y} = \sqrt{x} \pm \sqrt{y}$; hence if any proposed binomial surd can be put under the form $x \pm 2\sqrt{xy} + y$, its root may be found by inspection to be $\sqrt{x} \pm \sqrt{y}$. To show how to proceed in any proposed case, let us take the binomial $3 + 2\sqrt{2}$. To place this under the form $x + 2\sqrt{xy} + y$, we observe that $2\sqrt{2} = 2\sqrt{2} \times \sqrt{1}$, and the sum of the two numbers under the radical signs $2 + 1 = 3$, the rational term of the binomial; $\therefore 3 + 2\sqrt{2} = 2 + 2\sqrt{2} \times \sqrt{1} + 1$. Hence the square root of $3 + 2\sqrt{2} = \sqrt{2 + 2\sqrt{2} \times \sqrt{1} + 1} = \sqrt{2} + 1$.

Ex. 2. Required the square root of $7 - 2\sqrt{10}$.

Here $2\sqrt{10} = 2\sqrt{5} \times \sqrt{2}$.

Also, $5 + 2 = 7$, the rational term. Hence,

$7 - 2\sqrt{10} = 5 - 2\sqrt{5} \times \sqrt{2} + 2$; $\therefore$ root required is $\sqrt{5} - \sqrt{2}$.

Ex. 3. Required the square root of $11 - 6\sqrt{2}$.

Here $6\sqrt{2} = 2\sqrt{18} = 2\sqrt{9} \times \sqrt{2}$, or $2\sqrt{6} \times \sqrt{3}$; of which the former answers the condition that their sum $9 + 2 = 11$, the rational term; $\therefore 11 - 6\sqrt{2} = 9 - 2\sqrt{9} \times \sqrt{2} + 2$.

∴ the required root is $\sqrt{9} - \sqrt{2}$; that is, $3 - \sqrt{2}$.

These illustrations show the method to be, to *put the term which contains the surd into factors, of the form $2\sqrt{x} \times \sqrt{y}$, in such a manner that the sum, $x + y$, of the numbers under the two radicals may be equal to the rational term. Then the $\sqrt{x} \pm \sqrt{y}$ will be the required square root.*

Ex. 4. Required the square root of $7 + \sqrt{13}$.

Here $\sqrt{13} = 2\sqrt{\tfrac{13}{4}} = 2\sqrt{\tfrac{13}{2}} \times \sqrt{\tfrac{1}{2}}$.

Also, $\tfrac{13}{2} + \tfrac{1}{2} = 7$, the rational term.

$\therefore$ root required is $\sqrt{\tfrac{13}{2}} + \sqrt{\tfrac{1}{2}}$, or $\dfrac{\sqrt{13} + 1}{\sqrt{2}}$.

Examples—46.

Find the square roots of

1. $4+2\sqrt{3}$. 2. $11+6\sqrt{2}$. 3. $8-2\sqrt{15}$. 4. $38-12\sqrt{10}$.
5. $41-24\sqrt{2}$. 6. $2\frac{1}{4}-\sqrt{5}$. 7. $4\frac{1}{3}-\frac{1}{3}\sqrt{3}$.

222½. It is often required to *clear an equation of surds*. An equation may be cleared of a surd by *transposing the terms so that the surd shall form one side and the rational quantities the other side, and then raising both sides to that power which will rationalize the surd.*

In the case of quadratic surds we *square* both sides. We shall confine ourselves to clearing equations of quadratic surds.

Thus if $\sqrt{a+x}-b=c$, by transposition, $\sqrt{a+x}=b+c$; and, squaring both sides, $a+x=(b+c)^2$. We thus have an equation without surds.

If the equation contain *two* surds connected by the signs + or —, then the same operations must be repeated for the second surd.

Thus, if $\qquad \sqrt{a+x}+\sqrt{x}=b$,

by transposition, $\qquad \sqrt{a+x}=b-\sqrt{x}$;

squaring, $\qquad a+x=b^2-2b\sqrt{x}+x$;

reducing and transposing, $2b\sqrt{x}=b^2-a$;

squaring, $\qquad 4b^2x=(b^2-a)^2$,

an equation in which the surds do not appear.

Ex. 1. $\sqrt{5+x}+\sqrt{5-x}=2\sqrt{x}$; required x.

Transposing, $\qquad \sqrt{5+x}=2\sqrt{x}-\sqrt{5-x}$;

squaring, $\qquad 5+x=4x-4\sqrt{5x-x^2}+5-x$;

To clear an equation of surds.

reduc'g and transp'g, $4\sqrt{5x-x^2}=2x$;

$$2\sqrt{5x-x^2}= x;$$

squaring, $20x-4x^2=x^2$;

$$20x=5x^2;$$

$$\therefore 20=5x, \quad \text{and } x=4.$$

Examples—47.

Find x in the following equations:

1. $\sqrt{(4x)}+\sqrt{(4x-7)}=7.$ 2. $\sqrt{(x+14)}+\sqrt{(x-14)}=14.$
3. $\sqrt{(x+11)}+\sqrt{(x-9)}=10.$
4. $\sqrt{(9x+4)}+\sqrt{(9x-1)}=3.$
5. $\sqrt{(x+4ab)}=2a-\sqrt{x}.$
6. $\sqrt{(x-a)}+\sqrt{(x-b)}=\sqrt{(a-b)}.$
7. $a+x-\sqrt{(2ax+x^2)}=b.$ 8. $a+x+\sqrt{(a^2+bx+x^2)}=b.$

XXX. Quadratic Equations.

223. *Quadratic equations* are those in which the *square of the unknown quantity* is found, but no higher power of it. Of these there are two species:

1. *Pure* Quadratics, in which the square *only* of the unknown is found without the first power, as

$$x^2-9=0; \quad x^2-a^2=b^2, \&c.$$

2. *Affected* Quadratics, where the first power enters as well as the square, as

$$x^2-3x+2=0; \quad ax^2+bx=c; \&c.$$

224. Quadratic equations are (Art. 166) also called *Equations of the second degree*. The two species also are distinguished as, 1st, *Incomplete* equations of the second degree; and 2d, *Complete* equations of the second degree. We shall, however, generally use the notation of Art. 223.*

225. To solve a Pure Quadratic Equation:

Find the value of x^2 *by the rule for solving simple equations; then take the square root of both sides of this result, we thus find the value of* x, *to which we must prefix the double sign* $\pm$ (144).

Such equations will therefore have two equal roots with contrary signs.

Ex. 1. $\qquad x^2 - 9 = 0.$
Here $\qquad x^2 = 9,$ and $x = \pm 3.$

If we had put $\pm x = \pm 3$, we should still have had only these *two* different values of x, viz., $x = +3$, $x = -3$; since $-x = +3$ gives $x = -3$, and $-x = -3$ gives $x = +3$.

Ex. 2. $\qquad \frac{1}{5}(3x^2 + 5) - \frac{1}{3}(x^2 + 21) = 39 - 5x^2.$
Reducing, $\qquad 121x^2 = 1089;$
$\qquad \therefore x^2 = 9,$ and $x = \pm 3.$

Ex. 3. $\qquad \dfrac{x^2 + 2}{x^2 - 2} = \dfrac{9}{7}.$

To examples like this the principle of fractions, (Art. 134, vi), may be applied with advantage when the unknown quantity does not enter in *both* sides of it.

---

* The term *affected* was introduced by Vieta, about the year 1600. It is used to distinguish equations which involve or are *affected* with different powers of the unknown quantity from those which contain one power only. (LUND).

$$\frac{(x^2+2)+(x^2-2)}{(x^2+2)-(x^2-2)} = \frac{9+7}{9-7};$$

that is,
$$\frac{2x^2}{4} = \frac{16}{2} = 8.$$

$$\therefore x^2 = 16, \quad \text{and } x = \pm 4.$$

Ex. 4.
$$\frac{\sqrt{4+x^2}+x}{\sqrt{4+x^2}-x} = 4.$$

(134, vi)
$$\frac{\sqrt{4+x^2}}{x} = \frac{5}{3};$$

squaring,
$$\frac{4+x^2}{x^2} = \frac{25}{9};$$

again, (134, iv and i), $\quad \dfrac{x^2}{4} = \dfrac{9}{16}; \quad \therefore x^2 = \dfrac{9}{4}; \quad x = \pm\tfrac{3}{2}.$

Examples—48.

1. $\tfrac{1}{2}x^2 = 14 - 3x^2.$

2. $x^2 + 5 = 1\tfrac{2}{3}x^2 - 16.$

3. $(x+2)^2 = 4x + 5.$

4. $\dfrac{3}{1+x} + \dfrac{3}{1-x} = 8.$

5. $\dfrac{3}{4x^2} - \dfrac{1}{6x^2} = \dfrac{7}{3}.$

6. $8x + \dfrac{7}{x} = \dfrac{65x}{7}.$

7. $\dfrac{3x^2}{4} - \dfrac{15x^2+8}{6} = 2x^2 - 3.$

8. $\dfrac{x^2}{5} - \dfrac{x^2-10}{15} = 7 - \dfrac{50+x^2}{25}.$

9. $\dfrac{3x^2-27}{x^2+3} + \dfrac{90+4x^2}{x^2+9} = 7.$

10. $\dfrac{4x^2+5}{10} - \dfrac{2x^2-5}{15} = \dfrac{7x^2-25}{20}.$

11. $\dfrac{10x^2+17}{18} - \dfrac{12x^2+2}{11x^2-8} = \dfrac{5x^2-4}{9}.$

12. $\dfrac{14x^2+16}{21} - \dfrac{2x^2+8}{8x^2-11} = \dfrac{2x^2}{3}.$

13. $\dfrac{2}{x+\sqrt{(2-x^2)}} + \dfrac{2}{x-\sqrt{(2-x^2)}} = x.$

14. $\dfrac{\sqrt{16+x^2} - \sqrt{25-x^2}}{\sqrt{16+x^2} + \sqrt{25-x^2}} = \dfrac{1}{9}.$

226. An *affected quadratic,* or complete equation of the second degree, *may always be reduced to the form* $x^2+px+q=0$, *where the coefficient of* x^2 *is* $+1$, *and* p *and* q *represent known numbers, whole or fractional, positive or negative.*

For, let all the terms be brought to one side, and, if necessary, change the signs of all the terms, so that the coefficient of x^2 may be a positive number; then divide every term by this coefficient, and the equation takes the assigned form, $x^2+px+q=0.$

Now in this equation we have $x^2+px=-q$; and adding $(\tfrac{1}{2}p)^2$ to each side, we get $x^2+px+\tfrac{1}{4}p^2=\tfrac{1}{4}p^2-q$; by this step the first side becomes a complete square (Art. 153); and taking the square root of each side, prefixing, as before, the double sign to that of the second side, we have

$$x+\tfrac{1}{2}p = \pm\sqrt{\tfrac{1}{4}p^2-q};$$

$$\therefore x = -\tfrac{1}{2}p \pm \sqrt{\tfrac{1}{4}p^2-q},$$

which expression gives us, according as we take the upper or lower sign, two roots of the quadratic.

227. From the preceding we derive the following rule for the solution of equations containing an affected quadratic:

By reduction and transposition arrange the equation so that the terms involving x^2 *and* x *are alone on one side, and the coefficient of* x^2 *is* $+1$; *then add to each side the square of half the coefficient of* x, *and take the square root of each side, prefixing the double sign to the second.*

To what form may an affected quadratic always be reduced? Rule for the solution of equations containing an affected quadratic?

We thus obtain a simple equation from which x is readily found.

Ex. 1. $\qquad x^2 - 6x = 7.$

Here $\qquad x^2 - 6x + 9 = 7 + 9 = 16;$

whence $\qquad x - 3 = \pm 4,$

and $\qquad x = 3 + 4 = 7,\text{ or } x = 3 - 4 = -1;$

so that 7 and -1 are the two roots of the equation.

Ex. 2. $\qquad x^2 + 14x = 95.$

Here $\qquad x^2 + 14x + 49 = 95 + 49 = 144;$

whence $\qquad x + 7 = \pm 12,$

and $\qquad x = -7 \pm 12 = 5,\text{ or } -19.$

Examples—49.

Solve

1. $x^2 - 2x = 8.$ 2. $x^2 + 10x = -9.$ 3. $x^2 - 14x = 120.$
4. $x^2 - 12x = -35.$ 5. $x^2 + 32x = 320.$ 6. $x^2 + 100x = 1100.$

228. If the coefficient of x be *odd*, its half will be a fraction. Its square may be indicated on the first side by using brackets.

Ex. 1. $\qquad x^2 - 5x = -6.$

Here $\qquad x^2 - 5x + (\tfrac{5}{2})^2 = -6 + \tfrac{25}{4} = \tfrac{1}{4};$

whence $\qquad x - \tfrac{5}{2} = \pm \tfrac{1}{2},$

and $\qquad x = \tfrac{5}{2} + \tfrac{1}{2} = \tfrac{6}{2} = 3,\text{ or } x = \tfrac{5}{2} - \tfrac{1}{2} = \tfrac{4}{2} = 2.$

Ex. 2. $\qquad x^2 - x = \tfrac{3}{4}.$

Here $\qquad x^2 - x + (\tfrac{1}{2})^2 = \tfrac{3}{4} + \tfrac{1}{4} = 1;$

whence $\qquad x - \tfrac{1}{2} = \pm 1,$

and $\qquad x = \tfrac{1}{2} + 1 = 1\tfrac{1}{2};\text{ or } x = \tfrac{1}{2} - 1 = -\tfrac{1}{2}.$

QUADRATIC EQUATIONS. 205

Examples—50.

Solve

1. $x^2+7x=8$. 2. $x^2-13x=68$. 3. $x^2+25x=-100$.
4. $x^2+13x=-12$. 5. $x^2+19x=20$. 6. $x^2+111x=3400$.

229. If the coefficient of x be a fraction, its half will, of course, be found by halving the numerator, if possible; if not, by doubling the denominator.

Ex. 1. Solve $x^2+\frac{10}{3}x=19$.

Here $x^2+\frac{10}{3}x+(\frac{5}{3})^2=19+\frac{25}{9}=\frac{196}{9}$;

whence $x+\frac{5}{3}=\pm\frac{14}{3}$,

and $x=-\frac{5}{3}+\frac{14}{3}=3$, or $x=-\frac{5}{3}-\frac{14}{3}=-6\frac{1}{3}$.

Ex. 2. Solve $x^2+\frac{13}{5}x=74$.

Here $x^2+\frac{13}{5}x+(\frac{13}{10})^2=74+\frac{169}{100}=\frac{7569}{100}$;

whence $x+\frac{13}{10}=\pm\frac{87}{10}$,

and $x=-\frac{13}{10}+\frac{87}{10}=7\frac{2}{5}$, or $x=-\frac{13}{10}-\frac{87}{10}=-10$.

Examples—51.

Solve

1. $x^2-\frac{1}{3}x=34$. 2. $x^2-\frac{3}{5}x=27$. 3. $x^2+\frac{7}{3}x=86$.
4. $x^2-\frac{26}{7}x=144$. 5. $x^2+\frac{1}{12}x=145$. 6. $x^2-\frac{22}{13}x=147$.

230. In the following examples the equations will first require reduction; and since the rule requires that the coefficient of x^2 shall be $+1$, if it have any other coefficient we must first divide each term of the equation by it; and if its coefficient be negative we must change the signs of all the terms.

Ex. 1. Solve $-3x^2+20x+5=0$.

Here $3x^2-20x-5=0$,

and $x^2-\tfrac{20}{3}x=\tfrac{5}{3}$;

therefore, $x^2-\tfrac{20}{3}x+\tfrac{100}{9}=\tfrac{115}{9}$;

$\therefore x=\tfrac{1}{3}(10\pm\sqrt{115})$, the roots being here surd quantities.

Ex. 2. Solve $\dfrac{1}{2(x-1)}+\dfrac{3}{x^2-1}=\dfrac{1}{4}$.

Here we first clear of fractions by multiplying by $4(x^2-1)$, which is the least common multiple of the denominators.

Thus $2(x+1)+12=x^2-1$.

By transposition, $x^2-2x=15$;

adding 1^2, $x^2-2x+1=15+1=16$;

extracting the square root, $x-1=\pm 4$;

therefore, $x=1\pm 4=5,$ or -3.

Ex. 3. Solve $\dfrac{2x}{15}+\dfrac{3x-50}{3(10+x)}=\dfrac{12x+70}{190}$.

Multiplying by 570, which is the least common multiple of 15 and 190,

$$76x+\dfrac{190(3x-50)}{10+x}=3(12x+70);$$

whence $\dfrac{190(3x-50)}{10+x}=210-40x$;

and $190(3x-50)=(210-40x)(10+x)$;

that is, $570x-9500=2100-190x-40x^2$;

therefore, $40x^2+760x=11600$;

or $x^2+19x=290$;

adding $\left(\dfrac{19}{2}\right)^2$, $x^2+19x+\left(\dfrac{19}{2}\right)^2=290+\dfrac{361}{4}=\dfrac{1521}{4}$;

extracting the square root, $x+\frac{19}{2}=\pm\frac{39}{2}$;

whence $x=-\frac{19}{2}\pm\frac{39}{2}=10$, or -29.

Ex. 4. Solve $\frac{x+3}{x+2}+\frac{x-3}{x-2}=\frac{2x-3}{x-1}$.

Clearing of fractions,

$$(x+3)(x-2)(x-1)+(x-3)(x+2)(x-1)$$
$$=(2x-3)(x+2)(x-2);$$

that is, $x^3-7x+6+x^3-2x^2-5x+6=2x^3-3x^2-8x+12$;

or $2x^3-2x^2-12x+12=2x^3-3x^2-8x+12$;

therefore, $x^2-4x=0$;

adding 2^2, $x^2-4x+2^2=4$;

extracting the square root, $x-2=\pm 2$,

whence $x=2\pm 2=4$ or 0.

Remark.—We have given the last three lines in order to complete the solution of the equation in the same manner as in the former examples; but the results may be obtained more simply. For the equation $x^2-4x=0$ may be written $(x-4)x=0$; and in this form it is sufficiently obvious that we must have either $x-4=0$, or $x=0$, that is, $x=4$ or 0.

The student will observe that in this example $2x^3$ is found on both sides of the equation, after we have cleared of fractions; accordingly, it can be removed by subtraction, and so the equation remains a quadratic equation.

Examples—52.

1. $x = \frac{5}{6} + \frac{1}{15}x^2$.
2. $2x = 4 + \frac{6}{x}$.
3. $\frac{7}{11}x^2 - \frac{2}{3}x = \frac{1}{33}(11x+18)$.
4. $11x^2 - 9x = 11\frac{1}{4}$.
5. $\frac{3}{4}(x^2-3) = \frac{1}{2}(x-3)$.
6. $2x^2 + 1 = 11(x+2)$.

7. $x - \dfrac{x^3-8}{x^2+5} = 2.$ 8. $\dfrac{1}{3} + \dfrac{1}{3+x} + \dfrac{1}{3+2x} = 0.$

9. $\dfrac{x+22}{3} - \dfrac{4}{x} = \dfrac{9x-6}{2}.$ 10. $\dfrac{x+2}{x-1} - \dfrac{4-x}{2x} = 2\tfrac{1}{3}.$

11. $\dfrac{12}{5-x} + \dfrac{4}{4-x} = \dfrac{32}{x+2}.$ 12. $\dfrac{x}{x+1} + \dfrac{x+1}{x} = \dfrac{13}{6}.$

231. Sometimes, on completing the square, the second side of the equation becomes 0. For example, take the equation $x^2 - 14x = -49.$ This gives

$$x^2 - 14x + 49 = 0; \quad \therefore (x-7)^2 = 0; \quad \therefore x = 7.$$

In this case we say the quadratic equation has two *equal* roots.

232. Solve $x^2 - 6x + 13 = 0.$

By transposition, $\qquad x^2 - 6x = -13;$

adding 3^2, $\qquad x^2 - 6x + 9 = -13 + 9 = -4.$

If we try to extract the square root, we have

$$x - 3 = \pm\sqrt{-4}.$$

In this case the quadratic equation has no real root, and this is expressed by saying that the roots are *imaginary* or *impossible*.

233. An equation of the form $ax^2 + bx + c = 0$, or $ax^2 + bx = -c$ (where a, b, and c are any quantities whatever), may be solved by what is called the Hindoo method,* as follows, without dividing by the coefficient of x^2. *Multiply every term by* 4a, *that is,* 4 *times the coefficient of* x², *and add* b², *that is, the square of the coefficient of* x, *to both sides:* the first side will be a "complete square." Thus,

$$4a^2x^2 + 4abx + b^2 = b^2 - 4ac.$$

---

* This method is given in the Bija Ganita, a Hindoo treatise on Algebra.

QUADRATIC EQUATIONS. 209

Extracting the square root,
$$2ax+b=\pm\sqrt{b^2-4ac};$$
$$\therefore x=\frac{1}{2a}(-b\pm\sqrt{b^2-4ac}). \quad (1)$$

Ex. 1. If $3x^2+2x=85$, find x.

Multiplying by 4×3, or 12,	$36x^2+24x=1020;$
adding 2^2, or 4,	$36x^2+24x+4=1024;$
extracting root,	$6x+2=\pm 32;$
	$6x=\pm 32-2=30,\text{ or }-34;$
	$\therefore x=5,\text{ or }-5\tfrac{2}{3}.$

Ex. 2. If $5x^2-9x+2\tfrac{1}{4}=0$, find x.

Transposing,	$5x^2-9x=-2\tfrac{1}{4};$
multiplying by 4×5, or 20,	$100x^2-180x=-45;$
adding 9^2, or 81,	$100x^2-180x+81=81-45=36;$
extracting root,	$10x-9=\pm 6;$
whence,	$10x=9\pm 6=15,\text{ or }3;$
	$\therefore x=\dfrac{15}{10},\text{ or }\dfrac{3}{10};$
	$=1\tfrac{1}{2},\text{ or }\dfrac{3}{10}.$

The student will find it well to apply at once (by memory) the formula (1) above obtained for x.

Ex. 3. $(3x-2)(1-x)=4$, or $3x^2-5x+6=0$.

Here $x=\tfrac{1}{6}(5\pm\sqrt{25-72})=\tfrac{1}{6}(5\pm\sqrt{-47})$, the roots being impossible.

Or, since it appears that the equation $ax^2+bx=-c$ is reducible to the simple equation $2ax+b=\pm\sqrt{b^2-4ac}$, the

---

What two abbreviated forms of solution are suggested?

student may readily acquire the habit of writing down the simple equation from any proposed equation without the aid of any intermediate steps.

Ex. 4. Solve $3x^2+5x=42$.
$$6x+5=\pm\sqrt{25+12\times 42};$$
that is, $\quad 6x+5=\pm 23; \quad \therefore x=3,\text{ or }-4\tfrac{2}{3}.$

EXAMPLES—53.

1. $\dfrac{2x}{x-4}+\dfrac{2x-5}{x-3}=8\tfrac{1}{4}.$ 2. $\dfrac{2x+9}{9}+\dfrac{4x-3}{4x+3}=3+\dfrac{3x-16}{18}.$

3. $\dfrac{5x}{x+4}-\dfrac{3x-2}{2x-3}=2.$ 4. $\dfrac{4x+7}{19}+\dfrac{5-x}{3+x}=\dfrac{4x}{9}.$

5. $\dfrac{x-1}{x+1}+\dfrac{x-2}{x+2}=\dfrac{2x+13}{x+16}.$ 6. $\dfrac{x+1}{x-1}+\dfrac{x+2}{x-2}=\dfrac{2x+13}{x+1}.$

7. $\dfrac{2x-1}{x+1}+\dfrac{3x-1}{x+2}=\dfrac{5x-11}{x-1}.$ 8. $x-\dfrac{14x-9}{8x-3}=\dfrac{x^2-3}{x+1}.$

9. $a^2x^2-2a^2x+a^4-1=0.$ 10. $4a^2x=(a^2-b^2+x)^2.$

11. $\dfrac{x}{a}+\dfrac{a}{x}=\dfrac{x}{b}+\dfrac{b}{x}.$ 12. $\dfrac{1}{x}+\dfrac{1}{x+b}=\dfrac{1}{a}+\dfrac{1}{a+b}.$

234. If r, r' represent the two roots of $x^2+px+q=0$, then $-p=r+r'$, and $q=r\times r'$.

For $r=-\tfrac{1}{2}p+\sqrt{(\tfrac{1}{4}p^2-q)}, \quad r'=-\tfrac{1}{2}p-\sqrt{(\tfrac{1}{4}p^2-q)};$

$\therefore r+r'=-p, \quad$ and $r\times r'=\tfrac{1}{4}p^2-(\tfrac{1}{4}p^2-q)=q.$

Hence, *when any quadratic is reduced to the form* $x^2+px+q=0,$ *the coefficient of 2d term, with sign changed,* $=$ *sum of roots, and the 3d term* $=$ *product of roots.*

To what are the sum of the roots and the product of the roots of a quadratic equation, respectively, equal?

Thus, in (Ex. 1, 227) the equation, when expressed in this form, is $x^2-6x-7=0$, and the roots are there found, 7 and -1; and here $+6 = 7+(-1) =$ *sum* of roots, and $-7 = 7 \times (-1) =$ *product* of roots.

So, also, $ax^2+bx+c=0$, expressed in this form, becomes $x^2+\dfrac{b}{a}x+\dfrac{c}{a}=0$; $\therefore -\dfrac{b}{a} =$ *sum* of roots, $\dfrac{c}{a} =$ *product*.

235. *If r, r' be the roots of $x^2+px+q=0$, then*
$$x^2+px+q = (x-r)(x-r').$$
For, (236) $x^2+px+q = x^2 - (r+r')x + rr'$,
$$= x^2 - rx - r'x + rr' = (x-r)(x-r').$$
So, also, if r, r' be the roots of $ax^2+bx+c=0$,
that is, of $x^2 + \dfrac{b}{a}x + \dfrac{c}{a} = 0$,
we have $ax^2+bx+c = a\left(x^2 + \dfrac{b}{a}x + \dfrac{c}{a}\right) = a(x-r)(x-r')$.

236. Hence we may form a quadratic equation with any two given roots.

Thus with roots 2 and 3 we shall have
$$(x-2)(x-3) = x^2 - 5x + 6 = 0.$$

With roots -2 and $\tfrac{1}{4}$, we have $(x+2)(x-\tfrac{1}{4}) = x^2 + \tfrac{7}{4}x - \tfrac{1}{2} = 0$; or clearing it of fractions, $4x^2 + 7x - 2 = 0$.

If one of the roots be 0, the corresponding factor will be $x-0$, or x.

Thus with roots 0 and 4, we have $x(x-4) = 0$, or $x^2 - 4x = 0$. (Compare Ex. 4, Art. 230.) In such a case, then, x will occur in *every term* of the equation, and may be struck out of each; but we must notice, always, that when we thus strike out x from every term of an equation, $x=0$ satisfies the equation, and is therefore one of the roots.

A quadratic equation may be formed from any two given roots. $x=0$, a root.

Examples—54.

Form equations with the following roots:

1. 7 and -3.
2. $\frac{2}{3}$ and $-\frac{3}{8}$.
3. -6 and -5.
4. $2\frac{2}{3}$ and 0.
5. 10 and -10.
6. $a+\dfrac{1}{a}$ and $a-\dfrac{1}{a}$.
7. $-1+\sqrt{2}$ and $-1-\sqrt{2}$.

XXXI. Equations which may be solved like Quadratics.

237. There are many equations which are not strictly quadratics, but which may be solved by the method of *completing the square*. We will give some examples.

238. Ex. 1. Solve $x^6-7x^3=8$.

Adding $\left(\frac{7}{2}\right)^2$, $\quad x^6-7x^3+\left(\frac{7}{2}\right)^2=8+\frac{49}{4}=\frac{81}{4}$;

extracting the square root, $x^3-\frac{7}{2}=\pm\frac{9}{2}$;

whence, $\quad x^3=\frac{7}{2}\pm\frac{9}{2}=8$ or -1;

extracting the cube root, $\quad x=2$ or -1.

This method applies, evidently, in all cases where the *lowest* of the two exponents of the unknown quantity is one-half of the highest exponent.

Ex. 2. $x+4x^{\frac{1}{2}}=21$; required x.

$$x+4x^{\frac{1}{2}}+4=21+4=25;$$
$$x^{\frac{1}{2}}+2=\pm 5;$$
$$x^{\frac{1}{2}}=\pm 5-2=3 \text{ or } -7;$$
$$\therefore x=9 \text{ or } 49.$$

What other equations may be solved like quadratics?

QUADRATIC EQUATIONS. 213

Ex. 3. $x^{-1}+x^{-\frac{1}{2}}=6$; required x.

$$x^{-1}+x^{-\frac{1}{2}}+\tfrac{1}{4}=6+\tfrac{1}{4}=\tfrac{25}{4};$$

$$x^{-\frac{1}{2}}+\tfrac{1}{2}=\pm\tfrac{5}{2};$$

$$x^{-\frac{1}{2}}=\frac{-1\pm 5}{2}=2 \text{ or } -3;$$

$$\therefore x^{\frac{1}{2}}=\tfrac{1}{2} \text{ or } -\tfrac{1}{3};$$

$$\therefore x=\tfrac{1}{4} \text{ or } \tfrac{1}{9}.$$

239. Equations may be proposed containing quadratic surds, from which, by performing the operations of transposing and squaring, once or oftener (Art. 223), we obtain affected quadratic equations.

Ex. 1. $x+\sqrt{5x+10}=8$; to find x.

By transposition, $\sqrt{5x+10}=8-x;$

squaring, $5x+10=64-16x+x^2;$

$$x^2-21x=-54;$$

$$x^2-21x+\frac{441}{4}=\frac{441}{4}-54=\frac{225}{4};$$

$$x-\frac{21}{2}=\pm\frac{15}{2};$$

$$x=\frac{21\pm 15}{2}=18 \text{ or } 3.$$

We have thus found two values of x; but on trial we find that 18 does not satisfy the equation if we suppose that $\sqrt{5x+10}$ represents the positive square root. The value 18 satisfies the equation $x-\sqrt{5x+10}=8$.

Ex. 2. Solve $2x-\sqrt{(x^2-3x-3)}=9.$

Transposing, $2x-9=\sqrt{(x^2-3x-3)};$

squaring, $4x^2-36x+81=x^2-3x-3;$

transposing, $3x^2-33x+84=0;$

dividing by 3, $x^2-11x+28=0.$

By solving this quadratic we shall obtain $x=7$ or 4. The value 7 satisfies the original equation; the value 4 belongs strictly to the equation $2x+\sqrt{(x^2-3x-3)}=9$.

Ex. 3. Solve $\sqrt{(x+4)}+\sqrt{(2x+6)}=\sqrt{(8x+9)}$.

Squaring, $\quad x+4+2x+6+2\sqrt{(x+4)}\sqrt{(2x+6)}=8x+9$;

transposing, $\quad 2\sqrt{(x+4)}\sqrt{(2x+6)}=5x-1$;

squaring, $\quad 4(x+4)(2x+6)=25x^2-10x+1$;

that is, $\quad 8x^2+56x+96=25x^2-10x+1$;

transposing, $\quad 17x^2-66x-95=0$.

By solving this quadratic we shall obtain $x=5$, or $-\frac{19}{17}$. The value 5 satisfies the original equation; the value $-\frac{19}{17}$ belongs strictly to the equation

$$\sqrt{(2x+6)}-\sqrt{(x+4)}=\sqrt{(8x+9)}.$$

240. The student will see from the preceding examples that in cases in which we have to square in order to reduce an equation to the ordinary form, we cannot be certain, without trial, that the values finally obtained for the unknown quantity belong strictly to the original equation.

241. Solve $x^2+3x+3\sqrt{(x^2+3x-2)}=6$.

Subtracting 2 from both sides,

$$x^2+3x-2+3\sqrt{(x^2+3x-2)}=4.$$

Thus on the left-hand side we have two expressions, namely, $\sqrt{(x^2+3x-2)}$, and x^2+3x-2, and the latter is the square of the former; we can now *complete the square*.

Adding $(\frac{3}{2})^2$,

$$x^2+3x-2+3\sqrt{(x^2+3x-2)}+(\frac{3}{2})^2=4+\frac{9}{4}=\frac{25}{4};$$

extracting the square root,

$$\sqrt{(x^2+3x-2)}+\frac{3}{2}=\pm\frac{5}{2};$$

therefore, $\quad \sqrt{(x^2+3x-2)}=-\frac{3}{2}\pm\frac{5}{2}=1$ or -4.

First suppose $\sqrt{(x^2+3x-2)}=1$;
squaring both sides, $x^2+3x-2=1$.

This is an ordinary quadratic equation; by solving it we shall obtain
$$x=\frac{-3\pm\sqrt{21}}{2}.$$

Next, suppose $\sqrt{(x^2+3x-2)}=-4$.
Squaring both sides, $x^2+3x-2=16$.

This is an ordinary quadratic equation; by solving it we shall obtain $x=3$ or -6.

Thus on the whole we have four values for x, namely,
$$3 \text{ or } -6, \text{ or } \frac{-3\pm\sqrt{21}}{2}.$$

But we shall find, on trial, that only the values $\frac{-3\pm\sqrt{21}}{2}$ will satisfy the given equation
$$x^2+3x+3\sqrt{(x^2+3x-2)}=6,$$
but the values 3 or -6 satisfy the equation
$$x^2+3x-3\sqrt{(x^2+3x-2)}=6.$$

242. The method pursued in the example in the last article applies whenever an expression may be formed which, containing all the unknown terms outside of the surd, is the *same as the surd expression, or is a multiple of it.*

243. Equations of the third degree are sometimes proposed in which it is intended to find one of the roots by inspection or trial, and the two remaining roots by solving a quadratic equation.

Ex. 1. Solve $\dfrac{x+4}{x-4}-\dfrac{x-4}{x+4}=\dfrac{9+x}{9-x}-\dfrac{9-x}{9+x}.$

Bring the fractions on each side of the equation to a common denominator. Thus:

$$\frac{(x+4)^2-(x-4)^2}{x^2-16}=\frac{(9+x)^2-(9-x)^2}{81-x^2};$$

that is,
$$\frac{16x}{x^2-16}=\frac{36x}{81-x^2}.$$

Here it is obvious that $x=0$ is a root (Art. 236). To find the other roots we begin by dividing both sides of the equation by $4x$. Thus:

$$\frac{4}{x^2-16}=\frac{9}{81-x^2};$$

therefore, $\quad 4(81-x^2)=9(x^2-16);$

$\therefore\ 13x^2=324+144=468;$

$\therefore\ x^2=36; \qquad \therefore\ x=\pm 6.$

Thus there are three roots of the proposed equation, namely, 0, 6, -6.

Ex. 2. Solve $x^3-7xa^2+6a^3=0$.

Here it is obvious that $x=a$ is a root. We may write the equation,

$$x^3-a^3=7a^2(x-a);$$

and to find the other roots we begin by dividing by $x-a$.

Thus, $\qquad x^2+ax+a^2=7a^2.$

By solving this quadratic we obtain $x=2a$, or $-3a$. Thus there are three roots of the proposed equation, namely a, $2a$, $-3a$.

Examples—55.

1. $x^4-13x^2+36=0.$
2. $x-5\sqrt{x}-14=0.$
3. $x+\sqrt{(x+5)}=7.$
4. $x^2+\sqrt{(x^2+9)}=21.$
5. $2\sqrt{(x^2-2x+1)}+x^2=23+2x.$
6. $x^4-2x^3+x^2=36.$
7. $9\sqrt{(x^2-9x+28)}+9x=x^2+36.$

8. $2x^2+6x=226-\sqrt{(x^2+3x-8)}$.
9. $x^4-4x^2-2\sqrt{(x^4-4x^2+4)}=31$.
10. $x+2\sqrt{(x^2+5x+2)}=10$.
11. $3x+\sqrt{(x^2+7x+5)}=19$.
12. $\sqrt{(x+9)}=2\sqrt{x}-3$.   13. $5\sqrt{(1-x^2)}+5x=7$.
14. $\sqrt{(3x-3)}+\sqrt{(5x-19)}=\sqrt{(2x+8)}$.
15. $\dfrac{x+\sqrt{(12a^2-x)}}{x-\sqrt{(12a^2-x)}}=\dfrac{a+1}{a-1}$.
16. $\dfrac{1}{x+7}+\dfrac{1}{x-1}+\dfrac{1}{x+1}+\dfrac{1}{x-7}=0$.
17. $\dfrac{1}{x+\sqrt{(2-x^2)}}+\dfrac{1}{x-\sqrt{(2-x^2)}}=x$.
18. $\dfrac{x+\sqrt{(x^2-1)}}{x-\sqrt{(x^2-1)}}-\dfrac{x-\sqrt{(x^2-1)}}{x+\sqrt{(x^2-1)}}=8\sqrt{(x^2-1)}$.
19. $\dfrac{x+a}{x-a}-\dfrac{x-a}{x+a}=\dfrac{b+x}{b-x}-\dfrac{b-x}{b+x}$.
20. $x^3+3ax^2=4a^3$.

XXXII. Problems which lead to Quadratic Equations containing One Unknown Quantity.

214. In the solution of problems depending on quadratic and higher equations there may be two or more values of the root, and these values may be *real* quantities, or *impossible*. In the former case, we must consider if any of the roots are excluded by the nature of the question, which may altogether reject *fractional*, or *negative*, or *surd* answers; in the latter case, we conclude that the solution of the proposed question is arithmetically impossible.

PROB. 1. Find two numbers, such that their sum is 13, and their product is 42:

Let x be one of the numbers, then $13-x$ will be the other; and then,
$$x(13-x)=42;$$
$$x^2-13x=-42;$$
$$x=7 \text{ or } 6. \quad \therefore 13-x=6 \text{ or } 7.$$

Thus the two numbers are 7 and 6. Here, although the quadratic equation gives two values of x, yet there is really only one solution of the problem.

PROB. 2. What number, when added to 30, will be less than its square by 12?

Let $x =$ the number; then
$$30+x=x^2-12;$$
whence $\quad x=7 \text{ or } -6.$

And here the latter root would be excluded if we required only *positive* numbers.

PROB. 3. A person bought a number of oxen for \$600: if he had bought 3 more for the same money, he would have paid \$10 less for each. How many did he buy?

Let x be the number bought; then the price actually given for each was $\dfrac{600}{x}$, and therefore,
$$\frac{600}{x+3}=\frac{600}{x}-10;$$
whence $\quad x=12 \text{ or } -15,$

which latter root is rejected by the nature of the problem.

PROB. 4. There are four consecutive numbers, of which, if the first two be taken for the digits of a number, that number is the product of the other two.

Let x, $x+1$, $x+2$, $x+3$, be the four numbers required; then $10x+(x+1)=$ the number whose digits are x, and $x+1$.

Therefore, by the question, $(x+2)(x+3)=10x+(x+1);$

or $\quad x^2+5x+6=11x+1;$

whence $\quad x=5 \text{ or } 1.$

Hence the numbers required are 5, 6, 7, 8, or 1, 2, 3, 4, both of which results satisfy the conditions of the problem.

PROB. 5. Find two numbers whose difference is 10 and whose product is one-third of the square of their sum.

Let $x =$ the smaller, and $x + 10 =$ the greater; then,

$$x(x+10) = \tfrac{1}{3}(2x+10)^2,$$

whence
$$x = -5 \pm 5\sqrt{-3},$$

which values are *impossible*. And the solution of the question is arithmetically impossible, as may easily be shown, since it calls for two numbers whose product is equal to the sum of their squares.

245. The reason why results are sometimes obtained, as in Prob. 3, which do not apply to the problem proposed, seems to be that the algebraic language is more general than the ordinary language in which the problem is stated; and thus the equation which expresses the conditions of the problem will also apply to other conditions. It will be a profitable exercise for the student, when it is possible, by suitable changes in the statement of the problem, to form a new problem, corresponding to the result which was inapplicable to the original problem. Thus in Prob. 3 it will be found that "15" oxen is the answer of the following problem: Find the number of oxen bought for $600, when, if the person had bought 3 *fewer* oxen, he would have paid $10 more per head.

EXAMPLES—56.

1. Find the three consecutive numbers whose sum is equal to the product of the first two.

2. The sum of two numbers is 60, and the sum of their squares is 1872: find the numbers.

Why are some of the results obtained inapplicable?

3. The difference of two numbers is 6, and their product is 720: find the numbers.

4. Find three numbers, such that the second shall be two-thirds of the first, and the third one-half of the first, and that the sum of the squares of the numbers shall be 549.

5. Find the number which added to its square root will make 210.

6. There are two numbers, one of which is $\frac{4}{5}$ of the other, and the difference of their squares is 81: find them.

7. A and B together can perform a piece of work in $14\frac{2}{5}$ days, and A alone can perform it in 12 days less than B alone: find the time in which A alone can perform it.

8. In a certain court there are two square grass-plots, a side of one of which is 10 yards longer than a side of the other, and the area of the latter is $\frac{9}{25}$ of that of the former: what are the lengths of the sides?

9. A detachment of troops was arranged in a column with 5 more men in depth than in front; the arrangement was changed so as to increase the front by 845 men; this left the column 5 men deep: find the number of men in the detachment.

10. There is a rectangular field, whose length exceeds its breadth by 16 yards, and it contains 960 square yards: find its dimensions.

11. A person bought a certain number of oxen for $1200, and after losing 3, sold the rest for $40 a head more than they cost him, thus gaining $295 by the bargain: what number did he buy?

12. The fore-wheel of a carriage makes 6 revolutions more than the hind-wheel in going 120 yards; but if the circumference of each were increased by 3 feet, the fore-wheel would

make only 4 revolutions more than the hind one in the same space: what is the circumference of each?

13. By selling a horse for £24, I lose as much per cent. as it cost me: what was the prime cost of it?

14. Find the price of eggs per dozen, when two less in 24 cents' worth raises the price 2 cents per dozen.

15. There are three equal vessels, A, B, and C; the first contains water, the second brandy, and the third brandy and water. If the contents of B and C be put together, it is found that the mixture is nine times as strong as if the contents of A and C had been treated in like manner: find the proportion of brandy to water in the vessel C.

XXXIII. SIMULTANEOUS EQUATIONS INVOLVING QUADRATICS.

246. We shall now give some examples of simultaneous equations which may be solved by means of quadratics. There are three cases in which general rules can be given for the solution of these simultaneous equations of two unknown quantities.

247. I. When one of the equations is of the first degree, and the other is of the second degree:

RULE.—*From the equation of the first degree find the expression for either of the unknown quantities in terms of the other, and substitute this expression in the equation of the second degree.*

This will give a quadratic equation from which the value of one unknown is found.

Example. Given, $\left. \begin{array}{r} 3x+4y=18 \\ 5x^2-3xy=\ 2 \end{array} \right\}$ to find x and y.

Solution of Simultaneous Equations involving quadratics. Case I.

From the first equation, $y = \dfrac{18-3x}{4}$; substituting this value in the second equation,

$$5x^2 - \dfrac{3x(18-3x)}{4} = 2;$$

whence, $\qquad 20x^2 - 54x + 9x^2 = 8;$

that is, $\qquad 29x^2 - 54x = 8.$

From this quadratic we shall find that

$$x = 2, \text{ or } -\dfrac{4}{29};$$

and then by substituting these in the first equation we find that

$$y = 3, \text{ or } \dfrac{267}{58}.$$

248. II. When the two equations are of the second degree, and all those terms which contain x and y are homogeneous, with respect to these quantities:

RULE.—*Put* y=vx *in both equations; obtain by division an equation in which* v *is the only unknown;* v *being determined,* x *and* y *may then be found.*

Example. Solve $\quad \begin{matrix} 2x^2 - xy = 56 \\ 2xy - y^2 = 48 \end{matrix} \Big\}$

Putting $y = vx$ and substituting for y,

$$x^2(2-v) = 56, \text{ and } x^2(2v - v^2) = 48;$$

whence, by division,

$$\dfrac{2v - v^2}{2 - v} = \dfrac{48}{56} = \dfrac{6}{7};$$

whence, $v = \dfrac{6}{7}$, or, $v = 2$. The latter value is inapplicable; the first gives, $x = \pm 7, y = \pm 6$.

This method is also applicable to Case I.

Example. $\quad \begin{matrix} x^2 + xy + y^2 = 7 \\ 2x + 3y = 8 \end{matrix} \Big\}$

SIMULTANEOUS EQUATIONS.

Here putting vx for y,
$$x^2(1+v+v^2)=7 \quad (1);$$
$$x(2+3v)=8 \quad (2).$$

Therefore, by dividing (1) by the square of (2) x^2 disappears, and we have,
$$\frac{1+v+v^2}{(2+3v)^2}=\frac{7}{64};$$

whence, $v=2$, or 18; and, from (2),

$x(2+ 6)=8,$ that is, $\begin{cases} x=1, \\ \text{or } x=\frac{1}{7}; \end{cases}$ and $\begin{cases} y=vx=2; \\ \text{or } y=vx=2\frac{4}{7}. \end{cases}$
or $x(2+54)=8;$

249. III. *When each of the two equations is symmetrical with respect to x and y, put* $u+v$ *for* x, *and* $u-v$ *for* y.

[DEFINITION.—An expression is said to be *symmetrical* with respect to x and y when these quantities are similarly involved in it. Thus, each of the expressions,
$$x^3+x^2y^2+y^3, \qquad 4xy+5x+5y-1, \qquad 2x^4-3x^2y-3xy^2+2y^4,$$
is symmetrical with respect to x and y.]

Example. $\left.\begin{array}{r} x^3+y^3=18xy \\ x+y=12 \end{array}\right\}$ $\begin{array}{l}(1)\\(2).\end{array}$

Put $u+v$ for x, and $u-v$ for y;
then (1) becomes $(u+v)^3+(u-v)^3=18(u+v)(u-v),$
or, $u^3+3uv^2=9(u^2-v^2) \quad (3);$
and (2) becomes $(u+v)+(u-v)=12;$
whence, $u=6.$
Putting this for u in (3),
$$216+18v^2=9(36-v^2);$$
whence, $v=\pm 2;$
       $\therefore x=u+v=6\pm 2=8 \text{ or } 4;$
and, $y=u-v=6\mp 2=4 \text{ or } 8.$

Case III;—Symmetrical Equations.

250. The preceding are *general* methods for the solution of equations of the kind referred to, and will sometimes succeed also in other equations; yet in many of these cases a little ingenuity and experience will often suggest steps by which the roots may be found more simply.

Ex. 1. Solve $3x^2 - 2xy = 15$ (1)
$\qquad\qquad\quad 2x + 3y = 12$ (2)

Multiplying (1) by 3, $9x^2 - 6xy = 45$,

$\qquad$ (2) by $2x$, $4x^2 + 6xy = 24x$;

∴ adding, $13x^2 = 45 + 24x$, or $13x^2 - 24x = 45$, whence $x = 3$ or $-1\frac{2}{13}$. Equation (2) gives $y = \frac{1}{3}(12 - 2x) = 2$ or $4\frac{10}{13}$.

Ex. 2. Solve $x^2 + y^2 = 25$ (1)
$\qquad\qquad\quad 2xy = 24$ (2)

Here adding, $\qquad x^2 + 2xy + y^2 = 49$, whence $x + y = \pm 7$;

subtracting, $\qquad x^2 - 2xy + y^2 = 1$, whence $x - y = \pm 1$.

If $x + y = +7$ or, if $x + y = +7$
and $x - y = +1$ and $x - y = -1$

then $2x = 8$, and $x = 4$,   then $2x = 6$, and $x = 3$,

also $2y = 6$, and $y = 3$;   also $2y = 8$, and $y = 4$.

Similarly, by combining the equation $x + y = -7$ with each of the two $x - y = \pm 1$, we should get the other two pairs of roots,

$\qquad\qquad x = -4, \; y = -3,$ and $x = -3, \; y = -4$.

Ex. 3. Solve $x + y = 5$ (1)
$\qquad\qquad\quad x^3 + y^3 = 65$ (2)

This may be solved by the method of Art. 249, and also as follows:

By division, $\qquad \dfrac{x^3 + y^3}{x + y} = \dfrac{65}{5}$;

that is, $\qquad x^2 - xy + y^2 = 13$.   (3)

From this equation, combined with $x+y=5$, we can find x and y by the first case, or we may complete the solution thus:

$$x+y=5;$$

squaring, $\qquad x^2+2xy+y^2=25;\quad (4)$

also, (3) $\qquad x^2-xy+y^2=13;$

therefore, by subtraction, $3xy=12;$

or, $\qquad xy=4;$

and, $\qquad 4xy=16. \quad (5)$

Subtracting (5) from (4); $\quad x^2-2xy+y^2=9;$

extracting the square root, $\quad x-y=\pm 3.$

We have now to find x and y from the simple equations

$$x+y=5, \qquad x-y=\pm 3.$$

These give $\quad x=1$ or $4,\quad y=4$ or 1.

Ex. 4. Solve $x^2+xy+y^2=19,\quad x^4+x^2y^2+y^4=133.$

By division, $\qquad \dfrac{x^4+x^2y^2+y^4}{x^2+xy+y^2}=\dfrac{133}{19};$

that is, $\qquad x^2-xy+y^2=7.$

We have now to solve the equations

$$x^2+xy+y^2=19,\qquad x^2-xy+y^2=7.$$

By addition and subtraction we obtain successively

$$x^2+y^2=13,\qquad xy=6.$$

Then proceeding as in Ex. 2, we shall find

$$x=\pm 3 \text{ or } \pm 2, \qquad y=\pm 2 \text{ or } \pm 3.$$

Examples—57.

1. $\tfrac{1}{10}(3x+5y)+\tfrac{1}{6}(4x-3y)=6\tfrac{43}{30}$
   $3x^2+2y^2=179$

2. $x^2+y^2=25$
   $x+y=1$

3. $\left.\begin{array}{l}x^2+y^2=25\\4y+3x=24\end{array}\right\}$ 4. $\left.\begin{array}{l}2(x-y)=11\\xy=20\end{array}\right\}$ 5. $\left.\begin{array}{l}x^2+xy=66\\x^2-y^2=11\end{array}\right\}$

6. $\left.\begin{array}{l}x-y=2\\15(x^2-y^2)=16xy\end{array}\right\}$ 7. $\left.\begin{array}{l}x^2=\tfrac{8 5}{9}y^2-4xy\\x-y=2\end{array}\right\}$

8. $\left.\begin{array}{l}xy=(x-\tfrac{3}{4})(y+\tfrac{2}{3})\\x^2y^2=(x^2+3)(y^2-4)\end{array}\right\}$ 9. $\left.\begin{array}{l}x+y=6\\x^3+y^3=72\end{array}\right\}$

10. $\left.\begin{array}{l}3xy+2x+y=485\\3x=2y\end{array}\right\}$ 11. $\left.\begin{array}{l}x-y=1\\x^3-y^3=19\end{array}\right\}$

12. $\left.\begin{array}{l}x^3+y^3=189\\x^2y+xy^2=180\end{array}\right\}$ 13. $\left.\begin{array}{l}x+y=a\\x^2+y^2=b^2\end{array}\right\}$ 14. $\left.\begin{array}{l}xy=a^2\\x-y=b\end{array}\right\}$

15. $\left.\begin{array}{l}\sqrt{x}+\sqrt{y}=3\\x+y=9\end{array}\right\}$ 16. $\left.\begin{array}{l}x^2+xy=a^2\\y^2+xy=b^2\end{array}\right\}$

17. $18+9(x+y)=2(x+y)^2$, $6-(x-y)=(x-y)^2$.

18. $x^2-xy=a(x+1)+b+1$, $xy-y^2=ay+b$.

19. $\dfrac{a^2}{x^2}+\dfrac{y^2}{b^2}=18$, $\dfrac{ab}{xy}=1$.   20. $\dfrac{a^2}{x^2}-\dfrac{y^2}{b^2}=12$, $\dfrac{ab}{xy}=2$.

21. $x^2=ax+by$, $y^2=ay+bx$.

251. We shall now give some problems, to be solved by equations of the second degree, with more than one unknown quantity.

Ex. 1. The sum of the squares of the digits of a number of two places is 25, and the product of the digits is 12: find the number.

Let x, y be the digits, so that the number will be $10x+y$; then $x^2+y^2=25$, and $xy=12$, from which equations we get $x=3$, $y=4$, or $x=4$, $y=3$, and the number will be 34 or 43.

In this case both the roots give solutions.

Ex. 2. Find two numbers, such that their sum, their product, and the difference of their squares may be all equal.

Here assume $x+y$ and $x-y$ for the two numbers; [this step should be noticed, as it simplifies much the solution of problems of this kind:] then their sum $=2x$, their product $=x^2-y^2$, and the difference of their squares $=4xy$;

$$\therefore (1)\ 2x=4xy,\quad (2)\ 2x=x^2-y^2;$$

from (1), $y=\tfrac{1}{2}$; from (2), $2x=x^2-\tfrac{1}{4}$;

whence, $\qquad x=\tfrac{1}{2}(2\pm\sqrt{5});$

and, $\quad \therefore x+y=\tfrac{1}{2}(3\pm\sqrt{5}),\ x-y=\tfrac{1}{2}(1\pm\sqrt{5}),$

the numbers required.

Ex. 3. A man sets out from the foot of a mountain to walk to its summit. His rate of walking during the second half of the distance is half a mile per hour less than his rate during the first half, and he reaches the summit in $5\tfrac{1}{2}$ hours. He descends in $3\tfrac{3}{4}$ hours, by walking at a uniform rate, which is one mile per hour more than his rate during the first half of the ascent: find the distance to the summit, and his rates of walking.

Let $2x$ denote the number of miles to the summit, and suppose that during the first half of the ascent the man walked y miles per hour. Then he took $\dfrac{x}{y}$ hours for the first half of the ascent and $\dfrac{x}{y-\tfrac{1}{2}}$ hours for the second.

Therefore, $\qquad \dfrac{x}{y}+\dfrac{x}{y-\tfrac{1}{2}}=5\tfrac{1}{2}\quad (1).$

Similarly, $\qquad \dfrac{2x}{y+1}=3\tfrac{3}{4}\quad (2).$

From (2), $\qquad 2x=\dfrac{15}{4}(y+1);$

therefore, $\qquad x=\dfrac{15}{8}(y+1).$

From (1), $\quad x\left(2y-\dfrac{1}{2}\right)=\dfrac{11}{2}y\left(y-\dfrac{1}{2}\right).$

Therefore, by substitution,

$$\dfrac{15}{8}(y+1)\left(2y-\dfrac{1}{2}\right)=\dfrac{11}{2}y\left(y-\dfrac{1}{2}\right);$$

whence, $\quad 15(y+1)(4y-1)=44y(2y-1);$

and, $\quad 28y^2-89y+15=0.$

From this quadratic equation we obtain $y=3$, or $\dfrac{5}{28}$. The value $\dfrac{5}{28}$ is inapplicable, because, by supposition, y is greater than $\dfrac{1}{2}$. Therefore, $y=3$; and then $x=\dfrac{15}{2}$, so that the whole distance to the summit is 15 miles.

Examples—58.

1. The sum of the squares of two numbers is 170, and the difference of their squares is 72: find the numbers.

2. The product of two numbers is 192, and the sum of their squares is 640: find the numbers.

3. The product of two numbers is 60 times their difference, and the sum of their squares is 244: find the numbers.

4. Find two numbers, such that twice the first, with three times the second, may make 60, and twice the square of the first, with three times the square of the second, may make 840.

5. Find two numbers, such that their difference multiplied into the difference of their squares shall make 32, and their sum multiplied by the sum of their squares shall make 272.

6. Find two numbers, such that their difference added to the difference of their squares may make 14, and their sum added to the sum of their squares may make 26,

7. Find two numbers, such that their product is equal to their sum, and their sum added to the sum of their squares equal to 12.

8. The difference of two numbers is 3, and the difference of their cubes is 279: find the numbers.

9. A man has to travel a certain distance, and when he has travelled 40 miles he increases his speed 2 miles per hour. If he had travelled with his increased speed during the whole of his journey, he would have arrived at his destination 40 minutes earlier, but if he had continued at his original speed he would have arrived 20 minutes later: find the whole distance he had to travel.

10. A number consisting of two digits has one decimal place; the difference of the squares of the digits is 20, and if the digits be reversed, the sum of the two numbers is 11 · find the number.

11. A person buys a quantity of wheat, which he sells so as to gain 5 per cent. on his outlay, and thus clears £16. If he had sold it at a gain of 5 shillings per quarter, he would have cleared as many pounds as each quarter cost him shillings: find how many quarters he bought, and what each quarter cost.

12. Two trains start at the same time from two towns, and each proceeds at a uniform rate toward the other town. When they meet it is found that one train has run 108 miles more than the other, and that if they continue to run at the same rate they will finish the journey in 9 and 16 hours respectively: find the distance between the towns, and the rates of the trains.

13. A and B take shares in a concern to the amount, altogether, of $2500; they sell out at *par*—A at the end of 2 years, B at the end of 8 years—and each receives, in capital and profit, $1485: how much did each embark?

14. Find three numbers, such that if the first be multiplied by the sum of the second and third, the second by the sum of the first and third, and the third by the sum of the first and second, the products shall be 26, 50, and 56.

XXXIV. Ratio.

252. *Ratio* is the relation which one quantity bears to another with respect to magnitude, the comparison being made by considering what *multiple, part* or *parts,* the first is of the second; or, in other words, what *fraction* the first is of the second. Thus, if one quantity be two-thirds of another quantity, the former is said to be to the latter in the ratio of 2 to 3, for if both be divided into respectively equal parts, the former will contain two, and the latter three of these equal parts. And thus the ratio of 2 to 3 and the fraction $\frac{2}{3}$, express the same idea; for $\frac{2}{3}$ indicates that unity has been divided into 3 equal parts, and two of them are taken.

253. The ratio, then, of one quantity to another, is represented by the fraction obtained by dividing the former by the latter. Thus, the ratio of 6 to 3 is $\frac{6}{3}$, or 2; that of a to b is $\frac{a}{b}$; that of 15 to 40 is $\frac{15}{40}$, or $\frac{3}{8}$; that of $4a$ to $6b$ is $\frac{4a}{6b}$, or $\frac{2a}{3b}$. Of course the two quantities compared must be of the same kind, or one could not be a fraction of the other. (See Venable's Arithmetic, Art. 171.)

254. The ratio of a to b is expressed, either by two points placed between the quantities, as $a:b$, or for shortness, by its measure, $\frac{a}{b}$. The first of the quantities, $a:b$, is called the *antecedent* term of the *ratio*, and the latter the *consequent*.

255. A ratio is said to be of *greater* or *less inequality* according as the antecedent is greater or less than the consequent.

256. If the antecedents of any ratios are multiplied together, and also the consequents, a new ratio is obtained, which is said to be *compounded* of the former ratios. Thus, the ratio, $ac:bd$, is compounded of the two ratios, $a:b$, and $c:d$.

When the ratio $a:b$ is compounded with itself, the resulting ratio is $a^2:b^2$; this ratio is called the *duplicate* ratio of $a:b$; and the ratio $a^3:b^3$, is called the *triplicate* ratio of $a:b$.

257. Problems upon ratios are solved by representing them by their corresponding fractions, and then treating these fractions by the ordinary rules. Thus,

If the terms of a ratio be multiplied or divided by the same quantity, the ratio is not altered.

For, $$\frac{a}{b}=\frac{ma}{mb}.$$

Thus ratios are *compared* with one another by reducing the fractions which measure these ratios to common denominators, and comparing the numerators; and they are *compounded* by multiplying together the fractions which measure them. Thus, also, a ratio may be reduced to its lowest terms by dividing the numerator and denominator of its fraction by their G.C.D.

Ex. 1. Compare the ratios $5:7$ and $4:9$.

Ans. $\frac{45}{63}$, $\frac{28}{63}$; whence $5:7 > 4:9$.

Ex. 2. Find the ratio of $\frac{4}{5}:\frac{2}{3}$. Ans. $\frac{4}{5} \div \frac{2}{3} = \frac{4}{5} \times \frac{3}{2} = \frac{12}{10}$.

Ex. 3. What is the ratio compounded of $2:3$, $6:7$, $14:15$?

Ans. $\frac{2}{3} \times \frac{6}{7} \times \frac{14}{15} = \frac{8}{15}$, or $8:15$.

Ex. 4. Reduce to its lowest terms, $a^2-x^2 : a^2+2ax+x^2$.

Ans. $\dfrac{(a-x)}{(a+x)}\dfrac{(a+x)}{(a+x)} = \dfrac{a-x}{a+x}$, or $a-x : a+x$.

258. If to both terms of the ratio, $a:b$, the quantity x be added, that ratio will be increased or diminished according as a is *less* or *greater* than b.

For, $\qquad \dfrac{a}{b}$ is $>$ or $< \dfrac{a+x}{b+x}$;

if $\qquad \dfrac{ab+ax}{b(b+x)}$ is $>$ or $< \dfrac{ab+bx}{b(b+x)}$;

that is, if $\qquad ab+ax >$ or $< ab+bx$;

that is, if $\qquad ax >$ or $< bx$;

or if $\qquad a >$ or $< b$;

which shows the truth of the proposition.

Examples—59.

1. Compare the ratios $3:4$ and $4:5$; $13:14$ and $23:24$; $3:7$, $7:11$, and $11:15$.

2. Of $a+b : a-b$ and $a^2+b^2 : a^2-b^2$, which is greater, supposing $a > b$?

3. What is the ratio b inches to c yards?

4. Find the ratio compounded of $3:5, 10:21$, and $14:15$; of $7:9, 102:105$, and $15:17$.

5. Find the ratio compounded of $\dfrac{a^2+ax+x^2}{a^3-a^2x+ax^2-x^3}$ and $\dfrac{a^2-ax+x^2}{a+x}$.

6. Compound

$\qquad x^2-9x+20 : x^2-6x$ and $x^2-13x+42 : x^2-5x$.

7. Compound the ratios $a+b : a-b$, $a^2+b^2 : (a+b)^2$, $(a^2-b^2)^2 : a^4-b^4$.

8. What is the ratio compounded of the duplicate ratio of $a+b : a-b$, and the difference of the duplicate ratios of $a:a$ and $a:b$, supposing $a>b$?

9. What quantity must be added to each term of the ratio $a:b$, that it may become equal to the ratio $c:d$?

10. Show that $a-b : a+b \gtreqless a^2-b^2 : a^2+b^2$, according as $a:b$ is a ratio of less or greater inequality.

11. Find two numbers in the ratio of 3 to 4, such that their sum has to the sum of their squares the ratio of 7 to 50.

12. Find two numbers in the ratio of 5 to 6, such that their sum has to the difference of their squares the ratio of 1 to 7.

13. Find x so that the ratio $x:1$ may be the duplicate of the ratio $8:x$.

14. Find x so that the ratio $a-x : b-x$ may be the duplicate of the ratio $a:b$.

XXXV. Proportion.

259. When two ratios are equal, the four quantities composing them are said to be *proportional* to one another; thus, $a:b=c:d$; that is, if $\frac{a}{b}=\frac{c}{d}$, then a, b, c, d, are proportionals. Thus, four quantities are proportional when the first is the same multiple, part or parts of the second, as the third is of the fourth. This is expressed by saying a *is to* b as c *is to* d, and denoted thus, $a:b::c:d$; or thus, $a:b=c:d$; or thus, $\frac{a}{b}=\frac{c}{d}$.

The first and last terms in a proportion are called the *extremes*, the other two the *means*.

Problems on proportions, like those on ratios, are solved by the use of fractions.

260. (1.) *When four quantities are proportionals, the product of the extremes is equal to the product of the means.*

For if $\dfrac{a}{b} = \dfrac{c}{d}$, then $ad = bc$.

(2.) Hence, if three terms of a proportion are given, we can find the other from the equation $ad = bc$. Thus

$$a = \frac{bc}{d}, \quad b = \frac{ad}{c}, \quad c = \frac{ad}{b}, \quad d = \frac{bc}{a}.$$

(3.) If $a:b = b:d$, we have $ad = b^2$; that is, *if the first be to the second as the second is to the third, the product of the extremes is equal to the square of the mean.*

In this case a, b, d, are said to be in *continued proportion*.

261. *If the product of two quantities be equal to that of two others, the four are proportionals, the factors of either product being the extremes, and of the other the means.*

For, let $\qquad\qquad ad = bc$;

dividing by bd, $\qquad \dfrac{a}{b} = \dfrac{c}{d}$;

or $\qquad\qquad a:b = c:d$.

262. If $a:b = c:d$, and $c:d = e:f$, then $a:b = e:f$.

For $\qquad \dfrac{a}{b} = \dfrac{c}{d}$, and $\dfrac{c}{d} = \dfrac{e}{f}$;

therefore, $\qquad \dfrac{a}{b} = \dfrac{e}{f}$, or $a:b = e:f$.

263. If $a:b = c:d$, and $e:f = g:h$, then $ae:bf = cg:dh$.

Extremes. Means. Demonstrate Art. 260 (1), (2), and (3). Demonstrate Art. 261; Art. 262; Art. 263.

For $\dfrac{a}{b}=\dfrac{c}{d}$, and $\dfrac{e}{f}=\dfrac{g}{h}$;

$\therefore \dfrac{ae}{bf}=\dfrac{cg}{dh}$, or $ae:bf=cg:dh$.

This is called *compounding* the two proportions. And so we may compound any number of such proportions. Thus, if $a:b=c:d$, $a^2:b^2=c^2:d^2$, &c.

264. *If four quantities be proportionals, they are proportionals when taken inversely.* That is, if $a:b=c:d$, then $b:a=d:c$.

For (Art. 134, i), if $\dfrac{a}{b}=\dfrac{c}{d}$, $1\div\dfrac{a}{b}=1\div\dfrac{c}{d}$;

that is, $\dfrac{b}{a}=\dfrac{d}{c}$, or $b:a=d:c$.

265. *If four quantities be proportionals, they are proportionals when taken alternately.* That is, if $a:b=c:d$, then $a:c=b:d$.

For (Art. 134, ii), since $\dfrac{a}{b}=\dfrac{c}{d}$, $\dfrac{a}{b}\times\dfrac{b}{c}=\dfrac{c}{d}\times\dfrac{b}{c}$;

that is, $\dfrac{a}{c}=\dfrac{b}{d}$, or $a:c=b:d$.

266. *If four quantities are proportionals, the first together with the second is to the second, as the third together with the fourth is to the fourth.*

For $\dfrac{a}{b}=\dfrac{c}{d}$;

therefore (Art. 134, iii), $\dfrac{a+b}{b}=\dfrac{c+d}{d}$, or $a+b:b=c+d:d$.

267. Also, *the excess of the first above the second is to the second as the excess of the third above the fourth is to the fourth.*

Art. 264; Art. 265; Art. 266; Art. 267.

For $\frac{a}{b}=\frac{c}{d}$; therefore (Art. 134, iv), by subtracting 1 from each of these equals,

$$\frac{a-b}{b}=\frac{c-d}{d}, \text{ or } a-b:b=c-d:d.$$

268. We have also (134, v),

$$\frac{a\pm b}{b}\times\frac{b}{a}=\frac{c\pm d}{d}\times\frac{d}{c}; \quad \therefore \frac{a\pm b}{a}=\frac{c\pm d}{c};$$

or $a\pm b:a=c\pm d:c$, which, by inversion (264), gives

$$a:a\pm b=c:c\pm d.$$

269. *When four quantities are proportionals, the sum of the first and second is to their difference as the sum of the third and fourth is to their difference.*

For (Arts. 266 and 267),

$$\frac{a+b}{b}=\frac{c+d}{d}, \text{ and } \frac{a-b}{b}=\frac{c-d}{d};$$

therefore,
$$\frac{a+b}{b}\div\frac{a-b}{b}=\frac{c+d}{d}\div\frac{c-d}{d};$$

that is,
$$\frac{a+b}{a-b}=\frac{c+d}{c-d};$$

or $a+b:a-b=c+d:c-d.$

270. If four quantities form a proportion, we may derive from them many other proportions, all equally true.

Thus, if $\frac{a}{b}=\frac{c}{d}$, then $\frac{ma}{mb}=\frac{c}{d}$ or $ma:mb=c:d.$

Similarly, $ma:b=mc:d, \quad a:mb=c:md, \quad a:b=mc:md;$ and in like manner

$$\frac{a}{m}:\frac{b}{m}=c:d, \quad a:\frac{b}{m}=c:\frac{d}{m}, \text{ &c.}$$

That is, either the *first* or *fourth* terms of any proportion may be multiplied or divided by any quantity, provided that either the *second* or *third* be multiplied or divided by the same.

271. Again; if $a:b=c:d$, then $\dfrac{a}{b}=\dfrac{c}{d}$;

and $\dfrac{m}{n}\times\dfrac{a}{b}=\dfrac{m}{n}\times\dfrac{c}{d}$, or $\dfrac{ma}{nb}=\dfrac{mc}{nd}$;

or $ma:nb=mc:na$.

Then, by the preceding Articles, or by Art. 134,

$$\frac{ma\pm nb}{ma}=\frac{mc\pm nd}{mc};$$

whence, also, $\dfrac{ma\pm nb}{a}=\dfrac{mc\pm nd}{c}$;

or $ma\pm nb:a=mc\pm nd:c$.

Again (Art. 269); $\dfrac{ma+nb}{ma-nb}=\dfrac{mc+nd}{mc-nd}$;

or $ma+nb:ma-nb=mc+nd:mc-nd$.

272. (1) In like manner, if $a:b=c:d=e:f$, &c., by which it is meant $a:b=c:d$, or $a:b=e:f$, &c., so that $\dfrac{a}{b}=\dfrac{c}{d}=\dfrac{e}{f}$, &c. Then $a:b=a+c+e:b+d+f$, &c.

For, let $\dfrac{a}{b}=x=\dfrac{c}{d}=\dfrac{e}{f}$; then $a=bx$, $c=dx$, $e=fx$;

therefore, $a+c+e=bx+dx+fx=(b+d+f)x$.

$\therefore x$ or $\dfrac{a}{b}=\dfrac{a+c+e}{b+d+f}$, or $a:b=a+c+e:b+d+f$.

That is, *if there be any number of quantities in proportion, as one antecedent is to its consequent, so is the sum of all the antecedents to the sum of all the consequents.*

Again (2); the equations above derived from $\frac{a}{b}=x=\frac{c}{d}=\frac{e}{f}$, &c., give $ma=mbx$, $nc=ndx$, $pe=pfx$, &c.

$$\therefore ma+nc+pc=(mb+nd+pf)x;$$

therefore, x or $\dfrac{a}{b}=\dfrac{ma+nc+pe}{mb+nd+pf}$;

So also (3), since $\dfrac{a}{b}=\dfrac{c}{d}=\dfrac{e}{f}$, &c., $\dfrac{a^2}{b^2}=\dfrac{c^2}{d^2}=\dfrac{e^2}{f^2}$;

therefore, $\dfrac{a^2}{b^2}=\dfrac{a^2+c^2+e^2}{b^2+d^2+f^2}=\dfrac{ma^2+nc^2+pe^2}{mb^2+nd^2+pf^2}$;

$$\therefore \frac{a}{b}=\frac{\sqrt{a^2+c^2+e^2}}{\sqrt{b^2+d^2+f^2}}, \text{ or } a:b=\sqrt{a^2+c^2+e^2}:\sqrt{b^2+d^2+f^2};$$

and so on for any number of terms and any like powers.

Ex. 1. Find a fourth proportional to $\frac{1}{2}$, $\frac{1}{3}$, and $\frac{1}{4}$.

Since $d=\dfrac{bc}{a}$ (Art. 260), this is $\dfrac{\frac{1}{3}\times\frac{1}{4}}{\frac{1}{2}}=\frac{1}{6}$.

Ex. 2. Find a mean proportional to 2 and 8.

Since $b^2=ac$ (Art. 260), this is $\sqrt{(2\times 8)}=\sqrt{16}=4$.

Ex. 3. If $a:b=c:d$, express $(a+d)-(b+c)$ in terms of a, b, c only.

Here $(a+d)-(b+c)=\left(a+\dfrac{bc}{a}\right)-(b+c)$

$$=\frac{a^2-ab-ac+bc}{a}=\frac{(a-b)(a-c)}{a}.$$

Examples—61.

1. Find a fourth proportional to 3, 5, 6; to 12, 5, 10; to $\frac{2}{3}$, $\frac{1}{4}$, $\frac{1}{6}$.

2. Find a third proportional to 4, 6; to 2, 3; to $\frac{1}{3}$, $\frac{1}{4}$.

PROPORTION. 239

3. Find a mean proportional to 4, 9; to 4, $\frac{16}{25}$; to $1\frac{7}{9}$, $1\frac{9}{16}$.

4. If $a:b::b:c$, then, $a^2+b^2:a+c::a^2-b^2:a-c$.

5. If $\frac{a}{b}=\frac{c}{d}$, show that $(a+b)(c+d)=\frac{b}{d}(c+d)^2=\frac{d}{b}(a+b)^2$.

6. If $a:b::c:d$, and $m:n::p:q$,
then $ma+nb:ma-nb::pc+qd:pc-qd$.

7. If $a:b::b:c$, then $a^2-b^2:a::b^2-c^2:c$.

8. If $a:b::c:d::e:f$, then $a-e:b-f::c:d$.

9. If $a:b::b:c$,
then $ma^2-nb^2:ma-nc::pa^2+qb^2:pa+qc$.

Solve the equations,

10. $\sqrt{x}+\sqrt{b}:\sqrt{x}-\sqrt{b}=a:b$.

11. $x+a:2x-b=3x+b:4x-a$.

12. $x+y+1:x+y+2=6:7$
$y+2x:y-2x=12x+6y-3:6y-12x-1$.

13. $x:27=y:9=2:x-y$.

14. What number is that to which if 1, 5, and 13 be severally added, the first sum shall be to the second as the second to the third?

15. Find two numbers in the ratio of $2\frac{1}{2}:2$, such that, when diminished each by 5, they shall be in that of $1\frac{1}{3}:1$.

16. A railway passenger observes that a train passes him, moving in the opposite direction, in 2″, whereas, if it had been moving in the same direction with him, it would have passed him in 30″: compare the rates of the two trains.

17. A quantity of milk is increased by watering in the ratio of 4:5, and then three gallons are sold; the rest being mixed with three quarts of water, is increased in the ratio of 6:7: how many gallons of milk were there at first?

XXXVI. Arithmetical Progression.

273. Quantities are said to form a *Series* when they *proceed by a law*, *i. e.*, when any one quantity may be obtained from those which precede it by a rule, which is the *law* of the series.

274. Quantities are said to form an *Arithmetical Series*, or to be in *Arithmetical Progression*, when they proceed by a common difference.

Thus, the following series are in A. P.:

$$1, 3, 5, 7, 9, \ldots$$
$$12, 8, 4, 0, -4, \ldots$$
$$a, a+d, a+2d, a+3d, \ldots$$

In the first and third the quantities increase as the series proceeds; in the second, they decrease; the common differences being 2, -4, and d, respectively, which are found by *subtracting any term from the term following;* therefore, when the progression is a decreasing one, the common difference is negative.

275. *Given* a, *the first term, and* d, *the common difference of an Arithmetical Series, to find* l *the* n^{th} *term, and* S *the sum of* n *terms.*

Since a is the first term, and d the common difference, the second term is $a+d$; the third term is $a+2d$; the fourth term is $a+3d$; and so on, where the coefficient of d is *less by one* than the number of the term. So in the nth term we shall have $(n-1)d$; therefore, the nth term

$$l = a + (n-1)d. \quad (1)$$

Again, the sum of the terms,

$$S = a + (a+d) + (a+2d) + \&c., + (l-2d) + (l-d) + l;$$

Series. Arithmetical Series, or Progression. Common difference, how found; when negative. How to find the last term, and the sum of the series.

ARITHMETICAL PROGRESSION.

and by writing the series in the reverse order, we have also

$$S = l + (l-d) + (l-2d) + \&c. + (a+2d) + (a+d) + a.$$

Therefore, by addition,

$$2S = (a+l) + (a+l) + (a+l) \ \&c., \text{ to } n \text{ terms};$$

$$\therefore 2S = (a+l)n;$$

$$\therefore S = (a+l)\frac{n}{2}; \quad (2)$$

and since $\quad l = a + (n-1)d,$

we have also, $\quad S = [2a + (n-1)d]\frac{n}{2}. \quad (3)$

The equation (2) furnishes the following rule:

The sum of any number of terms in A. P. *is equal to the product of the number of terms into half the sum of the first and last terms.*

Ex. 1. Find the sum of 20 terms of the series 1, 2, 3, 4.

Here $a=1$, $d=1$, $n=20$; using formula (3),

$$S = [2 + (20-1)1]\tfrac{20}{2}, \text{ or } = (2+19)\tfrac{20}{2} = 21 \times 10 = 210.$$

Ex. 2. Find the 9th term, and the sum of 9 terms of 7, $5\tfrac{1}{2}$, 4, &c.

Here $\quad a=7, \ d=-\tfrac{3}{2}, \ n=9;$

$$\therefore l = 7 + (9-1) \times -\tfrac{3}{2} = 7 - 8 \times \tfrac{3}{2} = -5;$$

and $\quad S = \tfrac{9}{2}(7-5) = 9.$

Ex. 3. Find the 13th term of the series $-48, \ -44, \ -40,$ &c.

Here $\quad a = -48, \ d=4, \ n=13;$

$$\therefore l = -48 + (13-1)4 = 0.$$

Ex. 4. Find the sum of seven terms of $\tfrac{1}{2} + \tfrac{1}{3} + \tfrac{1}{4}$, &c.

Formulas (1), (2), (3).

242   ELEMENTARY ALGEBRA.

Here $a=\frac{1}{2}$, $d=-\frac{1}{6}$, $n=7$; here, as in Ex. 1, we are not required to find l; ∴ using formula (3),

$$S=(1+6\times -\tfrac{1}{6})\tfrac{7}{2}=(1-1)\tfrac{7}{2}=0.$$

The series continued to seven terms is $\frac{1}{2}$, $\frac{1}{3}$, $\frac{1}{6}$, 0, $-\frac{1}{6}$, $-\frac{1}{3}$, $-\frac{1}{2}$.

Examples—62.

Find the last term and the sum of

1. $2+4+6+$ &c. to 16 terms.
2. $1+3+5+$ &c. to 20 terms.
3. $3+9+15+$ &c. to 11 terms.
4. $1+8+15+$ &c. to 100 terms.
5. $-5-3-1-$ &c. to 8 terms.
6. $1+\frac{4}{3}+\frac{5}{3}+$ &c. to 15 terms.

Find the sum of

7. $\frac{2}{3}+\frac{7}{15}+\frac{4}{15}+$ &c. to 21 terms.
8. $4-3-10-$ &c. to 10 terms.
9. $\frac{1}{2}+\frac{3}{4}+1+$ &c. to 10 terms.
10. $\frac{1}{2}-\frac{2}{3}-1\frac{1}{6}-$ &c. to 13 terms.
11. $1+2\frac{2}{3}+4\frac{1}{3}+$ &c. to 20 terms.
12. $\frac{3}{5}-1\frac{4}{10}-\frac{11}{15}-$ &c. to 10 terms.

276. By means of the equations,

(1) $l=a+(n-1)d$, (2) $S=(a+l)\dfrac{n}{2}$,

and (3) $S=\{2a+(n-1)d\}\dfrac{n}{2}$,

when any three of the quantities a, d, l, n, S, are given, we may find the others.

We may also use these equations to solve many problems in Arithmetical Progression.

ARITHMETICAL PROGRESSION.

Ex. 1. The sum of 15 terms of an A. P. is 600, and the common difference is 5: find the first term.

Since $S=600$, $n=15$, and $d=5$, we have by (3),
$$600=(2a+14\times 5)\tfrac{15}{2};$$
$\therefore 600=(a+35)15;\quad \therefore a+35=40;\quad \therefore a=5.$

Ex. 2. What number of terms of the series 10, 8, 6, &c. must be taken to make 30?

$S=30,\ a=10,\ d=-2;\ \therefore$ by (3),
$$30=[20-2(n-1)]\tfrac{n}{2};$$
$$\therefore (22-2n)\tfrac{n}{2}=30;$$
that is, $\quad n^2-11n=-30,$

and the roots of this quadratic are 5 and 6, either of which satisfies the question, since the 6th term is 0.

Ex. 3. How many terms of the series 3, 5, 7, &c. make up 24?

Here $S=24,\ a=3,\ d=2$;

therefore, by (3), $\quad 24=[6+2(n-1)]\tfrac{n}{2};$

whence, $n=4$, or -6, of which the first only is admissible by the conditions of the question.

277. Ex. 4. Find *the Arithmetical Mean* between two quantities a and b.

Let x denote this mean; then since a, x, and b are in A. P.
$$x-a=b-x;$$
whence, $\quad x=\dfrac{a+b}{2};$

that is, the arithmetical mean between two quantities is half the *sum* of the quantities.

Ex. 5. Insert five arithmetical means between 11 and 23.

Here we have to obtain an A. P. consisting of *seven* terms, beginning with 11, and ending with 23.

Thus, $a=11$, $l=23$, $n=7$;

therefore, by (1), Art. 276, $23=11+6d$;

$$\therefore d=2.$$

Thus the whole series is 11, 13, 15, 17, 19, 21, 23.

278. Ex. 6. The sum of three numbers in A. P. is 21, and the sum of their squares is 155: find the numbers.

Let x = the middle number, and y the common difference; then $x-y$, x, $x+y$, represent the three numbers;

then $$(x-y)+x+(x+y)= 21$$
and $$(x-y)^2+x^2+(x+y)^2=155$$

or reducing,

$$3x= 21$$
$$3x^2+2y^2=155$$

whence, $x=7$, $y=\pm 2$;

and the numbers are 5, 7, 9.

Examples—63.

1. The first term in an A. P. is 2, the common difference 7, and the last term 79: find the number of terms.

2. The first term of an A. P. is $13\frac{1}{15}$, the common difference $-\frac{2}{3}$, and the last term $\frac{2}{3}$: find the number of terms.

3. The first and last of 40 numbers in A. P. are $1\frac{1}{8}$ and $1\frac{2}{3}$: find the other terms, and the sum of the series.

4. Insert 3 arithmetical means between 12 and 20.

5. Insert 5 arithmetical means between 14 and 16.

6. Insert 7 arithmetical means between 8 and -4.

7. Insert 8 arithmetical means between −1 and 5.

8. The first term of an arithmetical progression is 13, the second term is 11, the sum is 40: find the number of terms.

9. The first term of an arithmetical progression is 5, and the fifth term is 11: find the sum of 8 terms.

10. The sum of four terms in arithmetical progression is 44, and the last term is 17: find the terms.

11. The sum of five numbers in arithmetical progression is 15, and the sum of their squares is 55: find the numbers.

12. The seventh term of an arithmetical progression is 12, and the twelfth term is 7; the sum of the series is 171: find the number of terms.

13. A traveller has a journey of 140 miles to perform. He goes 26 miles the first day, 24 the second, 22 the third, and so on: in how many days does he perform the journey?

14. A sets out from a place and travels $2\frac{1}{2}$ miles an hour. B sets out 3 hours after A, and travels in the same direction, 3 miles the first hour, $3\frac{1}{2}$ miles the second, 4 miles the third, and so on: in how many hours will B overtake A.

XXXVII. Geometrical Progression.

279. Quantities are said to be in *Geometrical Progression* when they *proceed by a common factor;* that is, when each is equal to the product of the preceding by a common factor. This common factor is called the *common ratio,* or simply the *ratio.*

Thus the following series are in geometrical progression:

$$1, 3, 9, 27, 81, \ldots$$
$$4, 1, \tfrac{1}{4}, \tfrac{1}{16}, \tfrac{1}{64}, \ldots$$
$$-\tfrac{1}{3}, \tfrac{4}{15}, -\tfrac{16}{75} \ldots$$
$$a, ar, ar^2, \&c.$$

The *common ratios* being 3, $\tfrac{1}{4}$, $-\tfrac{4}{5}$, and r, respectively. The common ratio is found *by dividing any term by the term which immediately precedes it;* therefore, if the quantities are alternately + and −, the ratio is *negative*.

280. *Given* a *the first term and* r *the common ratio of a geometrical series, to find* l *the* nth *term, and* S *the sum of* n *terms.*

Here, since a is the first term and r the common ratio, the second term is ar, the third term is ar^2, the fourth term is ar^3, and so on; where the index of r in any term is *less by one* than the number of the term. Thus then the nth term
$$l = ar^{n-1}. \quad (1)$$

Again, $\quad S = a + ar + ar^2 + \&c., \; + ar^{n-1};$

and $\quad rS = ar + ar^2 + ar^3 + \&c., \; + ar^{n-1} + ar^n;$

therefore, by subtraction,
$$rS - S = ar^n - a,$$

the other terms disappearing. Hence,

$$S = \frac{ar^n - a}{r-1} = a \cdot \frac{(r^n - 1)}{r-1} \; (2); \text{ or } S = \frac{rl - a}{r-1} \; (3), \text{ since } rl = ar^n.$$

Ex. 1. Find the 6th term, and the sum of 6 terms of 1, 2, 4, &c.

Here $\qquad a = 1, \; r = 2, \; n = 6;$

$\therefore l = 1 \times 2^5 = 32;$ and $S = \dfrac{64 - 1}{2 - 1} = 63.$

Ex. 2. Find the 8th term, and the sum of 8 terms of 81, −27, 9, &c.

Here $\quad a=81,\ r=-\tfrac{1}{3},\ n=8;$

therefore, $\quad l=81\times\left(-\dfrac{1}{3}\right)^{7}=3^{4}\times -\dfrac{1}{3^{7}}=-\dfrac{1}{3^{3}}=-\tfrac{1}{27};$

and $\quad S=\dfrac{-\tfrac{1}{81}-81}{-\tfrac{1}{3}-1}=60\tfrac{20}{27}.$

Ex. 3. Find the sum of 8 terms of the series, 4, 2, 1, ½, &c.

Here $\quad a=4,\ r=\tfrac{1}{2},\ n=8;$

therefore, without finding l,

$$S=\dfrac{4\left(\dfrac{1}{2^{8}}-1\right)}{\tfrac{1}{2}-1}=\dfrac{4\left(1-\dfrac{1}{2^{8}}\right)}{1-\tfrac{1}{2}}=\dfrac{255}{64}\times\dfrac{2}{1}=\dfrac{255}{32}.$$

Ex. 4. Find the sum of $1-\tfrac{4}{3}+\tfrac{16}{9}-$&c. to 4 terms.

Here $\quad a=1,\ r=-\tfrac{4}{3},\ n=4;$

$$\therefore S=1\times\dfrac{\left(-\dfrac{4}{3}\right)^{4}-1}{-\tfrac{4}{3}-1}=\dfrac{\dfrac{4^{4}}{3^{4}}-1}{-\tfrac{4}{3}-1}=\dfrac{\dfrac{4^{4}-3^{4}}{3^{4}}}{-\tfrac{7}{3}}=-\dfrac{3}{7}\times\dfrac{256-81}{3^{4}}$$

$$=-\dfrac{175}{7.3^{3}}=-\dfrac{25}{27}.$$

Ex. 5. Find the sum of $2\tfrac{1}{2}-1+\tfrac{2}{5}-$&c. to 5 terms.

Here $\quad a=\tfrac{5}{2},\ r=-\tfrac{2}{5},\ n=5;$

$$\therefore S=\tfrac{5}{2}\cdot\dfrac{\left(-\dfrac{2}{5}\right)^{5}-1}{-\tfrac{2}{5}-1}=\dfrac{5}{2}\cdot\dfrac{-\dfrac{2^{5}}{5^{5}}-1}{-\tfrac{2}{5}-1}=\dfrac{5}{2}\cdot\dfrac{\dfrac{2^{5}+5^{5}}{5^{5}}}{\tfrac{7}{5}}$$

$$=\dfrac{5}{2}\cdot\dfrac{5}{7}\cdot\dfrac{32+3125}{5^{5}}=\dfrac{3157}{14.5^{3}}=1\tfrac{281}{875}.$$

Examples—64.

Find the last term and the sum of

1. $1+4+16+$&c. to 4 terms.   2. $5+20+80+$&c. to 5 terms.

Formulas (1), (2), (3).

3. $3+6+12+$ &c. to 6 terms.   4. $2-4+8-$ &c. to 8 terms.
5. $1-4+16-$ &c. to 7 terms.   6. $1-2+2^2-$ &c. to 10 terms.

Find the sum of

7. $\frac{1}{3}+\frac{1}{6}+\frac{1}{12}+$ &c. to 8 terms.   8. $\frac{1}{2}+\frac{1}{4}+\frac{3}{8}+$ &c. to 6 terms.
9. $\frac{3}{2}+1+\frac{2}{3}+$ &c. to 6 terms.   10. $3-\frac{1}{2}+\frac{1}{12}-$ &c. to 5 terms.

281. If the terms of a geometrical progression decrease numerically as the series proceeds, then the common ratio r is a proper fraction; that is, r is less than 1. Therefore the powers r^2, r^3, r^4, ... r^n, are still less than 1, and ar^n less than a. Both the numerator and denominator of the fraction $S=\dfrac{ar^n-a}{r-1}$ are then negative, and we may write it

$$S=\frac{a-ar^n}{1-r}=\frac{a}{1-r}-\frac{ar^n}{1-r}.$$

Now, the greater we take the number of terms n, the less will be the value of ar^n; and therefore, by taking n sufficiently great, we may make $\dfrac{ar^n}{1-r}$ as small as we please. Hence by making n sufficiently great, we render the value of S as near $\dfrac{a}{1-r}$ as we please.

This result we enunciate thus: *In a Geometrical Progression in which the common ratio is a proper fraction, by taking a sufficient number of terms the sum of the series can be made to differ as little as we please from* $\dfrac{a}{1-r}$.

$\dfrac{a}{1-r}$ is said then to be the *Limit* of the sum of the series a, ar, ar^2, &c., when $r<1$; or we say, for shortness (but not correctly), $S=\dfrac{a}{1-r}$ is the sum of the series *to infinity*. Using the same language, these series are called *infinite* Geometrical Progressions.

When the common ratio is a proper fraction. The limit of the sum of a series, when $r<1$. Infinite Geometrical Progressions.

GEOMETRICAL PROGRESSION.

It is common to denote the Limit of such a sum by Σ.

Ex. 1. Find the Limit of the sum of the series $1+\frac{1}{2}+\frac{1}{4}+$ &c.

Here $a=1$, $r=\frac{1}{2}$; $\therefore \Sigma=\dfrac{1}{1-\frac{1}{2}}=\dfrac{1}{\frac{1}{2}}=2$; that is, the more terms we take of this series, the more nearly will their sum $= 2$, but will never actually reach it.

Ex. 2. Find the sum of $2\frac{1}{2}-\frac{1}{2}+\frac{1}{10}-$ &c. *ad infinitum*.

Here $a=2\frac{1}{2}$, $r=-\frac{1}{5}$; $\therefore \Sigma=\dfrac{\frac{5}{2}}{1-(-\frac{1}{5})}=\dfrac{\frac{5}{2}}{1+\frac{1}{5}}=\dfrac{\frac{5}{2}}{\frac{6}{5}}=2\frac{1}{12}$.

282. Recurring Decimals are examples of infinite Geometrical Progressions. Thus, for example,

.3333 .... denotes $\frac{3}{10}+\frac{3}{100}+\frac{3}{1000}+$ &c.,

a G. P. of which the first term $a=\frac{3}{10}$ and the ratio $r=\frac{1}{10}$. Hence we may say that the Limit of this decimal is

$$\Sigma=\dfrac{\frac{3}{10}}{1-\frac{1}{10}}=\frac{3}{9}=\frac{1}{3}.$$

Again; .3242424 .... denotes $\frac{3}{10}+\frac{24}{1000}+\frac{24}{100000}+$ &c.

Here the terms after $\frac{3}{10}$ form a G. P. of which the first term $=\frac{24}{1000}$, and the common ratio is $\frac{1}{100}$. Hence the Limit of this series is $\dfrac{\frac{24}{1000}}{1-\frac{1}{100}}=\frac{24}{990}$. Therefore the limiting value of the recurring decimal is

$$\frac{3}{10}+\frac{24}{990}=\frac{3\times 99+24}{990}=\frac{3(100-1)+24}{990}=\frac{324-3}{990};$$

and this value accords with the rule in Arithmetic. (See Venable's Arithmetic, Recurring Decimals.)

EXAMPLES—65.

Find the Limits of the sums of the following series:

1. $4+2+1+$ &c. 2. $\frac{1}{2}+\frac{1}{3}+\frac{2}{9}+$ &c. 3. $\frac{1}{4}-\frac{1}{16}+\frac{1}{64}+$ &c.

4. $\frac{2}{3}-1+\frac{3}{2}-$&c.   5. $1-\frac{1}{2}+\frac{1}{4}-$&c.   6. $1-\frac{2}{5}+\frac{4}{25}-$&c.

7. $\frac{1}{5}+\frac{1}{15}+\frac{1}{45}+$&c.   8. $\frac{1}{3}+\frac{2}{9}+\frac{4}{27}+$&c.   9. $2-\frac{3}{4}+\frac{9}{32}-$&c.

Find the limiting values of the following recurring decimals:

10. $.151515....$ 11. $.123123123....$ 12. $.4282828....$

283. By means of the equations of Geometrical Progression, viz., $l = ar^{n-1}$, $S = \dfrac{lr-a}{r-1} = \dfrac{ar^n - a}{r-1}$, $\Sigma = \dfrac{a}{1-r}$, we may solve many problems respecting series of this kind. It is not, however, generally easy to find n from the other quantities, because it is an exponent. The method of logarithms will serve to find it in all cases.

Ex. 1. Find a geometrical series, whose 1st term is 2 and 7th term $\frac{1}{32}$.

Here $a=2$, $l=\frac{1}{32}$, $n=7$; $\therefore \frac{1}{32} = 2r^6$, and $r^6 = \frac{1}{64}$, whence $r = \pm\frac{1}{2}$, and the series is $2, \pm 1, \frac{1}{2}, \pm\frac{1}{4}$, &c.

Ex. 2. Given 6 the second term of a geometrical series and 54 the fourth, to find the first term.

Here $6 = ar$, $54 = ar^3$; $\therefore \dfrac{54}{6} = \dfrac{ar^3}{ar}$, or $9 = r^2$;

hence $r = \pm 3$, $a = \dfrac{6}{r} = \pm 2$.

Ex. 3. Insert three geometrical means between 2 and 32.

Here we have to obtain a geometrical progression consisting of *five* terms, beginning with 2 and ending with 32. Thus, $a=2$, $l=32$, $n=5$; therefore,

$$32 = 2r^4; \quad \therefore r^4 = 16; \quad \therefore r = 2.$$

Thus the series is $2, 4, 8, 16, 32$.

Ex. 4. How many terms of the series $2, -6, 18$, &c., must be taken to make -40?

Here $\quad a=2; \quad r=-3; \quad S=-40;$

therefore, $\quad -40 = \dfrac{2(-3)^n - 2}{-3 - 1};$

hence $\quad 2(-3)^n = 162;$

$\therefore (-3)^n = 81.$

But we know that $81 = 3^4$; therefore, $n = 4$.

Examples—66.

1. Insert 3 geometrical means between 1 and 256.

2. Insert 4 geometrical means between $5\frac{1}{3}$ and $40\frac{1}{2}$.

3. Insert 4 geometrical means between 3 and -729.

4. The sum of three terms in geometrical progression is 63, and the difference of the first and the third term is 45: find the terms.

5. The sum of the first four terms of a geometrical progression is 40, and the sum of the first eight terms is 3280: find the progression.

6. The population of a country increases annually in G. P., and in four years was raised from 10,000 to 14,641 souls: by what part of itself was it annually increased?

7. The sum of an infinite geometrical series is 3, and the sum of its first two terms is $2\frac{2}{3}$: find the series.

8. The sum of an infinite geometrical series is 2, and the second term is $-\frac{3}{2}$: find the series.

9. A body moves through 20 miles in the first one-millionth part of a second, 18 miles in the second millionth part of a second, and $16\frac{1}{5}$ miles in the third millionth part of a second, and so on forever: what is the limit of the distance from its point of departure, which it can attain?

XXXVIII. Harmonical Progression.

284. Quantities are said to be in *Harmonical Progression* when their reciprocals are in A. P. Thus, since 1, 3, 5, &c., $\frac{1}{2}$, $-\frac{1}{2}$, $-\frac{3}{2}$, &c., are in arithmetical progression, their reciprocals, 1, $\frac{1}{3}$, $\frac{1}{5}$, &c., 2, -2, $-\frac{2}{3}$, &c., are in Harmonical Progression.

The term *Harmonical* is applied to series of this character from the fact that musical strings of equal thickness and tension will produce harmony when sounded together, if their lengths be as the reciprocals of the arithmetical series of the natural numbers 1, 2, 3, 4, &c.

285. *If three quantities, A, B, and C, are in Harmonical Progression, then will* $A:C::A-B:B-C$.

For, by definition, $\frac{1}{A}$, $\frac{1}{B}$, and $\frac{1}{C}$ are in arithmetical progression; therefore,

$$\frac{1}{B} - \frac{1}{A} = \frac{1}{C} - \frac{1}{B};$$

multiplying by ABC, $\quad AC - BC = AB - AC$;

that is, $\quad\quad\quad\quad C(A-B) = A(B-C)$;

therefore, $A:C::A-B:B-C$, *which was to be proved.*

This property is sometimes given as the definition of Harmonical Progression, and the property given as the definition in Art. 284 deduced from it.

286. We cannot find a convenient expression for the sum of *any* number of terms of a harmonical series; but many problems with regard to such series may be solved by *inverting the terms*, and then treating these *reciprocals* as in arithmetical progression.

Harmonical Progression. Demonstrate Art. 285. To find the sum of the terms of a Harmonical Progression.

HARMONICAL PROGRESSION.

Ex. 1. Continue to three terms each way the H. P., 2, 3, 6.

Here, since $\frac{1}{2}$, $\frac{1}{3}$, $\frac{1}{6}$ are in A. P. with common difference $-\frac{1}{6}$, the arithmetical series continued each way is

$$1, \tfrac{5}{6}, \tfrac{2}{3}, \tfrac{1}{2}, \tfrac{1}{3}, \tfrac{1}{6}, 0, -\tfrac{1}{6}, -\tfrac{1}{3}$$

therefore the harmonical series is

$$1, \tfrac{6}{5}, \tfrac{3}{2}, 2, 3, 6, \text{infinity}, -6, -3.$$

Ex. 2. Insert five harmonical means between $\frac{2}{3}$ and $\frac{8}{15}$.

Here we have to insert five *arithmetical* means between $\frac{3}{2}$ and $\frac{15}{8}$. Hence by equation (1) Art. 275, $\tfrac{15}{8}=\tfrac{3}{2}+6d$; therefore, $6d=\tfrac{3}{8}$, and $d=\tfrac{1}{16}$; hence the A. P. is

$$\tfrac{3}{2}, \tfrac{25}{16}, \tfrac{26}{16}, \tfrac{27}{16}, \tfrac{28}{16}, \tfrac{29}{16}, \tfrac{15}{8};$$

and therefore the H. P. is

$$\tfrac{2}{3}, \tfrac{16}{25}, \tfrac{16}{26}, \tfrac{16}{27}, \tfrac{16}{28}, \tfrac{16}{29}, \tfrac{8}{15}.$$

287. The geometrical mean G between two quantities a and b is the geometrical mean between their arithmetical mean A and their harmonical mean H.

For, the arithmetical mean between a and b is (Art. 277),

$$A = \frac{a+b}{2}. \quad (1)$$

The geometrical mean G gives $\dfrac{b}{G} = \dfrac{G}{a}$; $\therefore G^2 = ab$ and $G = \sqrt{ab}$.

To find the harmonical mean H we have $\dfrac{1}{b} - \dfrac{1}{H} = \dfrac{1}{H} - \dfrac{1}{a}$;

therefore, $aH - ab = ab - bH$, or $H = \dfrac{2ab}{a+b}$; (2)

multiplying (1) and (2), we get

$$AH = \frac{a+b}{2} \times \frac{2ab}{a+b} = ab = G^2.$$

Therefore $G = \sqrt{AH}$, or G is the geometrical mean between A and H.

Demonstrate Art. 287.

Examples—67.

1. Continue the Harmonical Progression 6, 3, 2 for three terms.

2. Continue the Harmonical Progression 8, 2, $1\frac{1}{7}$ for three terms.

3. Insert 2 harmonical means between 4 and 2.

4. Insert 3 harmonical means between $\frac{1}{3}$ and $\frac{1}{21}$.

5. The arithmetical mean of two numbers is 9, and the harmonical mean is 8: find the numbers.

6. The geometrical mean of two numbers is 48, and the harmonical mean is $46\frac{2}{25}$: find the numbers.

7. Find two numbers, such that the sum of their arithmetical, geometrical, and harmonical means is $9\frac{1}{5}$, and the product of these means is 27.

8. Find two numbers, such that the product of their arithmetical and harmonical means is 27, and the excess of the arithmetical mean above the harmonical mean is $1\frac{1}{2}$.

XXXIX. Permutations and Combinations.

288. The *Permutations* of any number of things are the different arrangements which can be made of them by placing them in different orders, taking either all the things, or a certain number of them at a time, together.

Thus the *permutations* of a, b, c, taken *all* together, are abc, acb, bca, cba, cab, bac; taken two together, are ac, ca, ab, ba, bc, cb.

289. Note.—Some writers on Algebra restrict the word *permutations* to the case where the things are taken all together, and call the sets in all other cases *Variations*, or *Arrangements*. But this distinction is not always observed, and we shall use the word *permutations* in all cases.

290. *The number of permutations of* n *things, taken two together, is* $n(n-1)$; *taken three together, is* $n(n-1)(n-2)$.

Let there be n different things, a, b, c, d, &c. Remove one of them, a; there will be $n-1$ things, b, c, d, &c., left; now place a before each of these $n-1$ things; we thus get $n-1$ permutations, n things taken *two* together, in which a stands first. Next remove b from the n things; there will remain $n-1$ things, a, c, d, &c.; and placing b before each of these we get $n-1$ permutations of n things *taken two* together, in which b stands first. Similarly placing c before each one of the other letters, we find $n-1$ permutations, in which c stands first; and so on for the rest. Therefore, on the whole, *there are* $n(n-1)$ *permutations of* n *things taken two together, or two and two,* as is the usual phrase. Therefore there are also $(n-1)(n-2)$ permutations of $n-1$ things taken *two* together.

Let now a, one of the n things, be again removed; the remaining $n-1$ things, by what we have just proved, gives $(n-1)(n-2)$ permutations when taken *two* together; put a before each of these permutations; we thus get $(n-1)(n-2)$ permutations, each composed of three things, in which a stands first. Similarly, there are $(n-1)(n-2)$ permutations each, of three things in which b stands first; similarly, there are as many in which c stands first, and so on for the rest. *Therefore there are* $n(n-1)(n-2)$ *permutations of* n *things taken three together.*

291. We observe at once that the second term of the last factor of the product which expresses the number of permutations in each case of the preceding article, is *numerically less by one than the number of things taken together.* From these cases we might infer by induction that this is a general law, and that the number of permutations of n letters taken r together is $n(n-1)(n-2) \ldots (n-r+1)$, and this we can now demonstrate.

For, suppose this law to hold for the number of permutations of n things, a, b, c, d, &c., taken $r-1$ together, which would therefore be

$$n(n-1)(n-2) \ldots (n-(r-1)+1).$$

Now leave out a; there will be $n-1$ things, b, c, d, &c., and the permutations of these, taken $r-1$ together, will be, by the preceding result,

$$(n-1)(n-2) \ldots (n-1-(r-1)+1);$$

that is, $(n-1)(n-2) \ldots (n-r+1)$.

Set a before each of these permutations; we get thus $(n-1)(n-2) \ldots (n-r+1)$ permutations taken r together, in which a stands first. Similarly, we have as many in which b stands first; as many in which c stands first, and so of the rest; therefore on the whole there would be,

$$n(n-1)(n-2) \ldots (n-r+1)$$

permutations of n things taken r together.

If then the formula holds when the n things are taken $r-1$ together, it will hold when they are taken r together; but it has been proved true when they are taken 3 together; it holds, therefore, when they are taken 4 together; and therefore, when taken 5 together, and so on;

that is, $\quad n(n-1)(n-2) \ldots (n-r+1)$

represents the number of permutations of n things taken r together, for all values of r (these values being limited only by the definition).

General law for the number of Permutations of n letters taken r together.

292. Hence, denoting by P_1, P_2, P_3, &c., P_r, the number of permutations of n things taken 1, 2, 3, &c. r, together, we have from the preceding formula,

$$P_1 = n, \ P_2 = n(n-1), \ P_3 = n(n-1)(n-2), \ \&c.$$

$$P_r = n(n-1) \ldots \ldots (n-r+1).$$

293. If $r = n$, that is, if *all* the quantities are taken together, then the number of permutations (P) of n things is

$$n(n-1)(n-2) \ldots \ldots (n-n+1);$$

that is, $\quad n(n-1)(n-2) \ldots 1;$

or reversing the order of the factors, we have,

$$P = 1 \times 2 \times 3 \ldots \times n.$$

This result we may enunciate thus:

The number of Permutations of n *things, taken all together, is equal to the product of the natural numbers from* 1 *to* n, *inclusive.*

Thus the number of permutations of 8 letters, taken *all together*, is $1 \times 2 \times 3 \times 4 \times 5 \times 6 \times 7 \times 8$.

294. For the sake of shortness, the continued product, $1.2.3.4 \ldots n$, is often denoted by $\lfloor n$; thus $\lfloor n$ denotes the product of the natural numbers, from 1 to n inclusive. The symbol $\lfloor n$ may be read *factorial n*.

Ex. $\lfloor 8$, (read *factorial eight*), denotes the product

$$1 \times 2 \times 3 \times 4 \times 5 \times 6 \times 7 \times 8.$$

295. *To find the number of permutations of* n *things, which are not all different, taken* n, *i. e. all together.*

Express the formula by the use of the symbols P_1, P_2, P_3, etc. The number of Permutations where $r=n$. The symbol $\lfloor n$. Demonstrate Art. 295

Let there be n letters; and suppose p of them to be a's, q of them to be b's, r of them to be c's, &c.; the number of permutations of them, taken all together, will be,

$$\frac{1.2.3\ldots n}{1.2.3\ldots p \times 1.2.3\ldots q \times \&c.}$$

For let N be the number of such Permutations. Suppose now that in any *one* of them we change the p a's into *different* letters; then these letters might be arranged in $1.2.3\ldots p$ different ways, and so instead of this *one* permutation, in which p letters would have been a's, we shall now have $1.2.3\ldots p$ *different* permutations. The same would be true for *each* of the N permutations; hence, if the p a's were all changed to *different* letters, we should have all together $1.2.3\ldots p \times N$ different permutations of n letters, whereof still q are b's, r are c's, &c.

So, if in these the q b's were changed to different letters, we should have $1.2.3\ldots q \times 1.2.3\ldots p \times N$ different permutations of n things, whereof still r would be c's; and so we may go on, until *all* the n letters are different. But when this is the case we know that their whole number of permutations $= 1.2.3\ldots n$. Hence,

$$1.2.3\ldots p \times 1.2.3\ldots q \times \&c. \times N = 1.2.3\ldots n,$$

and
$$N = \frac{1.2.3\ldots n}{1.2.3\ldots p \times 1.2.3\ldots q \times \&c.}.$$

This value of N may be written by the notation of Art. 294; thus,

$$N = \frac{\lfloor n}{\lfloor p \ \lfloor q \ \lfloor r}.$$

Ex. 1. How many changes can be rung with 5 bells out of 8? How many with the whole peal?

Here $P_5 = 8.7.6.5.4 = 6720$; $P = 8.7.6.5.4.3.2\ 1 = 40320$.

Ex. 2. How many *different* words may be made with all the letters of the expression a^3b^2c?

Here are 6 letters, 3 a's, and 2 b's; $\therefore N = \dfrac{1.2.3.4.5.6}{1.2.3 \times 1.2} = 60$.

Examples—68.

1. How many changes may be rung with 5 bells out of 6, and how many with the whole peal?

2. In how many different orders may 7 persons seat themselves at table?

3. How many different words may be made of all the letters of the word *baccalaureus*?

4. How many different words may be made of all the letters of the word *Mississippi*?

5. How many different words may be made of all the letters of the word *Alabama*?

6. Of what number of things are the permutations 720?

7. There are 7 letters, of which a certain number are a's; and 210 different words can be made of them: how many a's are there?

8. If the number of permutations of n things taken 4 together is equal to twelve times the number of permutations of n things taken 2 together, find n.

296. The *Combinations* of any things are the *different* collections or sets that can be made of them, without regarding the order in which the things are placed. Thus the combinations of a, b, c, taken two together, are ab, ac, bc; of a, b, c, d, three together, are abc, abd, acd, bcd.

297. It is readily seen that each combination which contains r things will furnish $1.2.3 \ldots r$ permutations of these things taken all together. For we have seen, Art. 291, that n things give $1.2.3 \ldots n$ permutations.

Thus the combination abc supplies $1.2.3$, or 6 permutations, $abc, acb, bac, bca, cab, cba$.

298. *The number of combinations of* n *different things, taken* r *together, is*

$$\frac{n(n-1)(n-2)\ldots(n-r+1)}{1.2.3\ldots r}.$$

For, each combination of r things will supply $1.2.3\ldots r$ permutations of r things; hence, if C_r denotes the number of combinations of n things, r together, we have
$1.2.3 \ldots r \times C_r =$ number of permutations of n things, r together,

$$= V_r = n(n-1)(n-2)\ldots(n-r+1);$$

$$\therefore C_r = \frac{n(n-1)(n-2)\ldots(n-r+1)}{1.2.3\ldots r}.$$

Therefore, $C_1 = \frac{n}{1}$, $C_2 = \frac{(n-1)}{1.2}$, $C_3 = \frac{n(n-1)(n-2)}{1.2.3}$, &c.,

where C_1, C_2, C_3, &c., express the number of combinations of n letters taken one and one, two together, three together, &c.

299. The expression $C_r = \dfrac{n(n-1)(n-2)\ldots(n-r+1)}{1.2.3\ldots r}$ may be put in a very convenient form; for, by multiplying the numerator and denominator of the above fraction by $1.2.3\ldots(n-r)$, it becomes

$$\frac{n(n-1)(n-2)\ldots(n-r+1) \times (n-r)\ldots 3.2.1}{1.2.3\ldots r \quad \times 1.2.3\ldots(n-r)}$$

$$= \frac{1.2.3\ldots n}{1.2.3\ldots r \times 1.2.3\ldots(n-r)} = \frac{\lfloor n}{\lfloor r \lfloor n-r};$$

$$\therefore C^r = \frac{\lfloor n}{\lfloor r \lfloor n-r}\quad (1)$$

300. *The number of combinations of* n *things taken* r *together is the same as the number of combinations of* n *things taken* n−r *together.*

For, to find the number of combinations of n things taken $n-r$ together, we simply write $n-r$ for r in formula (1). We get thus

$$C_{n-r} = \frac{\lfloor n}{\lfloor n-r \lfloor n-(n-r)} = \frac{\lfloor n}{\lfloor n-r \lfloor r},$$

which is equal to C_r, which was to be proved.

The truth of this proposition is also evident from a very simple consideration, viz., that when we take r things from n things, $n-r$ things will be left; and for every different collection containing r things there will be a different collection left containing $n-r$ things; therefore the *number* of the former collections must be equal to that of the latter.

Ex. 1. Required the number of combinations of 20 things taken 18 together.

Here the number of combinations of 20 things taken 18 together is equal to the number of combinations of 20 things taken 2 together,

that is, $\quad C_{18} = C_2 = \dfrac{20 \times 19}{1 \times 2} = 10 \times 19 = 190.$

Ex. 2. Find the number of combinations of 10 things, 3 and 6 together.

Here $\quad C_3 = \dfrac{10.9.8}{1.2.3} = 120,$ and $C_6 = C_4 = \dfrac{10.9.8.7}{1.2.3.4} = 210.$

Ex. 3. How many words of 6 letters might be made out of the first 10 letters of the alphabet, with two vowels in each word?

In these 10 letters there are 7 consonants and 3 vowels; and in each of the required words there are to be 4 consonants and 2 vowels: now the 7 consonants can be combined four together in 35 ways, and the 3 vowels, two together, in 3 ways; hence there can be formed 35×3=105 different sets of 6 letters, of which 4 are consonants and 2 vowels: but each of these sets of 6 letters may be *permuted* 6.5.4.3.2.1 =720 ways, each of these forming a different *word*, though the whole 720 are composed of the same 6 letters; hence the number required=105×720=75600.

Examples—69.

1. How many combinations can be made of 9 things, 4 together? how many, 6 together? how many, 7 together?

2. How many combinations can be made of 11 things, 4 together? how many, 7 together? how many, 10 together?

3. A person having 15 friends, on how many days might he invite a different party of 10? or of 12?

4. Find the number of combinations of 100 things, taken 98 together.

5. Four persons are chosen by lot out of 10: in how many ways can this be done? on how many of these occasions would any given man be taken?

6. The number of combinations of $n+1$ things, 4 together, is 9 times the number of combinations of n things, 2 together: find n.

7. How often may a *different* guard be posted, of 6 men out of 60? on how many of these occasions would any given man be taken?

8. How many words may be formed, each consisting of three consonants and a vowel, out of 19 consonants and 5 vowels.

XL. Binomial Theorem.

301. The *Binomial Theorem* is the name given to a rule discovered by Sir Isaac Newton, by means of which any binomial may be raised to any given power much more expeditiously than by the process of repeated multiplication given in Involution.

302. *To prove the Binomial Theorem when the index of the power is a positive whole number.* (Bobillier's Proof.)

By actual multiplication the successive powers of the binomial $a+x$ are found to be as follows:

$$(a+x)^1 = a+x;$$
$$(a+x)^2 = a^2 + 2ax + x^2;$$
$$(a+x)^3 = a^3 + 3a^2x + 3ax^2 + x^3;$$
$$(a+x)^4 = a^4 + 4a^3x + 6a^2x^2 + 4ax^3 + x^4;$$

which, by dividing the first by 1, the second by 1.2, the third by 1.2.3, the fourth by 1.2.3.4, and using the *factorial* notation of the preceding chapter to denote the continued products 1.1, 1.2, 1.2.3, &c., may be written thus:

$$\frac{(a+x)^1}{\lfloor 1} = \frac{a^1}{\lfloor 1} + \frac{x^1}{\lfloor 1};$$

$$\frac{(a+x)^2}{\lfloor 2} = \frac{a^2}{\lfloor 2} + \frac{a^1\,x^1}{\lfloor 1\,\lfloor 1} + \frac{x^2}{\lfloor 2};$$

$$\frac{(a+x)^3}{\lfloor 3} = \frac{a^3}{\lfloor 3} + \frac{a^2\,x^1}{\lfloor 2\,\lfloor 1} + \frac{a^1\,x^2}{\lfloor 1\,\lfloor 2} + \frac{x^3}{\lfloor 3};$$

$$\frac{(a+x)^4}{\lfloor 4} = \frac{a^4}{\lfloor 4} + \frac{a^3\,x^1}{\lfloor 3\,\lfloor 1} + \frac{a^2\,x^2}{\lfloor 2\,\lfloor 2} + \frac{a^1\,x^3}{\lfloor 1\,\lfloor 3} + \frac{x^4}{\lfloor 4};$$

in which a *law* of formation is easily perceived in relation to the exponent of the power of the binomial. The same

---

Binomial Theorem. Proof of the Binomial Theorem, when the index of the power is a positive whole number.

law of formation of the terms of the expansion is found to hold for $(a+x)^6$, $(a+x)^6$, &c. Now the introduction of the new factor $a+x$ in order to convert $(a+x)^{n-1}$ into $(a+x)^n$, involves precisely the same processes as the introduction of the same factor $(a+x)$ to convert $(a+x)^5$ into $(a+x)^6$. It is reasonable then to assume that if the *law* is true for $(a+x)^{n-1}$, it is true for $(a+x)^n$; now we know by actual multiplication it is true for $(a+x)^6$; hence it is true for $(a+x)^7$, and hence for $(a+x)^8$, &c. Therefore the law holds *generally*—viz., for any positive whole number exponent we have

$$\frac{(x+a)^n}{\lfloor n} = \frac{x^n}{\lfloor n} + \frac{a\;x^{n-1}}{\lfloor 1\;\lfloor n-1} + \frac{a^2\;x^{n-2}}{\lfloor 2\;\lfloor n-2} + \frac{a^3\;x^{n-3}}{\lfloor 3\;\lfloor n-3} \cdots + \frac{a^n}{\lfloor n};$$

which may be written,

I. $(x+a)^n = x^n + \dfrac{\lfloor n}{\lfloor 1\;\lfloor n-1}\,a\,x^{n-1} + \dfrac{\lfloor n}{\lfloor 2\;\lfloor n-2}\,a^2 x^{n-2}$
$+ \dfrac{\lfloor n}{\lfloor 3\;\lfloor n-3}\,a^3 x^{n-3} + \cdots + \dfrac{\lfloor n}{\lfloor r\;\lfloor n-r}\,a^r x^{n-r} + \cdots + a^n.$

Or by cancelling the like factors in the coefficients,

II. $(x+a)^n = x^n + nax^{n-1} + \dfrac{n(n-1)}{\lfloor 2}\,a^2 x^{n-2} + \dfrac{n(n-1)(n-2)}{\lfloor 3}\,$
$a^3 x^{n-3} + \cdots + \dfrac{n(n-1)(n-2)\cdots(n-r+1)}{\lfloor r}\,a^r x^{n-r} \cdots + a^n.$

303. In these expressions I. and II. the corresponding terms

$$\frac{\lfloor n}{\lfloor r\;\lfloor n-r}\,a^r x^{n-r} \quad (1)$$

and $\quad \dfrac{n(n-1)(n-2)\cdots(n-r+1)}{\lfloor r}\,a^r x^{n-r} \quad (2)$

are the same, and they express the term which has r terms before it; that is, the $(r+1)^{\text{th}}$ term. This term is called the

General Term; and both forms of it, (1) and (2), should be carefully noted and remembered.

304. If the binomial is written $(a+x)^n$, the expansion I. would be

$$(a+x)^n = a^n + \frac{\lfloor n}{\lfloor 1 \lfloor n-1} a^{n-1}x + \frac{\lfloor n}{\lfloor 2 \lfloor n-2} a^{n-2}x^2 \, \&c. \ldots + x^n,$$

the general term being $\dfrac{\lfloor n}{\lfloor r \lfloor n-r} a^{n-r}x^r$, the exponents of a and x being interchanged. Similarly, II. becomes

$$(a+x)^n = a^n + na^{n-1}x + \frac{n(n-1)}{\lfloor 2} a^{n-2}x^2 + \ldots$$

$$+ \frac{n(n-1)(n-2)\ldots(n-r+1)}{\lfloor r} a^{n-r}x^r + \ldots x^n.$$

And if $a=1$, this last gives

III. $(1+x)^n = 1 + nx + \dfrac{n(n-1)}{\lfloor 2} x^2 + \dfrac{n(n-1)(n-2)}{\lfloor 3} x^3 \ldots$

$$+ \frac{n(n-1)(n-2)\ldots(n-r+1)}{\lfloor r} x^r + x^n.$$

305. I. The law of the exponents of the terms in the expansion of the binomial formula is, that the exponent of the leading letter of the binomial is in the first term n, and that of the second letter is o; and the former decreases by unity and the latter increases by unity, in each successive term to the last term, in which the exponent of the leading letter is o, and that of the second letter is n; and *the sum of the exponents of the two letters in any term is always* n, *the exponent of the binomial.* Moreover, the exponent of the second letter in any term expresses the number of terms which precede that term, and the exponent of the leading letter expresses the number of terms which follow it. Thus we can easily write the exponents of the letters in any required term.

II. The numerical coefficients of the first and last terms are 1; the coefficient of the second term is n, or the number of combinations of n things taken singly; the coefficient of the third term is the number of combinations of n things taken 2 and 2, &c., &c.; the coefficient of the $(r+1)^{\text{th}}$ term is the number of combinations of n things taken r together. And since the coefficient of the term which has r terms before it is $\dfrac{\lfloor n}{\lfloor r \; \lfloor n-r}$, and the coefficient of the term which has r terms after it or $n-r$ terms before it is $\dfrac{\lfloor n}{\lfloor n-r \; \lfloor r}$, it follows *that the numerical coefficients of any two terms equidistant from the beginning and end are the same.*

306. From the above it will be seen that to find the coefficient of any term we may use either of the following rules:

RULE I.—*The coefficient of any term is the exponent of the binomial, taken factorially, divided by the product of the exponents of the two letters in that term, taken also factorially, i. e., divided by the product of the number of terms which precede it and the number of terms which follow it, taken factorially.*

Examining Expansion II., Art. 302, we have for finding the coefficient of any term from the preceding term,

RULE II.—*Multiply the coefficient of the preceding term by the exponent of the leading letter in that term, and divide the product by the number of terms which precede the required term.*

NOTE.—The first rule is used always when we wish to find any term without finding the preceding terms.

Since from Art. 305 all the coefficients after the middle term, or (first middle term when there are two), repeat themselves, after having found all the terms as far as the middle, we may for the remaining terms simply write down the coefficients already found, in an inverted order, as in the following examples.

Ex. 1. $(a+x)^8$

$= a^8 + \dfrac{\underline{|8}}{\underline{|1}\ \underline{|7}}\, a^7 x + \dfrac{\underline{|8}}{\underline{|2}\ \underline{|6}}\, a^6 x^2 + \dfrac{\underline{|8}}{\underline{|3}\ \underline{|5}}\, a^5 x^3 + \dfrac{\underline{|8}}{\underline{|4}\ \underline{|4}}\, a^4 x^4 + \&c.;$

or,

$(a+x)^8 = a^8 + \dfrac{8}{1} a^7 x + \dfrac{8\cdot 7}{1\cdot 2} a^6 x^2 + \dfrac{8\cdot 7\cdot 6}{1\cdot 2\cdot 3} a^5 x^3 + \dfrac{8\cdot 7\cdot 6\cdot 5}{1\cdot 2\cdot 3\cdot 4} a^4 x^4 + \&c.,$

$= a^8 + 8a^7 x + 28a^6 x^2 + 56a^5 x^3 + 70a^4 x^4 + 56a^3 x^5$
$\qquad\qquad\qquad\qquad\qquad + 28a^2 x^6 + 8ax^7 + x^8.$

Ex. 2. $(a+x)^7 = a^7 + \dfrac{7}{1} a^6 x + \dfrac{7\cdot 6}{1\cdot 2} a^5 x^2 + \dfrac{7\cdot 6\cdot 5}{1\cdot 2\cdot 3} a^4 x^3 + \&c.,$

$= a^7 + 7a^6 x + 21a^5 x^2 + 35a^4 x^3 + 35a^3 x^4 + 21a^2 x^5 + 7ax^6 + x^7.$

307. If the second term of the binomial is negative, the second term of the expansion is negative, and every *alternate* term also negative, as is evident by the rule of signs of powers. Thus,

$(a-x)^7 = a^7 - 7a^6 x + 21a^5 x^2 - 35a^4 x^3 + 35a^3 x^4 - 21a^2 x^5 + 7ax^6 - x^7.$

Ex. 3. $(1-x)^7 = 1 - \dfrac{7}{1} x + \dfrac{7\cdot 6}{1\cdot 2} x^2 - \dfrac{7\cdot 6\cdot 5}{1\cdot 2\cdot 3} x^3 + \&c.$

$= 1 - 7x + 21x^2 - 35x^3 + 35x^4 - 21x^5 + 7x^6 - x^7.$

Ex. 4. $(3x - \tfrac{1}{2}y)^6$

$= (3x)^6 - \dfrac{6}{1}(3x)^5(\tfrac{1}{2}y) + \dfrac{6\cdot 5}{1\cdot 2}(3x)^4(\tfrac{1}{2}y)^2 - \dfrac{6\cdot 5\cdot 4}{1\cdot 2\cdot 3}(3x)^3(\tfrac{1}{2}y)^3 + \&c.$

$= 729x^6 - 6\times 243x^5 \times \tfrac{1}{2}y + 15\times 81x^4 \times \tfrac{1}{4}y^2 - 20\times 27x^3 \times \tfrac{1}{8}y^3$
$\qquad\qquad + 15\times 9x^2 \times \tfrac{1}{16}y^4 - 6\times 3x\times \tfrac{1}{32}y^5 + \tfrac{1}{64}y^6$

$= 729x^6 - 729x^5 y + \tfrac{1215}{4}x^4 y^2 - \tfrac{135}{2}x^3 y^3 + \tfrac{135}{16}x^2 y^4 - \tfrac{9}{16}xy^5 + \tfrac{1}{64}y^6.$

Ex. 5. Find the 8th term in the expansion $(x+a)^{11}$.

The exponents of 8th term give $x^7 a^4$.

Hence the term is $\dfrac{\lfloor 11}{\lfloor 7 \; \lfloor 4} x^7 a^4$;

or, cancelling out like factors,

$$\frac{8.9.10.11 \, x^7 a^4}{1.2.3.4} = 3.10.11 \, x^7 a^4 = 330 \, a^4 x^7.$$

Ex. 6. Find the middle term of $(a-b)^{12}$.

The middle term is the 7th. Hence it is

$$\frac{\lfloor 12}{\lfloor 6 \; \lfloor 6} a^6 b^6 = 924 a^6 b^6.$$

Examples—70.

1. $(1+x)^6$. 2. $(a-3x)^5$. 3. $(1-x)^8$. 4. $(a-x)^9$.
5. $(1+x)^{12}$. 6. $(1-2x)^{10}$. 7. $(a-3x)^6$. 8. $(2x+a)^6$.
9. $(2a-3x)^7$. 10. $(1-\tfrac{1}{2}x)^{10}$. 11. $(1-\tfrac{1}{3}x)^{11}$.

12. Find the 8th term (independently of the rest) in $(a-x)^9$.

13. Find the 98th term in $(a-b)^{100}$.

14. Find the 5th term in $(a^2-b^2)^{12}$.

15. Find the middle term of $(a+x)^{10}$.

16. $(x^4+x^2y^2)^5$. 17. $(a^3-x^3)^4$. 18. $(a^2+b^2)^6$.

308. The Binomial Theorem is true not only for n a positive integer, but for n *negative or fractional.* But the discussion in this case is not sufficiently elementary for this book.

XLI. Scales of Notation.

309. In the common system of Arithmetic numbers are expressed by the use of 9 figures called digits, and one cipher. This is effected, we know, by giving to each digit a *local*, as well as its intrinsic, value. The local values of the figures increase in a tenfold proportion in going from right to left; in other words, the local values of the digits *proceed according to the powers of* 10 *from right to left.*

Thus, 4296 may be expressed by

$$4000+200+90+6, \text{ or } 4\times 10^3+2\times 10^2+9\times 10+6.$$

A system of notation is called a *scale*. In the common system or *scale*, the number 10 is called the *radix* or *base* of the scale.

310. It is purely conventional that 10 should be the radix; and therefore there may be any number of different *scales*, each of which has its own *radix*. Notation is then the method of expressing numbers by means of a series of powers of some one fixed number, which is said to be the *base* of the scale in which the numbers are expressed. (We use the word *number* here in the sense of *whole number.*)

If the digits of a number N, of n digits (including 0 among the digits for convenience), be $a_0, a_1, a_2 \ldots a_{n-1}$, reckoning from right to left, and r be the radix, N may be expressed by the formula,

$$N = a_{n-1}r^{n-1} + a_{n-2}r^{n-2} + a_{n-3}r^{n-3} + \ldots + a_1 r + a_0.$$

Obs. 1.—It will be noted that since the units figure does not contain r, the highest power of r will be *one less than* the number of figures in the number expressed.

Obs. 2.—In any scale of notation every digit is necessarily less than r, therefore $r-1$ is the greatest digit, and $r-1$ expresses the number of digits, and the number of figures used in any scale including 0 is equal to r.

Arithmetical Notation. Scale. Radix, or Base. The general formula for expressing numbers.

311. If $r=2$ the scale is called the Binary;
$r=3$ .... Ternary;
$r=4$ .... Quaternary;
$r=5$ .... Quinary;
$r=6$ .... Senary;
&c., &c.
$r=10$ .... Denary;
$r=11$ .... Undenary;
$r=12$ .... Duodenary.

The digits, including the cipher, in the

Binary scale are 1, 0;
Ternary 1, 2, 0;
Quinary 1, 2, 3, 4, 0;
&c., &c.
Nonary 1, 2, 3, 4, 5, 6, 7, 8, 0;
Denary 1, 2, 3, 4, 5, 6, 7, 8, 9, 0;

but in the duodenary scale we must have two additional characters to express ten and eleven; we therefore put t for ten, and e for eleven.

∴ Duodenary digits are 1, 2, 3, 4, 5, 6, 7, 8, 9, t, e, 0;

also undenary .... 1, 2, 3, 4, 5, 6, 7, 8, 9, t, 0.

All numbers are supposed to be expressed in the common, or denary scale, unless otherwise stated.

312. *To express a given number in any proposed scale.*

Let N be the number, and r the radix of the proposed scale.

Then if a_0, a_1, a_2, &c. be the unknown digits,

$$N = a_{n-1}r^{n-1} + a_{n-2}r^{n-2} + \ldots + a_3r^3 + a_2r^2 + a_1r + a_0.$$

If now N be divided by r, the remainder is a_0.

If the quotient be divided by r, the remainder is a_1.

SCALES OF NOTATION.

If the second quotient be divided by r, the remainder is a_2; and so on, until there is no further quotient.

Hence the repeated divisions of the given number N, by the radix of the proposed scale, give as remainders the required digits of the number in the proposed scale.

Ex. 1. Express 1820 of the common or denary scale, in a scale whose base is 6.

```
6 | 1820
6 | 303......2   ∴ 1st remainder  a₀ = 2;
6 | 50.......3      2d     "      a₁ = 3;
6 | 8........2      3d     "      a₂ = 2;
6 | 1........2      4th    "      a₃ = 2;
```

∴ the number required is 12232.

This is easily verified, for

$$1\times 6^4 + 2\times 6^3 + 2\times 6^2 + 3\times 6 + 2 = 1820.$$

This verification gives the method of transforming a number from any other scale to the denary.

By the method of division given above, a number may be transformed from *any* given scale to any other of which the radix is given. It is only necessary to bear in mind throughout the process that the radix of the scale of the given numbers is not 10, but some other number. Or the same thing may be done by first expressing the number (as by verification above) in the *denary* scale, and then proceeding as in Ex. 1.

Ex. 2. Transform 12232 from the senary scale to the quaternary.

To transform a number from one scale to another.

(Observe, that in dividing 12 by 4, 12 does not mean *twelve*, but $1\times 6+2=8$; so also, 23 is *fifteen*, 32 is *twenty*, and so on; *i. e.* we must convert each partial dividend to the denary scale as we proceed.)

$$\begin{array}{r|l}
4 & 12232 \\ \hline
4 & 2035\ldots.0 \\ \hline
4 & 305\ldots.3 \\ \hline
4 & 44\ldots.1 \\ \hline
4 & 11\ldots.0 \\ \hline
 & 1\ldots.3
\end{array}$$

∴ 1st remainder $a_0=0$;
2d " $a_1=3$;
3d " $a_2=1$;
4th " $a_3=0$;
5th " $a_4=0$;

∴ the number required is 130130.

This number transformed to the denary scale is,

$$1\times 4^5+3\times 4^4+0\times 4^3+1\times 4^2+3\times 4+0=1820.$$

Ex. 3. Transform 3256 from a scale whose radix is 7, to the duodenary scale.

$$\begin{array}{r|l}
\text{twelve} & 3256 \\ \hline
\text{twelve} & 166\ldots..4 \\ \hline
 & 11\ldots..1
\end{array}$$

∴ 1st remainder $a_0=4$;
∴ 2d " $a_1=1$;

∴ the number required is 814.

(Observe in this division that 32 is *twenty-three*, and the remainder, *eleven*, is multiplied by 7 and added to the next figure, 5, giving *eighty-two* for the next partial dividend, &c.)

EXAMPLES—71.

1. Express the common number 300 in the scales of 2, 3, 4, 5, 6.

2. Express 10000 in the scales of 7, 8, 9, 11, 12.

3. Express a million in the duodenary scale.

SCALES OF NOTATION. 273

4. Transform $27t$ and 7007 from the undenary to the octenary scale.

5. If the number 803 is expressed by 30203, show that the new scale is the quaternary.

6. The number 95 is expressed in a different scale by 137: find the base of this scale.

313. The common processes of Arithmetic are all carried on with numbers expressed in any one of these scales as with ordinary numbers, observing that when we have to find what numbers we are to *carry* in Addition, &c., we must not divide by *ten*, but by the base of the scale in which the numbers are expressed.

	Addition.		Subtraction.	
	$r=4$	$r=7$	$r=3$	$r=12$
Ex. 1.	32123	65432	201210	$7t348$
	21003	54321	102221	$5e6\,t4$
	33012	43210	21212	$1t864$
	22033	1444		
	31102	65001		
	332011	326041		

Ex. 2. Multiply the numbers 1049 and $1e5$ together in the duodenary scale.

$$\begin{array}{r} 1049 \\ 1e5 \\ \hline 51e9 \\ e443 \\ 1049 \\ \hline 202329 \end{array}\text{—duodenary.}$$

∴ the product is

$202329 = 2 \times 12^5 + 2 \times 12^3 + 3 \times 12^2 + 2 \times 12 + 9$

$ = 501585$—denary.

12*

Ex. 3. Divide 234431 by 414 (quinary), and extract the square root of 122112 (senary).

```
 234431      414)234431(310     122112(252     122112
     41          2302                4             44
 234340           423            45)421        122024
                  414               401
                   41           542)2012
                                    1524
                                      44
```

314. *To find the greatest and least numbers expressed by a given number of figures in any proposed scale.*

Let r be the base of the scale, and n the number of digits; then the number will be *greatest* when every digit is as great as it can be, that is, $=r-1$. Thus the number will be

$$(r-1)r^{n-1}+(r-1)r^{n-2}+\ldots+(r-1)r^2+(r-1)r+r-1;$$

or, $(r-1)(r^{n-1}+r^{n-2}+\ldots+r^2+r+1)$.

But the quantity in the second parenthesis is the sum of the terms of a geometrical progression, of which the first term is r^{n-1}, the ratio r, and the last term 1. This is equal to $\frac{r^n-1}{r-1}$. We have then for our *greatest* number,

$$(r-1)\frac{r^n-1}{r-1}; \text{ or, } r^n-1.$$

Again, the number will be *least* when the digit on the left is 1, and all the other figures 0, in which case it will be equal to r^{n-1}.

Ex. 1. In the denary scale the greatest number of 3 figures is $10^3-1=999$; and the least is 10^2, or 100.

LOGARITHMS. 275

Ex. 2. In the senary scale the greatest number of 3 figures is $555 = 6^3 - 1 = 215$, denary; and the least number of 3 figures is $100 = 6^2 = 36$, denary.

Examples—72.

1. Extract the square root of 33224 in the scale of six.

2. Show that 144 is a perfect square, in any scale whose radix is greater than four.

3. Show that 12345654321 is divisible by 12321 in any scale greater than six.

4. Multiply the common numbers 64 and 33 in the binary and quaternary scales, and transform each result to the other scale.

5. Divide 51117344 by 675 (octenary), 37542627 by $42t$ (undenary), and $29t96580$ by $2tt9$ (duodenary).

6. Extract the square roots of 25400544 (senary), 47610370 (nonary), and $32e75721$ (duodenary).

7. Express in common numbers the greatest and least that can be formed with four figures in the scales of 6, 7, and 8.

8. Show that 1331 is a perfect cube in any scale of notation whose radix is greater than three.

XLII. Logarithms.

315. A geometrical progression whose first term is 1 and ratio any number, as a, may be written

$$a^0, a^1, a^2, a^3, a^4, a^5, a^6, a^7, a^8, \&c., a^n;$$

and the indices form the arithmetical progression

$$0, 1, 2, 3, 4, 5, 6, 7, 8 \ldots n.$$

In this A. P. each term measures the order of the ratio of the corresponding term in the geometrical progression to 1.* Hence these indices are called the *measures of the ratios* of the numbers in G. P. to 1, or the *Logarithms* of these numbers.

316. From the rules established in the earlier chapters, we know that to multiply or divide any two terms in the first series we have only to add or subtract their indices—*i. e.*, the corresponding terms in the second series; also, to raise a number of the first series to a given power, we multiply its index or corresponding term in the second series by the index of the power; also, to extract a given root of any number in the G. P., we divide its index or corresponding term in the A. P. by the index of the root.

317. It is evident from the above that if a geometrical progression can be formed which shall represent with a sufficiently close approximation all numbers from 1 to 10,000, and the terms of the arithmetical progression corresponding to this G. P., in the same manner as in Art. 315, be calculated, and both series be recorded in a table, that much trouble may be saved in arithmetical computation by operating solely on the terms of the A. P., and finding from the table the numbers of the G. P. corresponding to the results.

318. Such tables have been calculated, and are called *Tables of Logarithms*. To see how this may be effected, let $a=10$ in the system (Art. 315); we have then

$$10^0,\ 10^1,\ 10^2,\ 10^3,\ 10^4,\ 10^5,\ 10^6,\ 10^7,\ 10^8,\ 10^9,\ \&c.,\quad (1)$$
and $\quad 0,\ \ 1,\ \ 2,\ \ 3,\ \ 4,\ \ 5,\ \ 6,\ \ 7,\ \ 8,\ \ 9,\qquad (2)$
are the logarithms of the corresponding terms of the first series; that is, in a system of logarithms whose base is 10,

---

* The ratio of $a^2:1$ is the duplicate ratio of $a:1$.
The ratio of $a^3:1$ is the triplicate ratio of $a:1$.
And the ratio of $a^n:1$ is called n times the ratio of $a:1$.
Thus the indices *measure the ratios*.

LOGARITHMS.

$0 = \log. 10^0$ or log. 1;
$1 = \log. 10^1$ or log. 10;
$2 = \log. 10^2$ or log. 100;
$3 = \log. 10^3$ or log. 1000;
$4 = \log. 10^4$ or log. 10,000;
$5 = \log. 10^5$ or log. 100,000;
&c.,   &c.,   &c.

It is manifest now that the arithmetical mean between any two terms of the series (2) will be the logarithm of the geometrical mean between the two corresponding terms of the series (1).

The arithmetical mean of 0 and 1 is $\frac{0+1}{2} = .5$.

The geometrical mean between 1 and 10 is

$$\sqrt{1 \times 10} = 3.16227+;$$

and therefore .5 = the logarithm of 3.16227.

The arithmetical mean of .5 and 1 is .75.

The geometrical mean of 10 and 3.16227 is

$$\sqrt{10 \times 3.16227} = 5.62341+;$$

whence .75 = the logarithm of 5.62341.

The arithmetical mean of 1 and 2 is 1.5.

The geometrical mean of 10 and 100 is 31.62277+;
whence 1.5 = the logarithm of 31.62277.

And by repeating this process, with immense labor, the inventor of logarithms, Napier (A. D. 1618), and his successor in these calculations, Briggs (A. D. 1624), calculated tables of logarithms of natural numbers from 1 to 100,000. But the labor of calculating logarithms is much diminished by the use of series which cannot find place in an elementary work like the present; besides, as will be seen, the chief labor is with the prime numbers.

319. These logarithms in the common table of which 10 is the base, are the indices (entire or fractional) of the powers to which 10 is to be raised to obtain all natural numbers approximately. Thus, .30103 is the logarithm of 2, means that $10^{.30103} = 2$. And this may be verified by developing $10^{.30103} = (1+9)^{\frac{.30103}{100000}}$ by the binomial formula.

320. 10 is the most convenient base, but any positive number except 1 may be taken as the base. Napier took 2.71828 as his base. In general, by taking any positive number (except unity) for a base, we may express any positive number as some power of it. And thus logarithms may be defined to be *the indices of the powers (entire or fractional) to which we raise a fixed number, called the base, to obtain the series of natural numbers.* Each logarithm is the *representative* of its corresponding natural number.

321. In the common system, of which 10 is the base, it is clear that the logarithm of every number between 1 and 10 is a decimal fraction; that of every number between 10 and 100 is 1 with a decimal fraction annexed; that of any number between 100 and 1000 will be 2 with a decimal fraction annexed, &c. The integral part of a logarithm is called the *characteristic* of the logarithm; and the decimal part is called the Mantissa, or "handful." Thus 0 is the characteristic of the logarithms of numbers between 1 and 10; 1 is the characteristic of the logarithms of all numbers between 10 and 100; 2 that of the logarithms of all numbers between 100 and 1000, &c. And in general, the *characteristic of the logarithm of any number is always less by unity than the number of figures in the given number.*

322. Tables of logarithms, arranged in convenient form, are usually given in books on Trigonometry, and with them explanations of the mode of finding in the table the logarithms corresponding to a given number, or the number corresponding to a given logarithm. The table below is a portion of such a table of logarithms.

Logarithms, to base 10, of all Prime Numbers from 1 to 100.

No.	Logarithms.	No.	Logarithms.	No.	Logarithms.	No.	Logarithms.
2	0.3010300	19	1.2787536	43	1.6334685	71	1.8512583
3	0.4771213	23	1.3617278	47	1.6720979	73	1.8633229
7	0.8450980	29	1.4623980	53	1.7242759	79	1.8976271
11	1.0413927	31	1.4913617	59	1.7708520	83	1.9190781
13	1.1139434	37	1.5682017	61	1.7853298	89	1.9493900
17	1.2304489	41	1.6127839	67	1.8260748	97	1.9867717

323. We will now show more fully the properties of logarithms, which render them so useful in diminishing the labor of arithmetical calculations.

324. *In the same system, the sum of the logarithms of two numbers is the logarithm of their product; and the difference of the logarithms of two numbers is the logarithm of their quotient.*

Let m and n be the two numbers; let $x = $ log. m, and $y = $ log. n; let a be the base of the system; then $a^x = m$, and $a^y = n$; hence $a^{x+y} = mn$, and $a^{x-y} = \dfrac{m}{n}$; or $x+y$ is the log. mn, and $x-y$ is log. $\dfrac{m}{n}$; that is, log. m + log. n = log. mn; and log. m − log. n = log $\dfrac{m}{n}$.

Ex. 1. Log. 6 = log. 2 + log. 3 = .3010300 + .4771213
= .7781513.

Ex. 2. Log. mnp = log. mn + log. p = log. m + log. n + log. p.

Ex. 3. Log. 5 = log. 10 − log. 2 = 1 − log. 2 = .6989700.

Ex. 4. Log. $\frac{7}{5}$ = log. 7 − log. 5 = .1461280.

Ex. 5. Log. $.07 =$ log. $\frac{7}{100} =$ log. $7 -$ log. $100 = .8450980 - 2$, which is written thus, $\overline{2}.8450980$; it being understood that in this position of the negative sign it belongs only to the characteristic 2, and not to the mantissa, which is still positive.

Ex. 6. Log. $\frac{3}{97} = .4771213 - 1.9867717 = -1.5096504$, which may be written thus: $-2 + (1 - .5096504) = \overline{2}.4903496$.

325. *If the logarithm of a number be multiplied by* m, *the product is the logarithm of that number raised to the* m*th power.*

Let N be the number whose logarithm is x; then $a^x = N$; therefore $a^{mx} = N^m$; that is, mx is the log. of N^m; or log. $N^m = mx = m$ log. N.

Ex. 1. Log. $(13)^5 = 5 \times$ log. $13 = 5 \times 1.1139434 = 5.5697170$.

Ex. 2. Log. $b^y = y$ log. b.

Ex. 3. Log. $4 =$ log. $2^2 = 2$ log. $2 = .6020600$.

Ex. 4. Log. $(a^2 - x^2)^2 = 2$ log. $(a+x) + 2$ log. $(a-x)$.

Ex. 5. Log. $(a^m b^n c^p \ldots) = m$ log. $a + n$ log. $b + p$ log. $c + \ldots$

326. *If the logarithm of a number be divided by* m, *the quotient is the logarithm of the* m*th root of that number.*

Let $x =$ log. N, or $a^x = N$;

then $a^{\frac{x}{m}} = N^{\frac{1}{m}}$, or log. $N^{\frac{1}{m}} = \frac{x}{m} = \frac{\log. N}{m}$.

Ex. 1. Log. $5^{\frac{1}{4}} = \frac{\log. 5}{4} = \frac{.6989700}{4} = .1747425$.

Ex. 2. Log. $\sqrt{\frac{a}{b}} = \frac{1}{2}$ log. $a - \frac{1}{2}$ log. b.

Ex. 3. Log. $\sqrt{a^2 - x^2} = \frac{1}{2}$ log. $(a+x) + \frac{1}{2}$ log. $(a-x)$.

Ex. 4. Given log. 128=2.1072100 to extract the 7th root of 128.

Log. $\sqrt[7]{128} = \frac{1}{7}$ log. $128 = \frac{1}{7}$ (2.1072100) = .3010300 = log. 2.

$$\therefore \sqrt[7]{128} = 2.$$

Ex. 5. Log. $\sqrt[7]{\frac{1}{71}} = \frac{1}{7}$ log. $1 - \frac{1}{7}$ log. $71 = -\frac{1}{7}$ log. 71
$= \frac{1}{7} \times -1.8512583 = \frac{1}{7}(-2+(1-.8512583)) = \frac{1}{7}(\overline{2}.1487417)$.

Now in order to divide this log. by 7, we place it under the form $\overline{7} + 5.1487147$, so that the negative characteristic may become a multiple of 7; then

$$\tfrac{1}{7}(\overline{7} + 5.1487147) = \overline{1}.7355306.$$

327. We can now see how the work of computing a table of logarithms is facilitated by the application of the above properties of logarithms. For the logarithms of the composite numbers are all found by adding together the logarithms of their prime factors.

328. While we are at liberty to take any number except 1 as the base of a system of logarithms, we can now understand the great advantages of the system which has 10 as a base; that is, the advantages of having the base of the scale of notation the same as the base of the system of logarithms.

For, 1st, the characteristic of the logarithm of any whole number is always one less than the number of figures in the given number. Hence when the number of figures is given we know the characteristic; and when the characteristic of the logarithm is given, we know the number of figures in the required number.

2d. By every multiplication or division of a number by 10, the characteristic of its logarithm is increased or diminished by unity.

For log. 1280 = log. (128×10)
  = log. 128 + log. 10 = log. 128 + 1,

log. 12800 = log. 128 + log. 100 = log. 128 + 2,

log. 128000 = log. 128 + log. 1000 = log. 128 + 3,

log. 12.8 = log. (128 ÷ 10) = log. 128 − log. 10 = log. 128 − 1,

log. 1.28 = log. (128 ÷ 100) = log. 128 − log. 100 = log. 128 − 2,

log. .128 = log. 128 − log. 1000 = log. 128 − 3, &c.

From the tables of logarithms, log. 128 = 2.1072100.

Therefore,   log. 1280   = 3.1072100,
    log. 12800   = 4.1072100,
    log. 128000   = 5.1072100,
    log. 1280000 = 6.1072100,
    log. 12.8   = 1.1072100,
    log. 1.28   = 0.1072100,
    log. .128   = $\overline{1}$.1072100,
    log. .0128   = $\overline{2}$.1072100.

We observe that the logarithms of all numbers which contain the same significant figures, arranged in the same manner, have the same mantissa, or decimal parts; that is, the mantissa of the logarithm remains the same however we may change the corresponding number, by annexing ciphers or by inserting a decimal point in it, changing the position of its decimal point to the right or left.

Moreover, the logarithm of a decimal fraction has a negative characteristic greater by unity than the number of 0's between the decimal point and the first significant figure of the number.

329. *To find a fourth proportional to three given numbers, using logarithms.*

Let the numbers be a, b, and c; let $x =$ required fourth proportional. Then $a : b = c : x$; $\therefore x = \dfrac{bc}{a}$.

Therefore log. $x =$ log. $b +$ log. $c -$ log. a. Hence the rule:

From the sum of the logarithms of the second and third terms subtract the logarithm of the first term: the remainder will be the logarithm of the fourth proportional. The fourth proportional may then be found from the tables.

NOTE.—In the following examples use the table of logarithms given in Art. 322.

EXAMPLES—73.

1. Find the logarithms of 8, 9, 12, 20, 25, 60.

2. Find the logarithms of $\frac{1}{3}$, $\frac{1}{4}$, $\frac{2}{5}$, .03, $\frac{1}{30}$, .0033.

3. Required the logarithms of 168, 1.04, and 3690.

4. Given the logarithms of 3 and 7: find the logarithm of 14700.

5. Find the logarithm of 83349, from the logarithms of 3 and .21.

6. Determine the logarithms of $\sqrt[4]{\frac{24}{135}}$, and $\sqrt[4]{1.625}$, by means of those of 2, 3, 5, and 13.

7. Find a fourth proportional to the quantities 1.3, .0104, and 2.375, by logarithms.

8. Find by means of logarithms the number of figures in the results of the involutions of 2^{10} and 3^{12}.

9. Find the logarithm of $\sqrt[4]{\frac{1}{2}} \times \sqrt[3]{\frac{2}{3}} \times \sqrt{\frac{3}{4}}$.

ANSWERS TO EXAMPLES.

Examples—1.

1. 22. 2. 26. 3. 89. 4. 564. 5. 274. 6. 10.
7. 6. 8. 6. 9. 34. 10. 39. 11. 6. 12. 5. 13. 9.
14. 5. 16. $x+a+b$. 17. $x+x+a+x+a+b$. 18. $x-a$.
19. $S-x$. 20. $x-a+b$. 21. $x+x+2+x+2+3$.
22. $4 \times 10 + 5 + \frac{6}{10}$. 23. $100x+10y+z$, $100z+10y+x$.
24. $xn+bn$. 25. $11x+5$. 26. $\frac{S}{t}$. 27. $\frac{1}{x}$, $\frac{1}{x+3}$.
28. $\frac{N-r}{d}$.

Examples—2.

1. 55. 2. 81. 3. 94. 4. 8. 5. 27. 6. 81.
7. 12. 8. 11. 9. 21. 10. 15. 11. 10. 12. 3.
13. 2. 14. 127.

ANSWERS TO EXAMPLES.

EXAMPLES—4.

1. 5. 2. 16. 3. 9. 4. 224. 5. 459. 6. 7.
7. 74. 8. 12. 9. 8. 10. 238. 11. 420. 12. 144.
13. 43. 14. 15.

EXAMPLES—5.

1. $2a+2b$. 2. $2a$. 3. $2a-2b$. 4. $2a$. 5. $2a+2c$.
6. $2+m+n$. 7. $7m-1$. 8. $4xy+4x$. 9. $p-q+8$.
10. $6ab-bc$. 11. $15a-9b$. 12. $3x^2-3y^2$.
13. $9a+9b+9c$. 14. $4x+2y+4z$. 15. $a-b$.
16. $3x-3a-2b$. 17. $2a+2b$. 18. $a+b+c$.
19. $-2a+2b+2d$. 20. $2x^3-2x^2-8x+10$.
21. $5x^4+4x^3+3x^2+2x-9$. 22. $4a^3+2a^2b-4ab^2+b^3-7b^3$.
23. a^2x+3a^3. 24. $6ab-9a^2x+7ax^2+ax^3$. 25. $5x^2$.
26. $10x^3+8y^2+12x+12$.

EXAMPLES—6.

1. $3a+4b$. 2. $4a+2c$. 3. $a+5b+4c+d$.
4. $2x^2-2x-4$. 5. $3x^4-x^3-14x+18$. 6. $x^2-ax+2a^2$.
7. $-5xy-5xz+2y^2+yz$. 8. $3x^2+13xy-16xz-y^2-13yz$.
9. $2a^3-6a^2b+6ab^2-2b^3$. 10. $3x^3+4x+16$, x^2+8x^2.

Examples—7.

1. $4a-4x$.
2. $4a^2-4a^2c$.
3. $x^2-3y^2-3z^2$.
4. $2ax^2+2by^2+2cz^2$.
5. $a^2-3b^2+3c^2$.
6. $2ab+4b^2$.
7. 0.
8. $-3x-y+4z$.
9. $8x-8$.
10. $-4c+4d$.

Examples—8.

1. $(a-b+c)x^3-(b-c+d)x^2-(c+d+e)x$. 2. $2(ax-by)$.
3. $(a+b)x^2-(a-5b)xy+(a-c)y^2$.
4. $2(ax+cy)$, $2b(x+y)$.
5. $-(a-5b)x+(2a+3b+c)y$, $(a-4b-c)x+(a-3b-2c)y$, $(b-c)x+(3a-c)y$.
6. $(5a-b)x-(2a-3b-5c)y$, $-(a+c)x+(a-b+2c)y$, $(4a-b-c)x-(a-2b-7c)y$.

Examples—9.

1. abx^3y^4, $-mnx^6$, $2a^2cx^2y$, ab^2c^2, a^2bc^2, $-x^2y^2$.
2. $x^3-x^2y+xy^2$, $-a^2x+a^2x^2-ax^3$, $-abx^2+a^2bx^2-ab^2x$, $x^4y-3x^3y^2+3x^2y^3-xy^4$.
3. $2a^2+7ab+3b^2$, $2ac-bc-6ad+3bd$.
4. $6x^2+13xy+6y^2$, $6a^2b^2-ab^3-12b^4$.
5. x^3+6x^2+7x-6, $x^3-6x^2+11x-6$.
6. $a^4+a^3-2a^2+3a-1$, $a^4-a^3-8a^2+a+1$.

ANSWERS TO EXAMPLES.   287

7. $81x^4-y^4$.   8. a^5+32b^5.   9. $x^4-4a^3x+3a^4$.

10. $27a^3+b^3+8-18ab$.   11. $x^3-y^3+z^3+3xyz$.

12. a^4-1.   13. $a^3-8b^3-27c^3-18abc$.   14. $a^4+2a^2b^2+b^4$.

15. $x^3-(a+c)x^2+(ac+b)x-bc$;

$$x^4-(a^2-b+c)x^2+a(b+c)x-bc$$

16. $1-(a-1)x-(a-b+1)x^2+(a+b-c)x^3-(b+c)x^4+cx^5$.

Examples—10.

1. $a^2-2ax+x^2$, $1+4x^2+4x^4$, $4a^4+12a^2+9$, $9x^2-24xy+16y^2$.

2. $9+12x+4x^2$, $4x^2-12xy+9y^2$, $a^4-6a^3x+9a^2x^2$, $b^2x^4-2bcx^3y+c^2x^2y^2$.

3. $4a^2-1$, $9a^2x^2-b^2$, x^4-1.

4. x^2+4x+3, x^4+3x^2-4, a^2b^2-ab-6, $4a^2x^2-8abx+3b^2$.

5. $x^4-5a^2x^2+4a^4$.   6. $m^4x^4-13m^2n^2x^2y^2+36n^4y^4$.

7. $4x^2$.   8. x^4+4y^4, $4a^4-5a^2b^2+b^4$.

9. $a^2+2ab+b^2-c^2$, $a^2-b^2+2ac+c^2$, $a^2-b^2-2bc-c^2$.

10. $a^2-2ab+b^2-c^2$, $-a^2+2ab-b^2+c^2$, $-a^2+b^2-2bc+c^2$.

11. $4a^2-b^2+6bc-9c^2$, $-4a^2+12ac+b^2-9c^2$.

12. $4a^2-b^2-6bc-9c^2$, $-4a^2+4ab-b^2+9c^2$.

13. $a^2+2ac+c^2-b^2-2bd-d^2$, $a^2+2ad+d^2-b^2-2bc-c^2$, $b^2+2bc+c^2-a^2-2ad-d^2$.

14. $a^2+2ad+d^2-4b^2+12bc-9c^2$, $9c^2+6cd+d^2-a^2$ $+4ab-4b^2$, $a^2+6ac+9c^2-4b^2+4bd-d^2$.

Examples—11.

1. $5x^2$. 2. $-3a^3$. 3. $3xy$. 4. $-8a^2b^3c^2$.

5. $4a^4b^2y^2$. 6. x^2-2x+4. 7. $-a^2+4a-5$.

8. $x^2-3xy+4y^2$. 9. $5a^2b^2+ab-4$.

10. $15a^2b^2-12ab^2+9abc^2-5c^4$. 11. $x-4$. 12. $x-8$.

13. x^2+x+3. 14. $3x^2-2x+4$. 15. $3x^2+2x+1$.

16. x^2-3x+7. 17. $x^5+x^4+x^3+x^2+x+1$.

18. a^2+ab-b^2. 19. $x^3+3x^2y+9xy^2+27y^3$.

20. $x^3-x^2y+xy^2$. 21. $x^4+x^3y+x^2y^2+xy^3+y^4$.

22. $a^4-2a^3b+4a^2b^2-8ab^3+16b^4$.

23. $2a^3-6a^2b+18ab^2-27b^3$. 24. x^2+xy+y^2.

25. $x^2+2xy+3y^2$. 26. x^2-2x+2. 27. x^2-3x-1.

28. x^2-5x+6. 29. x^2-4x+8. 30. x^2+5x+6.

31. $x-c$. 32. x^2-px+q.

33. $y^4-(m-1)y^3-(m-n-1)y^2-(m-1)y+1$.

34. $a^2+b^2+c^2+ab-ac+bc$, $a^2+b^2+c^2+ab+ac-bc$.

35. $a-ax+ax^2-ax^3+\dfrac{ax^4}{1+x}$, $1+5x+15x^2+45x^3+\dfrac{135x^4}{1-3x}$.

36. $1+2x+3x^2+4x^3+\dfrac{5x^4-4x^5}{1-2x+x^2}$.

Examples—12.

1. $a-x$, $a^4+a^3x+a^2x^2+ax^3+x^4$, $a^5-a^4x+a^3x^2-a^2x^3+ax^4-x^5$.

2. $3x+1$, $5x-1$, $2x-3$.   3. $3mn-5$, $4m^2-n^2$.

4. $1-2x+4x^2$, $9x^2+3x+1$, $1-2x+4x^2-8x^3$.

5. $x^3+3x^2y+9xy^2+27y^3$, $a^4-2a^3b+4a^2b^2-8ab^3+16b^4$, $x^{15}-x^{12}y^2+x^9y^4-x^6y^6+x^3y^8-y^{10}$.

6. $\frac{1}{4}a^2-\frac{1}{2}ab+b^2$, $x^3y^3-x^2y^2z+xyz^2-z^3$.

7. $a+b+c$, $a+b-c$.

8. $(x+y)^2-(x+y)z+z^2=x^2+2xy+y^2-xz-yz+z^2$, $x^2+x(y-z)+(y-z)^2=x^2+xy-xz+y^2-2yz+z^2$.

Examples—13.

1. $(1-2x)(1+2x)$, $(a-3x)(a+3x)$, $(3m-2n)(3m+2n)$, $x^2(5a-2)(5a+2)$, $x^2y^2(4x-5y)(4x+5y)$.

2. $(x+y)(x^2-xy+y^2)$, $(x-y)(x^2+xy+y^2)$, $(1+xy)(1-xy+x^2y^2)$, $(x-1)(x+1)(x^2+1)$, $xy(ay-x^2)(ay+x^2)$, $2ab^2c(a-2c)(a+2c)$.

3. $x^2(5x-a)(5x+a)$, $a^4(a-3b^2)(a+3b^2)$, $(2x-3)(4x^2+6x+9)$, $(a-2b)(a^2+2ab+4b^2)$, $x^2y(a+3y)(a^2-3ay+9y^2)$.

4. $(x+2)(x^4-2x^3+4x^2-8x+16)$, $x^3(a+3x)(a^2-3ax+9x^2)$, $(2x^2+y^2)(4x^6-2x^2y^2+y^4)$, $(ab^3+c^3)(ab^3-c^3)(a^2b^6+c^6)$, $abc(a+c)^2$.

5. $(3x-1)(3x+1)(9x^2+1)$, $(x-2)(x+2)(x^2+2x+4)(x^2-2x+4)$, $x^2(x-b)^2$, $x^2(x-a)^2(x+a)^2$.

6. $(4x-5)(2x+1)$, $(a+3b)(a-b)$, $7(x-y)(x+y)$.

7. $(x-y)^2(x+y)^2$, $(c+a-b)(c-a+b)$, $8ab$.

8. $(x+y)^2$, $mn(m-n)$, $5b(a-b)$.

9. $2(x+y)(4x-y)$, $2(x-y)(4y-x)$, $4y(x+y)$.

10. $(a+b)(a^2+ab+b^2)$, $(a-b)^2$, 0.

Examples—14.

1. $(x+1)(x+5)$, $(x+4)(x+5)$, $(x-2)(x-3)$, $(x-3)(x-5)$, $(x+1)(x+7)$, $(x-1)(x-9)$.

2. $(x+3)(x-2)$, $(x-3)(x+2)$, $(x-3)(x+1)$, $(x+5)(x-3)$, $(x+8)(x-1)$, $(x-9)(x+1)$.

3. $(2x+3)(2x+1)$, $(4x+1)(x+3)$, $(4x-1)(x+3)$, $(2x-3)(2x+1)$, $(3x-2)(x+2)$, $(3x+4)(2x-1)$.

4. $(4x+1)(3x-2)$, $2(6x-1)(x-1)$, $(4x+1)(3x-1)$, $(x+4)(x-3)$, $(3x-5)(x+1)$.

5. $a^2(x-a)(x-2a)$, $a(a-3x)(a+2x)$, $ab(3a-2b)(a+b)$, $(2a+x)(2a-x)(3a^2+x^2)$.

6. $xy(2x+y)(x+2y)$, $3y^2(3x+2y)(x-y)$, $a^2(3ax-1)(2ax+1)$, $x^2(2b-3x)(3b+x)$.

Examples—15.

1. $2x^2(a+x)^2$.
2. $x^2(a+x)^2$.
3. $ab(a-b)^2$.
4. $2(x-1)$.
5. $x^2(x+1)$.
6. $2(x+a)$.
7. $a^2(x+1)$.
8. $3(ax+2)$.
9. $x-7$.
10. $x+5$.
11. $x-10$.
12. x^2-x+1.
13. $x+3y$.

Examples—16.

1. $3x-2$.
2. $2x+3$.
3. $3x+5$.
4. $8x^2+14x-15$.
5. $4x-5$.
6. x^2+2x-3.

Examples—17.

1. $3x-2$.
2. $3x-2$.
3. $2(x^2+2x+1)$.
4. $y-2$.
5. $x-2a$.
6. $x+3$.
7. $3(x+3)$.
8. $x^2 \div y^2$.
9. $a(a+b)$.
10. $a(a^2-b^2)$.
11. $x^2-2xy+y^2$.
12. x^2+4x+4.

Examples—18.

1. $12a^2b^2c$, $36x^3y^3$, ax^2y-axy^2, ab^2-ad^2.
2. $120a^4b^2$, $10a^5b^6$, $1800a^3x^3$.

3. $6(a^2-b^2)$, $12a(a^2-1)$, $120xy(x^2-y^2)$.

4. $24a^2b^2(a^2-b^2)$, $36xy^2(x^2-y^2)$.

5. $(x+1)(x+3)(x-4)$.   **6.** $(x+2)(x+4)(x^2+3x+1)$.

7. $x(2x+1)(3x-1)(4x+3)$.

8. $(x^2-5x+6)(x-1)(x-4)$.

9. $(x^2+3x+2)(x-3)(x+5)$.

10. $(x^2+x+1)(x^2+1)(x+1)(x-1)$.

11. $36a^3b^3c^2$.   **12.** $120(a+b)^2(a-b)^2$.

13. $24(a-b)(a^2+b^2)$.   **14.** $105ab^2(a+b)(a-b)$.

15. x^6-1.   **16.** x^9-1.   **17.** $x^{12}-1$.

18. $(x+1)(x+2)(x+3)$.

Examples—19.

1. $3x + \dfrac{4x}{7}$.   **2.** $4ac + \dfrac{4c}{9}$.   **3.** $2a + \dfrac{3b}{4a}$.   **4.** $2x - \dfrac{5y}{6x}$.

5. $x + \dfrac{2}{x+3}$.   **6.** $2x - \dfrac{1}{x-3}$.   **7.** $x^2 + 3ax + 3a^2 + \dfrac{3a^3}{x-2a}$.

8. $x - 1 - \dfrac{2x-1}{x^2-x+1}$.   **9.** $x^3 + x^2 + x + 1 + \dfrac{2}{x-1}$.

10. $x^3 - x^2 + x - 1$.   **11.** $\dfrac{4a^2}{3b}$.   **12.** $\dfrac{8(a^2+b^2)}{3(a+b)}$.

13. $\dfrac{3(a-b)}{2(a+b)}$.   **14.** $\dfrac{x^2}{(x-1)^2(x+1)}$.   **15.** $\dfrac{4x}{3y}$.

16. $\dfrac{3a+2b}{a+b}$.   17. $\dfrac{2(a-b)}{3(a+b)}$.   18. $\dfrac{(x^3-1)(x+1)}{x^2+1}$.

Examples—20.

1. $\dfrac{2a^2x}{3y}$.   2. $\dfrac{a+b}{2b}$.   3. $\dfrac{a+b}{a-b}$.   4. $\dfrac{2ax}{ax-3y}$.

5. $\dfrac{4(a+b)}{5(a-b)}$.   6. $\dfrac{a^2-ab+b^2}{a-b}$.   7. $\dfrac{x+2}{x+5}$.

8. $\dfrac{x+7}{x-5}$.   9. $\dfrac{x+3}{x-7}$.   10. $\dfrac{x+b}{x+c}$.   11. $\dfrac{x-b}{x+c}$.

12. $\dfrac{3x-4}{4x-3}$.   13. $\dfrac{x+a-b-c}{x+b-a-c}$.   14. $\dfrac{x+3}{x^2-2x+5}$.

15. $\dfrac{x-3}{x^2+7x+3}$.   16. $\dfrac{x+5}{x^2+3x+2}$.   17. $\dfrac{1}{x^2-a^2}$.

18. $\dfrac{y^{n-1}}{x^{m+1}}$.

19. $\dfrac{x-1}{a}$, $\dfrac{x^2+a^2}{x^2}$, $\dfrac{a^4+a^2b^2+b^4}{a^2+b^2}$, $\dfrac{x^2-bx}{x+b}$, $\dfrac{a-b}{a+b}$.

20. $\dfrac{9x^2}{12x^3}$, $\dfrac{8x}{12x^3}$, $\dfrac{5}{12x^3}$.

21. $\dfrac{4(x-1)}{4(x^2-1)}$, $\dfrac{3(x-1)}{4(x^2-1)}$, $\dfrac{4x}{4(x^2-1)}$.

22. $\dfrac{a(x+a)}{x^2-a^2}$, $\dfrac{-x(x+a)}{x^2-a^2}$, $\dfrac{x^2}{x^2-a^2}$, $\dfrac{-ax}{x^2-a^2}$.

23. $\left(\dfrac{a(a+b)}{a^2-b^2}, \dfrac{b(a-b)}{a^2-b^2}, \dfrac{ab}{a^2-b^2}, \dfrac{b^2}{a^2+b^2}\right) = \dfrac{a(a+b)(a^2+b^2)}{a^4-b^4},$

$\dfrac{b(a-b)(a^2+b^2)}{a^4-b^4}, \dfrac{ab(a^2+b^2)}{a^4-b^4}, \dfrac{b^2(a^2-b^2)}{a^4-b^4}.$

24. $\dfrac{(x-1)(x+1)^2}{(x-1)^2(x+1)^2}, \dfrac{x(x+1)^2}{(x-1)^2(x+1)^2}, \dfrac{3(x-1)(x+1)^2}{(x-1)^2(x+1)^2},$

$\dfrac{4(x-1)^2}{(x-1)^2(x+1)^2}, \dfrac{5(x-1)(x+1)}{(x-1)^2(x+1)^2}.$

25. $\dfrac{a(x^2+ax+a^2)}{x^3-a^3}, \dfrac{a^2-x^2}{x^3-a^3}, \dfrac{ax}{x^3-a^3}.$

26. $\dfrac{x^2+ax+a^2}{x^4+a^2x^2+a^4}, \dfrac{x^2-ax+a^2}{x^4+a^2x^2+a^4}, \dfrac{a^2}{x^4+a^2x^2+a^4}.$

Examples—21.

1. $\dfrac{a^2+b^2}{2(a+b)b}, \dfrac{3a^2-ab+2b^2}{6(a-b)b}, \dfrac{25a-20b}{12}.$

2. $\dfrac{ab}{a-b}, \dfrac{a^2+b^2}{a^2-b^2}, \dfrac{a^2+b^2}{a^2-b^2}, \dfrac{a^2-ab+b^2}{a^2-b^2}.$

ANSWERS TO EXAMPLES. 295

3. $\dfrac{a+bx}{c+dx}$, $\dfrac{2a^2-2ab+2b^2}{a^2-b^2}$, $\dfrac{2ab}{a^2-b^2}$, $\dfrac{x-y}{x}$.

4. $\dfrac{2a^2}{a^4-x^4}$, 0. 5. $\dfrac{1}{x^2(x^2-1)}$. 6. $\dfrac{a}{4a^2-b^2}$.

7. $\dfrac{a+bx}{b+ax}$. 8. $\dfrac{1+x^3+x^6}{x^2(x^2+1)^2}$. 9. $\dfrac{2x}{x+y}$.

10. $\dfrac{4x^3y-x^2y^2-y^4}{x^4-y^4}$. 11. $\dfrac{a^2+x^2}{a^2(a+x)}$.

12. $\dfrac{2x^4+4x^2y^2-2y^4}{x^4-y^4}$. 13. $\dfrac{a^2+x^2}{a^2(x-a)}$. 14. $\dfrac{y}{x+y}$.

15. $\dfrac{x-3x^2+3x^3}{(1-x)^3}$. 16. $\dfrac{1+2x+3x^2}{4(1-x^4)}$.

Examples—22.

1. $\dfrac{x}{(x-a)(x-b)}$. 2. $\dfrac{x(a+b)-ab}{(x-a)(x-b)}$.

3. $\dfrac{1}{(a-c)(c-b)}$. 4. $\dfrac{c-a-b}{(c-a)(c-b)}$. 5. 0.

6. $-\dfrac{1}{c(c-a)(c-b)}$. 7. 1.

Examples—23.

1. $\dfrac{4c}{5a}$. 2. 1. 3. $\dfrac{a^2b^3c^2}{x^2y^3z^2}$. 4. $\dfrac{1}{(x-1)(x+2)}$.

5. $x-a$.

6. $\dfrac{a^4-b^4}{ab}$.

7. $\dfrac{a^2b^2}{a^2-b^2}$.

8. $\dfrac{ax}{a^2-x^2}$.

9. $\dfrac{(x+y)^2}{x^2+y^2}$.

10. $\dfrac{x+c}{x+b}$.

11. $\dfrac{x}{x-y}$.

12. $\dfrac{(a-c)^2-b^2}{abc}$.

13. $\dfrac{x^6-a x^4+a^2x-a^3}{a^2x^3}$.

14. $\dfrac{x^2}{a^2}+\dfrac{a^2}{x^2}-\dfrac{y^2}{b^2}-\dfrac{b^2}{y^2}$.

15. 1.

Examples—24.

1. $\dfrac{6ay}{bx}$.

2. $\dfrac{9c^2x^2}{16a^2z^2}$.

3. $\dfrac{1}{x+y}$.

4. $\dfrac{3(a-b)^2}{b(a+b)}$.

5. $\dfrac{x(a+2x)}{a^2}$.

6. $\dfrac{2x}{x-y}$.

7. $\dfrac{a+x}{x+y}$.

8. $\dfrac{x-b}{x-a}$.

9. $\dfrac{a+b-c}{c+a-b}$.

10. $\dfrac{1}{x^2-y^2}$.

11. $\left(\dfrac{x-1}{x-3}\right)^2$.

12. $\dfrac{y^4-x^4}{y^3}$.

13. $5x-1$.

14. $\dfrac{a^4+a^2+1}{a^2}$.

15. $\dfrac{(x^2+a^2)(x^4+a^4)}{x^3a^3}$.

16. $\dfrac{x^2-6a^2}{xa}$.

17. $\dfrac{x-y}{y}$.

18. $\dfrac{x^2+ax+a^2}{ax}$.

Examples—25.

1. $\dfrac{1}{x}$.

2. 1.

3. $\dfrac{1}{x+1}$.

4. $x+1$.

ANSWERS TO EXAMPLES.

5. 1.   6. $\dfrac{x-4}{x-5}$.   7. $\dfrac{b}{a}$.   8. 0.

9. $\tfrac{4}{5}$.   10. $2\tfrac{4}{7}$.   11. 0.   12. 0.   13. a.

Examples—26.

1. $4a^2b^4$, $-27a^6b^6c^{12}$, $\dfrac{81a^4b^8}{256c^{12}}$, $-\dfrac{x^{10}y^{15}z^{20}}{32}$.

2. $x^3+6x^2+12x+8$.   3. $x^4-8x^3+24x^2-32x+16$.

4. $x^5+15x^4+90x^3+270x^2+405x+243$.

5. $1+10x+40x^2+80x^3+80x^4+32x^5$.

6. $8m^3-12m^2+6m-1$.

7. $81x^4+108x^3+54x^2+12x+1$.

8. $16x^4-32ax^3+24a^2x^2-8a^3x+a^4$.

9. $243x^5+810ax^4+1080a^2x^3+720a^3x^2+240a^4x+32a^5$.

10. $64a^3-144a^2b+108ab^2-27b^3$.

11. $a^3x^3-3a^2x^2y^2+3axy^4-y^6$.

12. $a^4x^4+4a^3x^5+6a^2x^6+4ax^7+x^8$.

13. $32a^5m^5-80a^4m^6+80a^3m^7-40a^2m^8+10am^9-m^{10}$.

14. $a^3-3a^2b+3a^2c+3ab^2-6abc+3ac^2-b^3+3b^2c-3bc^2+c^3$.

15. $1-3x+6x^2-7x^3+6x^4-3x^5+x^6$.

Examples—27

1. $4(ab+ad+bc+cd)$.
2. $2(a^2+2ac+c^2+b^2+2bd+d^2)$.
3. $1+2x+3x^2+2x^3+x^4$.
4. $1-2x+3x^2-2x^3+x^4$.
5. $1+2x-x^2-2x^3+x^4$.
6. $1+6x+13x^2+12x^3+4x^4$.
7. $1-6x+15x^2-18x^3+9x^4$.
8. $2(4+25x^2+16x^4)$.
9. $1-2x+3x^2-x^4+2x^5+x^6$.
10. $1+4x+10x^2+20x^3+25x^4+24x^5+16x^6$.

Examples—28.

1. $\pm 2ab^2c^3$, $\pm 7x^3y^2z$, $\pm 10a^4b^5c^6$.
2. $\pm\dfrac{3ax^2y^3}{5z}$, $\pm\dfrac{7xy^2}{8a}$, $\pm\dfrac{5x^2y^3}{4ab^2}$.
3. $\pm\dfrac{a^2x^2y}{2}$, $-\dfrac{2ay^2}{3x^3}$, $\dfrac{4b^2c^2}{5a^4}$, $-\dfrac{6abc^3}{7}$.
4. $\dfrac{3a}{bc}$, $\dfrac{a}{2b^2}$, $\pm\dfrac{2ab^2}{c^4}$.

Examples—29.

1. x^2+x+1.
2. $1-x+2x^2$.
3. x^2+3x+8.
4. x^2-2x-2.
5. $1-2x+3x^2$.
6. $2x^4-x^2-2$.
7. $x^2-ax+2a^2$.
8. x^2-ax+b^2.
9. $x^3-6x^2+12x-8$.

10. $x^3+2ax^2-2a^2x-a^3$. 11. $1-x+x^2-x^3+x^4$.

12. $\dfrac{2x}{3y}-\dfrac{4x}{5z}-\dfrac{3y}{4z}$. 13. $1-x, a-2$. 14. $2a-3b$.

15. x^2-xy+y^2.

Examples—30.

1. 421, 347, 69.4, 737, 1046, 4321.

2. 2082, 20.92, 1011, 20.22, 129.63.

3. 1.5811, 44.721, .54772, .17320, 10.535, .03331, .06324, .07071.

Examples—31.

1. $x+2y$. 2. $a-3$. 3. $x+4$. 4. $2a-3b$.
5. $a+8b$. 6. $2x-7y$. 7. $m-4nx$. 8. $ax-5bx$.
9. a^2+2a+1. 10. x^2-4x+2. 11. a^2-ab+b^2.
12. $a-b+c$.

Examples—32.

1. 21, 23, 25, 32, 4.7, 48, 64, 9.6.

2. 114, 11.7, 125, 108, 1.41, 192.

3. 1.357, .5848, .2154, 1.587.

Examples—33.

1. 5.　　2. 2.　　3. 3.　　4. $\frac{4}{7}$.　　5. $-\frac{1}{2}$.

6. $\frac{d-a}{m-n}$.　　7. 2.　　8. 1.　　9. 4.　　10. $-\frac{1}{3}a$.

11. -4.　　12. $\frac{4}{5}$.　　13. $-\frac{2}{3}$.　　14. $\frac{m^2}{n}$.　　15. $x=5$.

Examples—34.

1. 42.　　2. 12.　　3. 12.　　4. 5.　　5. 7.　　6. 4.
7. 5.　　8. $\frac{2}{3}$.　　9. 7.　　10. $\frac{1}{13}(25a-18b)$.
11. 7.　　12. $1\frac{1}{5}$.　　13. 11.　　14. 5.　　15. $2\frac{1}{5}$.　　16. 3.
17. 2.　　18. 4.　　19. 2.

Examples—35.

1. 10.　　2. 8.　　3. 12.　　4. 6.　　5. -7.
6. 16.　　7. 5.　　8. $3\frac{1}{7}$.　　9. -6.　　10. 5.
11. 8.　　12. $\frac{7}{4}$.　　13. 3.　　14. 2.　　15. 7.
16. $1\frac{4}{5}$.　　17. $\frac{1}{5}$.　　18. 1.　　19. 17.　　20. 2.
21. 4.　　22. 2.　　23. 18.　　24. 8.　　25. $x=2$.
26. $x=\frac{5\,0}{2\,3}$.　　27. $x=7$.　　28. $x=4$.　　29. $x=-1$.
30. 20.　　31. 3.　　32. 5.　　33. $a-b$.

ANSWERS TO EXAMPLES.

34. $b-a$. **35.** $\dfrac{2ab}{a+b}$. **36.** $\dfrac{a^2+ab+b^2}{a+b}$.

37. $\dfrac{ab}{a+b-c}$. **38.** $\dfrac{2ab}{a+b}$. **39.** $\dfrac{a+b}{2}$.

40. $\dfrac{a+b+c+d}{m+n}$. **41.** c. **42.** $\dfrac{a^2}{b-a}$.

43. $\tfrac{1}{2}(a+b+3)$.

Examples—36.

1. 12.   **2.** 9.   **3.** 120.   **4.** $1.75.
5. 35, 13.   **6.** 513, 466.   **7.** 15.   **8.** 31, 18.
9. 15.   **10.** 90, 60.   **11.** November 20th.
12. 16.   **13.** 37, 30, 20.   **14.** 20.   **15.** 41.
16. 88.   **17.** $36, $12, $16.   **18.** 5.
19. £45, £57, £63, £65.   **20.** 15, 5.
21. 98⅔ miles from B; 10⅔ hours.
22. 10, 14, 18, 22, 26, 30.   **23.** 28, 14.   **24.** 88, 44.
25. 5, 6.   **26.** 22, 7, 12 gallons.   **27.** 3000.
28. 18, 3, 3.   **29.** 24000.   **30.** £140.

Examples—37.

1. 45 gallons.   **2.** 2450, 196, 98.   **3.** 84.
4. 15 feet by 11 feet.   **5.** 20 lbs., 15 lbs., 15 lbs.

6. $240.　　7. $3\frac{1}{3}$ days.　　8. 75.　　9. 1504.

10. 1540, 880, 616.　　11. 10 lbs.

12. 18, $10\frac{1}{5}$, $6\frac{3}{4}$ days.　　13. $1.05, $1.17.　　14. $6\frac{2}{3}$ oz.

15. 654.　16. 76, 30.　17. $21\frac{9}{11}$ hrs., $10\frac{10}{23}$ hrs.　18. 12, 16.

19. 10, 15, 3, 60.　　20. 240, 180, 144 days.　　21. 12.

22. 20, 80.　23. $5\frac{5}{17}$.　24. 240.　25. 24.　26. 60.

27. 25.　　　　28. 7 hours, $5\frac{5}{11}'$, 6 hours, $16\frac{4}{11}'$.

29. 40 minutes past eleven.　　　　30. $100000000.

31. 7, 15, 48.　　32. 189.

Examples—38.

1. $\dfrac{mna}{m+n}$.

2. $\dfrac{m(nb-a)}{n-m}$, $\dfrac{n(a-mb)}{n-m}$.

3. $\dfrac{ma}{m+n}$, $\dfrac{na}{m+n}$.

4. $\dfrac{mpa}{mp+np+nq}$, $\dfrac{npa}{mp+np+nq}$, $\dfrac{nqa}{mp+np+nq}$.

5. $\dfrac{mb-na}{n-m}$.　　6. $\dfrac{abc}{ab+ac+bc}$.　　7. $\dfrac{d}{b+c}$.

8. $\dfrac{bc}{b+c}$.

Examples—39.

1. 10; 7. 2. 17; 19. 3. 2; 13. 4. 4; 1.
5. 5; 5. 6. 21; 12. 7. 19; 2. 8. $38\frac{1}{2}$; 70.
9. 6; 12. 10. $\frac{349}{157}$; $\frac{169}{157}$. 11. 5; 7. 12. $2\frac{1}{2}$; 1.
13. $x=1$, $y=7$. 14. $x=10$, $y=24$.
15. $x=144$, $y=216$. 16. .2; .2. 17. 10; 8.
18. 12; 3. 19. 3; 2. 20. a; b. 21. a; b.
22. $\frac{ab}{a+b}$; $\frac{ab}{a-b}$. 23. b; a. 24. $\frac{ab^2c}{a^2+b^2}$; $\frac{a^2bc}{a^2+b^2}$.
25. $\frac{ac}{a+b}$; $\frac{bc}{a+b}$. 26. $\frac{1}{a+b}$; 0. 27. a; b.

Examples—40.

1. $x=1$, $y=2$, $z=3$. 2. $x=7$, $y=10$, $z=9$.
3. $x=5$, $y=6$, $z=7$. 4. $x=4$, $y=-5$, $z=6$.
5. $x=-5$, $y=6$, $z=-2$. 6. $x=1\frac{5}{7}$, $y=2\frac{3}{7}$, $z=-12$.
7. $x=2$, $y=-3$, $z=4$. 8. $x=12$, $y=12$, $z=12$.
9. $x=5$, $y=7$, $z=-3$. 10. $\frac{2}{3}$; $\frac{3}{4}$; $\frac{2}{5}$.
11. $x=\frac{1}{2}(b+c-a)$, &c. 12. $x=\frac{2}{3}(a+b+c)-a$, &c.
13. $x=\frac{1}{2}(b+c)$, &c. 14. $x=y=z=\dfrac{abc}{ab+bc+ca}$.

Examples—41.

1. $\frac{2}{15}$.   2. 48.   3. 108 sq. ft.   4. 4 hours, 6 hours.
5. 20, 30, 60.   6. 24, 72.   7. 49; 21.
8. 45; 63.   9. $\frac{3}{5}$.   10. $(24-1)20$.
11. 1; 2.   12. 50 yards; rates 4 and 5 yards per minute.
13. 11, and 5, gallons.   14. A. D. 1752.   15. 50; 75.
16. 90; 72; 60.   17. 4; 2.   18. 8; 5.
19. 4 miles walking, 3 miles rowing, at first.
20. 30; 50 miles per hour.
21. 60 miles; passenger train 30 miles per hour.
22. 150; 120; 90.   23. $x=40$, $y=160$, $z=480$.
24. $\dfrac{a+b}{2}$, $\dfrac{a-b}{2}$.

25. $\dfrac{mc-ah+am(n-b)}{mb-an}$; $\dfrac{bh-nc+bn(a-m)}{mb-an}$.

26. $\dfrac{b+a^2}{2a}$, $\dfrac{a^2-b}{2a}$.   27. $\dfrac{2n}{m-1}$, $\dfrac{2n}{m+1}$.

Examples—42.

1. $x^{\frac{2}{3}}+x^{\frac{4}{3}}$, $+x^{\frac{2}{3}}$, $+x^{\frac{3}{3}}$; $ab^{\frac{4}{3}}+a^{\frac{2}{3}}b^{\frac{2}{3}}+a^{\frac{3}{3}}b^2+a^{\frac{5}{3}}b$.

2. $ab^{\frac{2}{3}}+a^{\frac{4}{3}}+a^2b^{\frac{2}{3}}+ab^{\frac{4}{3}}$; $a^{\frac{1}{2}}b^2+ab^2+a^{\frac{3}{2}}b^2+a^{\frac{2}{3}}b^2$.

3. $a^{-1}+2b^{-2}+3c^{-3}+4ab^{-1}+5a^{-1}b$;

   $a^2b^{-3}+3a^2b^{-1}+5ab^{-2}+4a^{-2}b+2a^{-3}b^2$;

   $\dfrac{1}{a}+\dfrac{2}{b^2}+\dfrac{3}{c^3}+\dfrac{4}{a^{-1}b}+\dfrac{5}{ab^{-1}}$;

   $\dfrac{1}{a^{-3}b^3}+\dfrac{3}{a^{-2}b}+\dfrac{5}{a^{-1}b^2}+\dfrac{4}{a^2b^{-1}}+\dfrac{2}{a^3b^{-2}}$.

4. $\tfrac{1}{3}a^3b^{-2}c^{-2}+4a^{-2}b^{-1}c^2+2a^{-1}bc+\tfrac{1}{3}a^{-1}b^{-1}c^{-1}$,

   $\tfrac{1}{2}abc^{-\tfrac{1}{3}}+\tfrac{2}{3}a^{-\tfrac{3}{2}}b^2c^2+\tfrac{3}{4}a^{-\tfrac{3}{3}}b^{-\tfrac{1}{3}}c^{-\tfrac{2}{3}}+5a^{-1}b^{-\tfrac{3}{4}}c$;

   and $\dfrac{1}{3a^{-3}b^2c^2}+\dfrac{4}{a^2bc^{-2}}+\dfrac{2}{ab^{-1}c^{-1}}+\dfrac{1}{3abc}$;

   $\dfrac{1}{2a^{-1}b^{-1}c^{\tfrac{1}{3}}}+\dfrac{2}{3a^{\tfrac{3}{2}}b^{-2}c^{-2}}+\dfrac{3}{4a^{\tfrac{2}{3}}b^{\tfrac{1}{3}}c^{\tfrac{2}{3}}}+\dfrac{5}{ab^{\tfrac{3}{4}}c^{-1}}$.

5. $\sqrt{a}+2\sqrt[3]{a^2}+3\sqrt[4]{a^3}+4\sqrt[5]{a}+\sqrt[6]{a^5}$,

   $\dfrac{\sqrt[4]{a}}{\sqrt[5]{b^3}}+\dfrac{\sqrt[3]{(a^2b)}}{2\sqrt{c}}+\dfrac{2\sqrt{(ac^3)}}{3\sqrt{b^3}}+\dfrac{\sqrt[5]{(b^2c^2)}}{4\sqrt[3]{a}}+\dfrac{\sqrt[6]{(bc^5)}}{5\sqrt[4]{a^3}}$.

6. $\dfrac{bc}{a}+\dfrac{ac}{b^2}+\dfrac{1}{abc}+\dfrac{c^2}{ab^2}$, $\dfrac{1}{\sqrt{a^2}}+\dfrac{\sqrt{a}}{\sqrt[3]{b^4}}+\dfrac{\sqrt[3]{b^2}}{\sqrt{a^3}}+\dfrac{1}{\sqrt[3]{b^5}}$.

7. $\dfrac{c}{a^2b^2}+2abc+\dfrac{3a^3}{bc^2}+ab^2c^3$; $\dfrac{\sqrt[3]{b}}{a^2}+\dfrac{\sqrt{a^3}}{\sqrt[3]{b^2}}+\dfrac{\sqrt[4]{a^2}}{\sqrt[3]{b^3}}+\dfrac{b^2}{\sqrt{a}}$.

Examples—43.

1. $\tfrac{1}{3}$.   2. $\tfrac{1}{8}$.   3. $\tfrac{1}{10}$.   4. 100.   5. $\tfrac{1}{27}$.

6. a^{-6}.   7. a^6.   8. a^{-2}.   9. a^{-1}.   10. $a^{\tfrac{7}{12}}$.

11. $x^{\tfrac{3}{2}}-y^{\tfrac{3}{2}}$.   12. $a-b$.   13. $x^2+2x^{\tfrac{3}{2}}+x-4$.

14. x^4+1+x^{-4}.   15. $a^{-1}-1$.   16. $a^2-3a^{\frac{2}{3}}+3a^{-\frac{2}{3}}-a^{-2}$.

17. $a^2+2a^{\frac{3}{2}}b^{\frac{1}{2}}+ab-x^{\frac{2}{3}}y^{\frac{4}{3}}$.   18. $x^{\frac{3}{2}}+x^{\frac{3}{2}}y^{\frac{1}{6}}+x^{\frac{1}{6}}y^{\frac{3}{2}}+y^{\frac{3}{2}}$.

19. $a^{\frac{2}{3}}+a^{\frac{1}{3}}b^{\frac{1}{3}}+b^{\frac{2}{3}}$.   20. $16x^{-\frac{2}{3}}-12x^{-\frac{1}{3}}y^{-\frac{1}{3}}+9y^{-\frac{2}{3}}$.

21. $x+y$.   22. $a^{\frac{1}{3}}-a^{\frac{1}{6}}b^{\frac{1}{6}}+b^{\frac{1}{3}}$.   23. $a^{\frac{1}{3}}+b^{\frac{1}{3}}-c^{\frac{1}{3}}$.

24. $x^{\frac{3}{2}}+2x^{\frac{3}{2}}a^{\frac{1}{2}}+3x^{\frac{1}{2}}a+2x^{\frac{1}{2}}a^{\frac{3}{2}}+a^2$.

25. $x^{\frac{1}{3}}-2x^{-\frac{1}{3}}$.   26. $x-2-x^{-1}$.   27. $ab^{-1}+1+a^{-1}b$.

Examples—44.

1. $64^{\frac{2}{3}}$, $81^{\frac{1}{2}}$, $(\frac{1}{4})^{\frac{3}{2}}$, $(\frac{1}{8})^{\frac{2}{3}}$, $(\frac{2}{3})^{\frac{1}{2}}$, $8^{\frac{1}{3}}$.

2. $25^{\frac{1}{2}}$, $(\frac{25}{4})^{\frac{1}{2}}$, $(\frac{4}{9}a^4)^{\frac{1}{2}}$, $(\frac{9}{4}a^4)^{\frac{1}{2}}$, $\{\frac{1}{4}(a^2+2ab+b^2)\}^{\frac{1}{2}}$;

   $125^{\frac{1}{3}}$, $(1\frac{27}{8})^{\frac{1}{3}}$, $(\frac{8}{27}a^9)^{\frac{1}{3}}$, $(\frac{27}{8}a^9)^{\frac{1}{3}}$, $\{\frac{1}{8}(a^3+3a^2b+3ab^2+b^3)\}^{\frac{1}{3}}$.

3. $(\frac{1}{125})^{\frac{1}{3}}$, $(\frac{27}{1000})^{\frac{1}{3}}$, $\left(\frac{1}{a^6}\right)^{\frac{1}{3}}$, $\left(\frac{a^3}{b^3c^6}\right)^{\frac{1}{3}}$;

   $6561^{-\frac{1}{4}}$, $(\frac{10000}{81})^{-\frac{1}{4}}$, $(a^8)^{-\frac{1}{4}}$, $\left(\frac{b^4c^8}{a^4}\right)^{-\frac{1}{4}}$.

4. $\sqrt{125}$, $\sqrt{3}$, $\sqrt{12}$, $\sqrt{\frac{3}{5}}$, $\sqrt{\frac{1}{3}}$, $\sqrt{320}$.

5. $\sqrt[3]{54}$, $\sqrt[3]{256}$, $\sqrt[3]{2048}$, $\sqrt[3]{3}$, $\sqrt[3]{\frac{2}{3}}$, $\sqrt[3]{\frac{1}{18}}$.

6. $\sqrt{(4a)}$, $\sqrt{(98a^2x)}$, $\sqrt{\dfrac{a+b}{a-b}}$.

7. $\sqrt[3]{(2ab)}$, $\sqrt[3]{(6a^2x)}$, $\sqrt[3]{\dfrac{4a^2}{9b^2}}$, $\sqrt[3]{\dfrac{2a}{3}}$, $\sqrt[3]{(a^3-x^3)}$.

ANSWERS TO EXAMPLES. 307

8. $3\sqrt{5},\ 5\sqrt{5},\ 36\sqrt{3},\ 3\sqrt[3]{5},\ 18\sqrt[3]{2},\ \frac{1}{2}\sqrt{6},\ \sqrt[3]{12},\ \sqrt[3]{54},\ 6.$

9. $4\sqrt[3]{2},\ 8\sqrt[3]{2},\ 6\sqrt[3]{48},\ \frac{2}{3}\sqrt{2},\ \frac{2}{27}\sqrt{2},\ \frac{2}{3}\sqrt[3]{2},\ \frac{3}{7}\sqrt{21},\ \frac{3}{5}\sqrt[3]{150},\ \sqrt[5]{375}.$

10. $2\sqrt{3},\ 15\sqrt{3},\ \frac{7}{2}\sqrt{3},\ \frac{4}{15}\sqrt{3},\ \frac{1}{2}\sqrt{3},\ \frac{1}{6}\sqrt{3}.$

Examples—45.

1. $\sqrt{108},\ \sqrt{112};\ \sqrt[3]{81},\ \sqrt[3]{80};\ \sqrt[3]{120},\ \sqrt[3]{128},\ \sqrt[3]{135}.$

2. $7\sqrt{2}.$ 3. $9\sqrt[3]{4}.$ 4. $\frac{2}{3}\sqrt{3}.$ 5. $\frac{\sqrt[3]{4}}{4}.$

6. $\frac{13\sqrt{15}}{10}.$ 7. $\frac{5\sqrt[3]{2}}{2}.$ 8. $2+2\sqrt{2}-2\sqrt{3}.$

9. $2+\frac{5}{6}\sqrt{6}.$

10. $\frac{1}{6}(\sqrt{2}+\sqrt{3}+\sqrt{5}),\ \frac{1}{3}\sqrt{6}+\frac{1}{2}\sqrt[3]{32}+\frac{1}{6}\sqrt[3]{120}.$

11. $\frac{1}{5}(2\sqrt{2}+\sqrt{3}),\ \sqrt{5}+1,\ \sqrt{5}-\sqrt{2},\ 4+\sqrt{2},\ \frac{1}{2}(7+3\sqrt{5}).$

12. $\dfrac{a+\sqrt{a^2-x^2}}{x}.$

Examples—46.

1. $\sqrt{3}+1.$ 2. $3+\sqrt{2}.$ 3. $\sqrt{5}-\sqrt{3}.$

4. $2\sqrt{5}-3\sqrt{2}.$ 5. $4\sqrt{2}-3.$ 6. $\frac{1}{2}\sqrt{5}-1.$

7. $2-\frac{1}{3}\sqrt{3}.$

Examples—47.

1. 4.   2. 50.   3. 25.   4. $1\frac{3}{8\frac{1}{4}}$.   5. $(a-b)^2$.

6. a.   7. $\dfrac{(a-b)^2}{2b}$.   8. $\dfrac{b(b-2a)}{3b-2a}$.

Examples—48.

1. ± 2.   2. ± 3.   3. ± 1.   4. $\pm \frac{1}{2}$.

5. $\pm \frac{1}{2}$.   6. $\pm 2\frac{1}{3}$.   7. $\pm \frac{2}{3}$.   8. ± 5.

9. ± 3.   10. ± 5.   11. ± 2.   12. ± 2.

13. $\pm \sqrt{3}$.   14. $x = \pm 3$.

Examples—49.

1. 4, −2.   2. −1, −9.   3. 20, −6.

4. 7, 5.   5. 8, −40.   6. 10, −110.

Examples—50.

1. 1, −8.   2. 17, −4.   3. −5, −20.

4. −1, −12.   5. 1, −20.   6. 25, −136.

ANSWERS TO EXAMPLES. 309

Examples—51.

1. $6, -5\frac{2}{3}$.
2. $6, -4\frac{1}{2}$.
3. $8\frac{1}{3}, -10$.
4. $14, -10\frac{2}{7}$.
5. $12, -12\frac{1}{12}$.
6. $13, -11\frac{4}{13}$.

Examples—52.

1. $10, 2$.
2. $3, -1$.
3. $2, -\frac{3}{4}$.
4. $1\frac{1}{2}, -1\frac{5}{12}$.
5. $1\frac{2}{3}, -1\frac{1}{2}$.
6. $7, -1\frac{1}{2}$.
7. $2, \frac{1}{2}$.
8. $\frac{1}{2}(-9 \pm 3\sqrt{3})$.
9. $2, 1\frac{2}{5}$.
10. $3, -\frac{1}{5}$.
11. $\frac{1}{8}(27 \pm \sqrt{57})$.
12. $2, -3$.

Examples—53.

1. $6, 3\frac{1}{13}$.
2. $6, -4\frac{3}{4}$.
3. $1, 10\frac{2}{3}$.
4. $3, -8\frac{7}{10}$.
5. $5, -1\frac{5}{13}$.
6. $5, 1\frac{1}{5}$.
7. $5, -1\frac{1}{4}$.
8. $2\frac{2}{3}, 0$.
9. $a \pm \dfrac{1}{a}$.
10. $(a \pm b)^2$.
11. $\pm \sqrt{(ab)}$.
12. $a, -\dfrac{o(a+b)}{2a+b}$.

Examples—54.

1. $x^2-4x-21=0.$
2. $6x^2+5x-6=0.$
3. $x^2+11x+30=0.$
4. $3x^2-8x=0.$
5. $x^2-100=0.$
6. $x^2-2ax+a^2-\dfrac{1}{a^2}=0.$
7. $x^2+2x-1=0.$

Examples—55.

1. $\pm 2, \pm 3.$
2. 49.
3. 4.
4. $\pm 4.$
5. 5, −3.
6. 3, −2.
7. 12, −3.
8. 9, −12.
9. $\pm 3.$
10. 2.
11. 4.
12. 16.
13. $\frac{3}{5}, \frac{4}{5}.$
14. 4.
15. $3a^2.$
16. 0, $\pm 5.$
17. 0, $\pm\sqrt{2}.$
18. 2, $\pm 1.$
19. 0, $\pm\sqrt{(ab)}.$
20. $a, -2a, -2a.$

Examples—56.

1. 3, 4, 5.
2. 36, 24.
3. 30, 24.
4. 18, 12, 9.
5. 196.
6. $\pm 12, \pm 15.$
7. 24.
8. 15 yards, 25 yards.
9. 4550.
10. 40 yds. by 24.

ANSWERS TO EXAMPLES. 311

11. 16.   12. 4 yards, 5 yards.   13. £60, or £40.
14. 8d.   15. Equal.

Examples—57.

1. $x=7,\ y=\pm 4.$

2. $\left.\begin{array}{l} x=4,\ y=-3, \\ x=-3,\ y=4. \end{array}\right\}$

3. $\left.\begin{array}{l} x=4,\ y=3, \\ x=1\frac{1\ 2}{2\ 3},\ y=4\frac{1\ 7}{2\ 3}. \end{array}\right\}$

4. $\left.\begin{array}{l} x=8,\ y=2\frac{1}{2}, \\ x=-2\frac{1}{2},\ y=-8. \end{array}\right\}$

5. $\left.\begin{array}{l} x=6,\ y=5, \\ x=-6,\ y=-5. \end{array}\right\}$

6. $\left.\begin{array}{l} x=5,\ y=3, \\ x=\frac{3}{4},\ y=-1\frac{1}{4}. \end{array}\right\}$

7. $\left.\begin{array}{l} x=5,\ y=3, \\ x=1\frac{7}{10},\ y=-\frac{3}{10}. \end{array}\right\}$

8. $\left.\begin{array}{l} x=3,\ y=4, \\ x=-1\frac{1}{11},\ y=-2\frac{4}{11}. \end{array}\right\}$

9. $\left.\begin{array}{l} x=4,\ y=2, \\ x=2,\ y=4. \end{array}\right\}$

10. $\left.\begin{array}{l} x=10,\ y=15, \\ x=-10\frac{7}{8},\ y=-16\frac{1}{4}. \end{array}\right\}$

11. $\left.\begin{array}{l} x=3,\ y=2, \\ x=-2,\ y=-3. \end{array}\right\}$

12. $\left.\begin{array}{l} x=5,\ y=4, \\ x=4,\ y=5. \end{array}\right\}$

13. $\left.\begin{array}{l} x=\tfrac{1}{2}\{a\mp\sqrt{(2b^2-a^2)}\}, \\ y=\tfrac{1}{2}\{a\pm\sqrt{(2b^2-a^2)}\}. \end{array}\right\}$

14. $\left.\begin{array}{l} x=\tfrac{1}{2}\{\pm\sqrt{(4a^2+b^2)}+b\}, \\ y=\tfrac{1}{2}\{\pm\sqrt{(4a^2+b^2)}-b\}. \end{array}\right\}$

15. $\left.\begin{array}{l} x=8,\ y=1, \\ x=1,\ y=8. \end{array}\right\}$

16. $x=\pm\dfrac{a^2}{\sqrt{(a^2+b^2)}},\ y=\pm\dfrac{b^2}{\sqrt{(a^2+b^2)}}.$

17. $4, \frac{3}{5}; \frac{1}{4}, -\frac{9}{4}; 2, \frac{3}{2}; -\frac{7}{4}, \frac{9}{4}.$

18. $a+b+1, -\dfrac{a+b+1}{a+1}; \ b, -\dfrac{b}{a+1}.$

19. $\pm\dfrac{a}{3}; \ \pm 3b.$ 20. $\pm\dfrac{a}{4}; \ \pm 2b.$

21. $0, \ a+b, \ \frac{1}{2}(a-b) \pm \frac{1}{2}\sqrt{\{(a+3b)(a-b)\}}.$

Examples—58.

1. 11; 7. **2.** 8; 24. **3.** 10; 12. **4.** 18; 8: 6; 16.

5. 5; 3. **6.** 4; 2. **7.** 2; 2. **8.** 7; 4.

9. 60. **10.** 6, .4. **11.** 160; £2.

12. 756; 36; 27. **13.** £275, £225. **14.** 2, 5, 8.

Examples—59.

1. $\frac{15}{20}, \frac{16}{20}; \frac{158}{188}, \frac{181}{188}; \frac{495}{1155}, \frac{735}{1155}, \frac{847}{1155}.$

2. $\dfrac{a+b}{a-b}.$ **3.** $\dfrac{b}{36c}.$ **4.** $\frac{4}{15}, \frac{3}{8}.$

5. $\dfrac{a^4+a^2x^2+x^4}{a^4-x^4}.$ **6.** $\dfrac{x^2-11x+28}{x^2}.$ **7.** 1.

ANSWERS TO EXAMPLES.

8. $\dfrac{(a+b)^2}{b^2(a-b)}$.   9. $\dfrac{ad-bc}{c-d}$.   11. 6, 8.

12. 35, 42.   13. 4.   14. $\dfrac{ab}{a+b}$.

Examples—61.

1. 10, $4\frac{1}{6}$, $2\frac{3}{16}$.   2. 9, $4\frac{1}{2}$, $1\frac{1}{4}$.   3. 6, $1\frac{3}{5}$, $1\frac{2}{3}$.

10. $b\left(\dfrac{a+b}{a-b}\right)^2$;   11. $a+b$, or $\frac{1}{2}(a-b)$.   12. $x=1$, $y=4$;

13. $x=\pm 9$, $y=\pm 3$.   14. 3.   15. 25, 20.

16. 8 : 7.   17. 6.

Examples—62.

1. 32, 272.   2. 39, 400.   3. 63, 363.

4. 694, 34750.   5. 9, 16.   6. -1, 0.   7. -28.

8. -275.   9. $16\frac{1}{4}$.   10. $-84\frac{1}{2}$.   11. $336\frac{2}{3}$.

12. -84.

Examples—63.

1. 12.   2. 20.   3. $1\frac{40}{117}$, $1\frac{41}{117}$, &c., &c.; $S=60$.

4. 14, 16, 18.   5. $14\frac{1}{3}$, $14\frac{2}{3}$, ...   6. $6\frac{1}{2}$, 5, ...

7. $-\frac{1}{5}, \frac{1}{5}, \ldots$ 8. 10, 4.   9. 82.   10. 5, 9, 13, 17.
11. 1, 2, 3, 4, 5.   12. 18, 19.   13. 7.   14. 5.

Examples—64.

1. 64, 85.   2. 1280, 1705.   3. 96, 189.
4. −256, −170.   5. 4096, 3277.   6. −512, −341.
7. $\frac{85}{125}$.   8. $1\frac{173}{486}$.   9. $4\frac{17}{108}$.   10. $2\frac{243}{434}$.

Examples—65.

1. 8.   2. $1\frac{1}{2}$.   3. $\frac{1}{5}$.   4. $\frac{9}{10}$.   5. $\frac{3}{8}$.
6. $\frac{4}{7}$.   7. $\frac{3}{10}$.   8. 1.   9. $1\frac{5}{11}$.   10. $\frac{6}{33}$.
11. $\frac{41}{333}$.   12. $\frac{213}{405}$.

Examples—66.

1. 4, 16, 64.   2. 8, 12, 18, 27.   3. −9, 27, −81, 243.
4. 3, 12, 48; or 81, −54, 36.   5. 1, 3, 9, . .

ANSWERS TO EXAMPLES.   315

6. $\frac{1}{10}$.   7. $2+\frac{2}{3}+\frac{2}{5}+$&c. ; or $4-\frac{4}{3}+\frac{4}{5}-$&c

8. $3-\frac{3}{2}+\frac{3}{4}-$&c.   9. 200 miles.

EXAMPLES—67.

1. $\frac{3}{2}$, $\frac{6}{5}$, 1.   2. $\frac{4}{5}$, $\frac{8}{13}$, 2.   3. 3, $1\frac{2}{5}$.

4. $\frac{2}{15}$, $\frac{1}{12}$, $\frac{2}{33}$.   5. 6, 12.   6. 36, 64.

7. 1, 9.   8. 3, 9.

EXAMPLES—68.

1. 720, 720.   2. 5040.   3. 19958400.

4. 34650.   5. 210.   6. 6.   7. 4.   8. 6.

EXAMPLES—69.

1. 126, 84, 36.   2. 330, 330, 11.   3. 3003, 455.

4. 4950.   5. 210, 84.   6. 11.

7. 50063860, 5006386.   8. 116280.

EXAMPLES—70.

1. $1+6x+15x^2+20x^3+15x^4+6x^5+x^6$.

2. $a^6-15a^4x+90a^3x^2-270a^2x^3+405ax^4-243x^5$.

3. $1 - 8x + 28x^2 - 56x^3 + 70x^4 - 56x^5 + 28x^6 - 8x^7 + x^8$.

4. $a^9 - 9a^8x + 36a^7x^2 - 84a^6x^3 + 126a^5x^4 - 126a^4x^5 + 84a^3x^6 - 36a^2x^7 + 9ax^8 - x^9$.

5. $1 + 12x + 66x^2 + 220x^3 + 495x^4 + 792x^5 + 924x^6 + 792x^7 + 495x^8 + 220x^9 + 66x^{10} + 12x^{11} + x^{12}$.

6. $1 - 20x + 180x^2 - 960x^3 + 3360x^4 - 8064x^5 + 13440x^6 - 15360x^7 + 11520x^8 - 5120x^9 + 1024x^{10}$.

7. $a^6 - 18a^5x + 135a^4x^2 - 540a^3x^3 + 1215a^2x^4 - 1458ax^5 + 729x^6$.

8. $256x^8 + 1024ax^7 + 1792a^2x^6 + 1792a^3x^5 + 1120a^4x^4 + 448a^5x^3 + 112a^6x^2 + 16a^7x + a^8$.

9. $128a^7 - 1344a^6x + 6048a^5x^2 - 15120a^4x^3 + 22680a^3x^4 - 20412a^2x^5 + 10206ax^6 - 2187x^7$.

10. $1 - 5x + \tfrac{45}{4}x^2 - 15x^3 + \tfrac{105}{8}x^4 - \tfrac{63}{8}x^5 + \tfrac{105}{32}x^6 - \tfrac{15}{16}x^7 + \tfrac{45}{256}x^8 - \tfrac{5}{256}x^9 + \tfrac{1}{1024}x^{10}$.

11. $1 - \tfrac{11}{3}x + \tfrac{55}{9}x^2 - \tfrac{55}{9}x^3 + \tfrac{110}{27}x^4 - \tfrac{154}{81}x^5 + \tfrac{154}{243}x^6 - \tfrac{110}{729}x^7 + \tfrac{55}{2187}x^8 - \tfrac{55}{19683}x^9 + \tfrac{11}{59049}x^{10} - \tfrac{1}{177147}x^{11}$.

12. $36a^2x^7$.

13. $-\dfrac{100 \times 98 \times 99}{1 . 2 . 3} a^3 y^{97}$.

14. $495a^{10}b^8$.

15. $\dfrac{\lfloor 10}{\lfloor 5 \;\lfloor 5} a^5 x^5$.

Examples—71.

1. 100101100, 102010, 10230, 2200, 1220.

2. 41104, 23420, 14641, 7571, 5954.

3. 402854.   4. 511, 22154.   6. 8.

Examples—72.

1. 152.   4. 100001000000 (binary) = 201000 (quat.).

5. 57264, 95494, e7t8.   6. 4112, 6543, 62te.

7. 1295, 216; 2400, 343; 4095, 512.

Examples—73.

1. .9030900, .9542426, 1.0791813, 1.3010300, 1.3979400, 1.7781513.

2. $\overline{1}$.5228787, $\overline{1}$.3979400, $\overline{1}$.6020600, $\overline{2}$.4771213, $\overline{2}$.5228787, $\overline{3}$.5185140.

3. 2.2253093, .0170334, 3.5670265.

4. $2 + \log. 3 + 2 \log. 7$.

5. $6 + 2 \log. 3 + 3 \log. .21$.

6. $2 \log. 2 - \frac{2}{3} \log. 3 + \frac{2}{3} \log. 5 - 1$, and $\frac{1}{2} \log. 13 - \frac{3}{2} \log. 2$

7. $.019$.   8. 4 and 6.   9. $\overline{1}.8035760$.

www.ingramcontent.com/pod-product-compliance
Lightning Source LLC
Chambersburg PA
CBHW030016240426
43672CB00007B/978